SHAKESPEARE SURVEY

(1951)

ADVISORY BOARD

SHAKESPEARE SURVEY

AN ANNUAL SURVEY OF
SHAKESPEARIAN STUDY & PRODUCTION

4

EDITED BY
ALLARDYCE NICOLL

Issued under the Sponsorship of

THE UNIVERSITY OF BIRMINGHAM
THE UNIVERSITY OF MANCHESTER
THE SHAKESPEARE MEMORIAL THEATRE
THE SHAKESPEARE BIRTHPLACE TRUST

CAMBRIDGE
AT THE UNIVERSITY PRESS
1968

Published by the Syndics of the Cambridge University Press
Bentley House, 200 Euston Road, London, N.W.1
American Branch: 32 East 57th Street, New York, N.Y. 10022

Standard Book Number: 521 06417 1

Shakespeare Survey was first published in 1948. For the first eighteen volumes it was edited by Allardyce Nicoll under the sponsorship of the University of Birmingham, the University of Manchester, the Royal Shakespeare Theatre and the Shakespeare Birthplace Trust.

First published 1951
Reprinted 1968

First printed in Great Britain
at the University Printing House, Cambridge

Reprinted in Great Britain
by William Lewis (Printers) Ltd, Cardiff

PREFACE

Criticism, or appreciation, of Shakespeare's works is, of course, the chief and indeed the all-embracing theme of *Shakespeare Survey*, and it seems appropriate that, after the Retrospects dealing with the twentieth century's contribution to the study of his life and theatre and to the production of his plays, there should now appear a general article attempting to assess the various approaches which our age has made to his works. Kenneth Muir's Retrospect is thus designed to provide a broad conspectus of the most noteworthy trends in Shakespeare interpretation during the last fifty years. It is accompanied by two other articles, by Hardin Craig and Muriel C. Bradbrook, which suggest how much—despite all that has been done in the meticulous study of the plays—remains for further fruitful exploration. D. S. Bland's essay dealing with certain aspects of Shakespeare's use of language, anticipates a theme which will be the 'core' of a later volume of *Shakespeare Survey*.

Several of the other contributions in this volume form parts of a series already represented in earlier issues of the *Survey*. Slovakia and Yugoslavia take their place among the countries whose Shakespearian activities have been examined; the Bodleian Library joins the Folger Shakespeare Library, Shakespeare's Birthplace and the British Museum in the descriptions of great collections of Shakespeariana. The theatre is represented not only by Richard David's analytical review of two selected recent productions, but also by articles on the Elizabethan stage (by G. F. Reynolds) and (by John Gielgud) on modern stage tradition. J. Dover Wilson essays to solve the puzzles arising from the very first allusion to Shakespeare as a dramatist, and Levi Fox examines the earliest transcript of his will, rediscovered only a few months ago.

In the next, the fifth, volume of the *Survey*, it is planned to take as a central theme the question of the editing of Shakespeare's works and to demonstrate why, after so many generations of editors have laboured at his writings, fresh advances must still be made in the attempt to provide for modern readers a text which shall come as close as possible to what the author intended. Among other material to be included in this volume, special attention may be drawn to a hitherto unreproduced sketch showing the front of Shakespeare's New Place—the only representation, made with any authority, of this house as it stood before its demolition in 1702.

Contributions offered for publication in *Shakespeare Survey* should be addressed to:
The Editor, The University, Edmund Street, Birmingham 3.

A*

CONTRIBUTORS

D. S. BLAND
Staff Tutor, Extra-Mural Department, King's College, University of Durham

M. C. BRADBROOK
Fellow of Girton College and Lecturer in English, Cambridge University

HARDIN CRAIG
Professor of English, University of Missouri, U.S.A.

RICHARD DAVID
London Manager, Cambridge University Press

LEVI FOX
Director, Shakespeare's Birthplace Trust

JOHN GIELGUD
Actor and Producer

L. W. HANSON
Keeper of Printed Books, Bodleian Library, Oxford

CLIFFORD LEECH
Senior Lecturer in English, University of Durham

JAMES G. McMANAWAY
Consultant in Literature and Bibliography, Folger Shakespeare Library, Washington, U.S.A.

KENNETH MUIR
Senior Lecturer in English, University of Leeds

VLADETA POPOVIĆ
Professor of English, University of Belgrade, Yugoslavia

GEORGE F. REYNOLDS
Emeritus Professor of English Literature, University of Colorado, U.S.A.

JÁN ŠIMKO
Lecturer in English, Slovak University, Bratislava

J. I. M. STEWART
Fellow of Christ Church College, Oxford University

J. DOVER WILSON
Emeritus Professor of English, University of Edinburgh

CONTENTS

Notes are placed at the end of each contribution

LIST OF PLATES

LIST OF PLATES

FIFTY YEARS OF SHAKESPEARIAN CRITICISM: 1900–1950

BY

KENNETH MUIR

This survey of twentieth-century criticism will be mainly confined to works of interpretation. Bibliographical and textual works will be entirely excluded; biographical works will be discussed only in so far as they contain criticism, so that for the present purpose E. K. Chambers's *Shakespeare: A Survey* is more relevant than his imposing and indispensable *Shakespeare: A Study of Facts and Problems*; works of scholarship which deal with special problems, such as authenticity or sources, will be mentioned only incidentally; and little attempt will be made to do justice to the many valuable books which have appeared during the last fifty years on such subjects as the Elizabethan Stage—books which have profoundly affected our understanding of Shakespeare's own works. Impressive as much of the interpretative criticism of the period has been, it might be argued that it has not been the literary critics who have added most to our understanding of the plays but rather the textual critics who have brought us nearer to what Shakespeare wrote, the scholars who have increased our knowledge of the stage and audience for which he wrote and of the mental climate in which he lived, and the producers who have given us a chance of seeing Shakespeare's plays more or less as they were written, so that we can see that many of their alleged faults vanish when they are performed with some understanding of Elizabethan conventions. As a last *caveat*, it should be mentioned that although an attempt will be made to consider all important English-speaking critics only occasional reference will be made to those who have written in other languages. To deal with them adequately would have doubled the length of the article, and in any case the important contributions to Shakespearian criticism made in other countries are being surveyed by other hands.[1]

THE SITUATION IN 1900

The situation at the end of the nineteenth century may be roughly summarized. There were signs in the last quarter of the century of a revival of Shakespearian criticism after the barrenness of the period that followed the death of Coleridge. The Victorian period had seen the settlement of the chronology of Shakespeare's plays; it produced a textual orthodoxy which remained undisturbed for many years;[2] it started many lines of investigation; but it produced no major Shakespearian critic. Arnold preferred to say 'Others abide our question', and leave it at that. Dowden's famous book, *Shakespeare, A Critical Study of his Mind and Art*, which appeared in 1875, was still the standard work a generation later. It was followed by Swinburne's *Study*, in which, like his master Hugo, he was perpetually losing himself in a cloud of superlatives, and by Moulton's *Shakespeare as a Dramatic Artist*. There was Sidney Lee's *Life* and Brandes's voluminous *William Shakespeare*. These are the only critics of the period who are likely to be consulted to-day. Dowden and Brandes believed that Shakespeare's works were in some measure a reflexion of his inner development; Lee, on the other hand, assumed that there was a complete separation between Shakespeare the Man and Shakespeare the Artist, for the odd reason—amongst better ones—that Shakespeare was prosperous, and therefore happy, when he wrote his tragedies. The chief outcome of Shakespeare's toil was to Dowden the building up of the poet's moral nature and the fortifying himself for the conduct of life, but Lee declared that Shakespeare's "literary attainments and successes were chiefly valued as serving the prosaic end of making a permanent provision for himself and his daughters". Dowden's description of Shakespeare 'in the depths' and 'on the heights' proved irresistibly comic to Lytton Strachey who in his famous essay on 'Shakespeare's Final Period' (1903) argued that the poet's 'ultimate mood of grave serenity' was a sentimental myth invented by Victorian critics, and that his real mood was one of boredom and disgust, alleviated only by 'visions of loveliness'. Dowden was certainly a sentimentalist, but it is nevertheless arguable that he was nearer to the truth than his critic and that the influence of Strachey's brilliant essay was for many years disastrous. Its effect was reinforced by Thorndike's valuable study of *The Influence of Beaumont and Fletcher on Shakespeare* (1901), in which he pointed out, for example, many resemblances between *Philaster* and *Cymbeline*, and explained the characteristics of the plays of the last period by the popularity of Beaumont and Fletcher. The chronology of their plays is still unsettled, and we cannot be certain that *Philaster* preceded *Cymbeline*. In any case, we can see from *Pericles* that Shakespeare had already broken new ground, and that although some cross-fertilization was natural Shakespeare's development might not have been very different if Beaumont and Fletcher had never lived. But Thorndike's theory led later critics to adopt an apologetic attitude to the Romances as being pot-boilers, and this prevented them from attempting to find out what Shakespeare was really trying to do when he wrote *Cymbeline*.

Another subject that was exercising critics at this time was Shakespeare's morality. R. G. Moulton clung to the belief that Shakespeare was a teacher, and he tended to forget that he was this only incidentally. His book on *The Moral System of Shakespeare* (1903) suffers from a somewhat rigid systematization, and also from his abstraction of plot from the play as an artistic whole. W. B. Yeats, reacting against the Victorian conception of Shakespeare as a worshipper of success, wrote an essay on the historical plays, published in *Ideas of Good and Evil* (1903), in which he denies that Shakespeare preferred Prince Hal and Bolingbroke to the 'sweet lovely rose', Richard II. Yeats's essay derives partly from Pater, and in its denigration of Prince Hal and in its sympathy with failure it was to influence Masefield a few years later. Another book of the period, T. R. Lounsbury's *Shakespeare as a Dramatic Artist* (1902), has a misleading title, for it is mainly an account of the gradual breaking down of the assumption that Shakespeare was a barbarian of genius. It contains little positive criticism of Shakespeare's artistry, and the author is unduly disturbed by the quibbling and indecency to be found in the plays. But the classic exhibition of this disturbance is to be found in 'The Influence of the Audience on Shakespeare's Dramas' (1906) in which Robert Bridges complained bitterly of the bad taste and low morals of those wretched beings, the groundlings, "who can never be forgiven their share in preventing the greatest poet and dramatist of the world from being the best artist". It can, on the contrary, be said that Shakespeare's original audience, if only because it took an intelligent and informed delight in poetry, made possible the great tragedies. But, like Lounsbury, Bridges complained of obscenity and quibbling; he argued that Shakespeare pardoned the wicked (such as Angelo) to please his audience; and above all he accused the poet of sacrificing coherent psychology for the sake of striking situations. This last point was later to be developed by Stoll, and we shall return to it in discussing J. I. M. Stewart's book. It is odd that in Bridges's own plays, which were uncontaminated by the taste of any audience, and had indeed few readers, he continually sacrificed psychology to situation. His essay was, in fact, a kind of pendant to Bradley's *Shakespearean Tragedy*, to which we must now turn.

BRADLEY AND THE BRADLEYITES

Bradley's *Shakespearean Tragedy* (1904) was at once the culmination of the kind of criticism which had started a hundred years before—that of Morgann and the great Romantics—and it was also to be for a whole generation the truest and most profound book ever written on Shakespeare. Indeed, when all deductions have been made, it probably retains that high position to-day with the majority of readers. Bradley is not without weaknesses, though they are mostly those of his age and not peculiar to himself. The catalogue he gives of Shakespeare's faults, for example, seems now as presumptuous as Johnson's similar list in his great Preface. He complains of the stringing together of short scenes, as in the middle part of *Antony and Cleopatra*; of the introduction of irrelevant anachronisms; of the direct addressing of the audience in soliloquies; of the excessive use of metaphor and bombastic language; of Shakespeare's failure to distinguish between the speech of different characters; and of the use of 'gnomic' passages. There is not one of these accusations which would be supported by a competent modern critic, at least without many qualifications. And this fact is not, of course, due to the superiority of modern critics, but rather to the fact that the conventions of the Elizabethan stage are now better understood and appreciated.

Bradley was very conscious of the imperfections of even the best stage performance compared with the ideal performance in the critic's mind; and unfortunately the actors of his day never gave him an opportunity of seeing a play uncut and unhampered by the elaborate scenery which was supposed to be indispensable to success, even though it slowed down the action to an intolerable degree. Yet Bradley's avowed object was to examine each play more or less as if he were an actor who had to study all the parts. This—and the example of Coleridge and Hazlitt—led him to devote two-thirds of his space to a consideration of the characters of the plays. It is not quite fair to say that he substituted an interest in psychology for the dramatic interest, for he was well aware that "the psychological point of view is not the equivalent of the tragic"; but it may be said fairly enough that he was sometimes led to consider the characters as real people rather than as imaginary characters in a drama. His discussion of what Cordelia would have done in Desdemona's place, his musings on the childhood of Cordelia, which remind one of Mrs Jameson and Mary Cowden Clarke, and the notorious note on "How many children had Lady Macbeth?" are examples of Bradley's weaker side. On the other hand, his Hegelianism is comparatively harmless, and the frequent accusation that is made against him that he read into the plays subtleties that would have astonished their author is seldom true. His interpretations of the chief characters, developed as many of them are from those of previous critics, especially from Coleridge, have remained the standard. We may feel, with Lily Campbell, that he ignores the Elizabethan acceptance of certain "abnormal states of mind as resulting from the unchecked domination of passion over reason". We may think that he passes too lightly over Hamlet's faults; that he makes too little of Iago's motives; and that he credits to Macbeth's character the poetical genius of his creator. But when all is said the main characters of the great tragedies have never before or since been analysed so brilliantly or so convincingly; we diverge from him, as we often must, at our peril. His other Shakespearian essays in *Oxford Lectures* and *A Miscellany* possess the same qualities, though he perhaps sentimentalizes the rejection of Falstaff and fails to appreciate the wonderful constructive power displayed in *Antony and Cleopatra*.

Nearly all recent critics have been influenced by Bradley in one way or another, not least when they have reacted against his methods. Three books which are mainly concerned with the analysis of character may conveniently be mentioned here: Agnes Mure Mackenzie's *The Women in Shakespeare's Plays* (1924) and John Palmer's *Political Characters* and *Comic Characters of Shakespeare* (1945–6). Palmer is particularly good in his defence of the Tribunes in *Coriolanus*, while his understanding of how modern politicians behave frequently enables him to reveal unnoticed touches of realism in Shakespeare's characters. Palmer's knowledge of the world and his unpedantic understanding of drama, displayed in his books on Jonson and Molière, combine to make both his Shakespearian books excellent of their kind.

H. B. Charlton's *Shakespearian Tragedy* (1948) was avowedly written as a kind of supplement to Bradley's book on the same subject. With needless modesty Charlton speaks of himself as 'a mere scholar' who can only hope by an examination of sources and a study of the 'cosmic framework' of each play to add a little to the truth about Shakespeare which is contained in its purest form in the pages of Bradley. One might complain that his discussion of Saxo Grammaticus and of some of the earlier versions of the Lear story is not strictly relevant to his purpose, especially as he seems to think that *The Mirror for Magistrates* and *The Faerie Queene* contributed nothing to *King Lear*, and as he misses the opportunity of examining Shakespeare's indebtedness to Sidney's *Arcadia*. But he has a useful discussion of the way Shakespeare transformed the sources of *Macbeth* and *Othello*, and some interesting remarks on the background of all four tragedies.

His companion volume, *Shakespearian Comedy* (1937), is one of the surprisingly few books devoted to its subject, and it contains a generally plausible and certainly erudite account of how Shakespeare learned from his various experiments to write the three masterpieces. But Charlton is so anxious to believe that Shakespeare went from strength to strength that he plays fast and loose with chronology, and assumes that the 'dark comedies' were written before *Much Ado*, merely because he would like to have it so. He does much the same thing in his book on the tragedies, where he states that *King Lear* was written after *Macbeth*. In both books, too, he expresses an abnormally low opinion of the Romances, arguing that though the poetry is as great as ever Shakespeare's power of imaginative vision is blunted. There would seem to be a contradiction here, for it would have been impossible for great poetry to have been written by the ageing sentimentalist of Charlton's description, a man who was almost, we are led to understand, like Johnson's Polonius, declining into dotage.

It will be convenient to mention here two other books on Shakespearian Comedy. George Gordon's book of this title (1944) is Bradleian only in the sense that he approaches the comedies mainly through the characters; he is nearer to Raleigh in spirit. It is unfair to judge the author by this posthumous book, as he prepared only one chapter, on Shakespeare's English, for publication. There are chapters on *King Lear* and *Othello*, and scattered through the chapters on the comedies there are flashes of wit and humour which made his lectures delightful to listen to, and which deepen our regret that he left no book on the subject worthy of his talents. Some of his most attractive criticism is contained in school editions of nine of the plays.

Very different is *Shakespearean Comedy* (1949) by the veteran Thomas Marc Parrott, the learned editor of Chapman's plays. The work is intended for the general reader rather than the scholar, though it is more likely to be read by the student than either. Parrott believes that "it is neither in action nor in speech that Shakespeare attains the height of his art, but in character creation". Although, therefore, he discusses Shakespeare's sources at some length, his main concern is with the characters. He refers to a number of modern performances of the comedies, and he obviously enjoys them; but his long commentary, sensible as it is, seldom startles the reader with a new critical insight. Sometimes his statements are questionable, as when he asserts that "*A Midsummer Night's Dream* has never enjoyed great success on the stage"; that Poor Tom was a comic character; and that "the vulgar dissertation of the effects of drink" in *Macbeth* was not written by Shakespeare. In spite of the books of Palmer, Charlton and Parrott, there is still no interpretation of the comedies as outstanding as Bradley's on the tragedies.

APPROACHES TO SHAKESPEARE

All through the period under review there has been a continuous stream of short surveys of Shakespeare, ranging from Swinburne's shrill eulogy to Hardin Craig's solid and sensible *Interpretation of Shakespeare* (1948). Some of them were intended for students, and some for the general reader; most of them contain points of originality; but as they cover such a wide field they are very difficult to classify. Stopford Brooke's *Ten Plays* (1905) and *Ten More Plays* (1913) no longer mean very much to us. Walter Raleigh's *Shakespeare* (1907) is still one of the most popular introductions, because of its sensible tone and its pleasant style. George Saintsbury's account in *The Cambridge History of English Literature* (1910) is still worth glancing at, in spite of its style. John Masefield's little book (1911) is brilliant, aphoristic and original, but sometimes spoilt by the author's imposition on Shakespeare of his own moral views. His later lecture 'Shakespeare and Spiritual Life' is notable for eloquent passages on *Julius Caesar* and *Macbeth*; but *A Macbeth Production* (1945) contains only elementary, if admirable, advice to the players.

The various volumes of E. K. Chambers form perhaps the most impressive achievement of literary scholarship in our time, but he has also given us in *Shakespeare: A Survey* (1925) his personal interpretations of the plays. Among his notable points are his discussion of Richard III as an actor, his suggestion that the interlude of Pyramus and Thisbe is a burlesque of *Romeo and Juliet*, his mention of the "temper of the inquisitor" displayed by Shakespeare in *Measure for Measure*, and his remarks on the egotism of Coriolanus. These essays appeared originally as introductions to the separate plays, and they may be compared with M. R. Ridley's book, written after he had edited the New Temple Shakespeare. Two other brief introductions may be mentioned here: John Bailey's *Shakespeare* (1929), which is the work of a cultured man but of one who is apt to be offended by certain characteristics of the poet—as when he complains that *Venus and Adonis* is "without reserve or reticence, dignity or manliness or morals"—and J. W. Mackail's *The Approach to Shakespeare* (1930) which is excellent in its traditional style.

More substantial and more original are two books which appeared in 1939. Peter Alexander's *Shakespeare's Life and Art*, as Tillyard remarks, "makes the strategic error of uniting in one treatment the most severely factual with the delicately critical". But Alexander, by a judicious use of the great critics of the past, exhibits old problems in a fresh light; and where he permits himself to be original he is often illuminating. He suggests, for example, that "the great comic artists are even more ruthless with men's virtues than with their vices"; that Shakespeare's ironic reserve about his religious convictions "is itself an artistic device that gives an added force to the evidence his work affords us about the ultimate nature of things"; and, in reference to Isabella, that "the charity of Shakespeare's art embraces the virtuous as well as the sinner". His defence of Shakespeare as a dramatic artist would have been strengthened if he had taken more note of Elizabethan conventions.

Mark Van Doren's *Shakespeare* is remarkably independent and original. In some respects the author reminds us of the critic he most admires, Samuel Johnson. He is not afraid to say that the seventy-first sonnet alone "maintains its music to the ending syllable"; that the sonnets are addressed to Shakespeare's own poetry—an aberration of which Johnson would hardly have approved; that *Venus and Adonis* contains 'desperate rhetoric'; and that Constance is the "last and most terrible of Shakespeare's wailing women". He even dares to speak of the melodramatic inferiority of Macbeth's speech beginning "Come, seeling night". But, on the other hand, there is hardly a page without an illuminating comment, as when he links Cleopatra's 'immortal longings' with the Clown's use of 'immortal' just before, when he speaks of Gloucester and Lear as having "learned too much, too late", or when he remarks that Imogen's devotion, being complete, "has its pressing tendernesses, its urgent delicacies, its passionate reserves". The book is particularly valuable for its comments on the development of Shakespeare's verse, and on the way verse and prose are used to differentiate character. Sometimes, however, he falls into the mistake of forgetting that verse is only a medium, and that we should not say that Imogen made Iachimo a great poet, any more than we should say that Hamlet in his address to the players "may be a little proud of the nobility which knows its way so well among the short words and the long ones, the epigrams and the periods". It is Shakespeare, rather than Iachimo and Hamlet, who is the poet and the stylist.

Finally, a word is due to Charles Williams's interpretation of *Troilus and Cressida* and *Hamlet* in *The English Poetic Mind* (1932).

PERSONAL AND IMPERSONAL SHAKESPEARES

In the nineteenth century, as we have seen, critical opinion was divided between the view that Shakespeare's life was reflected in his plays and the view that his art was absolutely impersonal. Frank Harris's *Shakespeare the Man* (1909) gave a portrait of the poet as a neurotic, obsessed with sex; his views still occasionally appear in a modified form, as, for example, in the books of Hesketh Pearson and Ivor Brown. Wyndham Lewis's study of the role of the hero in Shakespeare's plays, entitled *The Lion and the Fox*, is a violent attack on the idea that Shakespeare was impersonal. Lewis argued that the poet was an executioner who identified himself with his victims, and that all the tragedies were a criticism of the assumption that action is the end of existence. The book, which is brilliant, intemperate and amateurish, deals also with the impact of Machiavelli's supposed views on Elizabethan dramatists. It is difficult to accept without qualification the portrait of Shakespeare that emerges, though a suffering bard is at least more acceptable than the Smilesian pachyderm of Lee's biography.

G. L. Kittredge's tercentenary address, Sisson's lecture on 'The Mythical Sorrows of Shakespeare' (1934) and R. W. Chambers's on 'The Jacobean Shakespeare' (1937) persuasively argue the danger of deducing anything about the poet's biography from his plays. No doubt the danger is there, even if we assume that the sonnets were not entirely fictitious. Eliot once declared that "the greater the artist, the wider the gulf between the heart that suffers and the mind that creates". This aphorism implies the existence of a suffering heart, and Shakespeare had obviously experienced

> The heartache and the thousand natural shocks
> That flesh is heir to—

even if we can never know the details.

DISINTEGRATION AND REINTEGRATION

J. M. Robertson's chief contribution to Shakespeare criticism—what he wrote on Montaigne's influence has been superseded—was his attempt to give away to other dramatists, such as Marlowe, Greene, Peele and Chapman, those plays, scenes and passages which he regarded as unworthy of Shakespeare himself. All his work in this field is rendered nugatory by the simple probabilities that Shakespeare in his youth imitated Marlowe and others, that he did not always write well, and that he sometimes wrote excellently without earning Robertson's approval. The New Cambridge editors also detected other hands or the signs of revision when they came across passages they disliked. Dugdale Sykes used some of Robertson's methods in his *Sidelights on Shakespeare* in discussing the authorship of *The Two Noble Kinsmen* and *Pericles*; and Alfred Hart in *Shakespeare and the Homilies* supported Shakespeare's partial authorship of *Edward III* and *The Two Noble Kinsmen* by more reliable vocabulary tests than those employed by Robertson and Sykes.

E. K. Chambers made effective counter-attacks on the disintegrators in his British Academy lecture on 'The Disintegration of Shakespeare' and in his *Shakespeare: A Study of Facts and Problems*. Peter Alexander, by his overwhelming demonstration that *The Contention* and *The True Tragedy* were bad quartos of the second and third parts of *Henry VI*, shattered the orthodox conception, on which Robertson largely relied, that Shakespeare began his career as a reviser of plays written by one or more of the University Wits. A third critic, Lascelles Abercrombie, in his 'Plea for the Liberty of Interpreting' (1930) rightly claimed that if Shakespeare incorporated other men's work into his own, we should still judge the result as a work of art for the whole of which Shakespeare must be held responsible. There are only one or two cases where Shakespeare's work was completed or altered by other dramatists—*Macbeth* certainly, and *Timon of Athens* possibly. Abercrombie urged that we should judge by results, rather than by intentions, because knowledge of the conditions of the time cannot confer any right to say what was intended. By 'liberty of interpreting' Abercrombie did not mean the liberty "to read into a play of Shakespeare's whatever feeling or idea a modern reader may loosely and accidentally

B

associate with its subject", but rather "anything which may be found in that art, even if it is only the modern reader who can find it there, may legitimately be taken as its meaning". This is to open the door wide for cranks of all kinds; but if reasonable discretion is maintained Abercrombie's plea is at least a useful antidote to those critics who would circumscribe Shakespeare's genius by the poetasters of his own age.

Abercrombie's own book, *The Idea of Great Poetry* (1925), illustrates the way he used the liberty he claimed. He addresses himself to the question of why we enjoy in tragedy what seems a version of the mere evil of life, and argues that Shakespeare finds the good in the character which creates and endures the evil. Macbeth's personality, for example, "towers into its loftiest grandeur" by experiencing to the full the imbecile futility of life, and in that very act personal life "superbly signifies itself". It may be argued, however, that Macbeth should not be credited with the poetical power of his creator, and that significance is restored to life not, surely, by the character but by the revelation of moral order in the play as a whole. Abercrombie's analysis of *Hamlet* is equally interesting, and perhaps more convincing. He thinks that Hamlet's delay, for which he is continually upbraiding himself, exists only in his own mind.

SCHOLARSHIP AND CRITICISM

Some eminent Shakespearians can best be judged by their profound influence on their pupils. G. L. Kittredge, for example, though he produced an excellent one-volume edition of Shakespeare (1936) and annotated editions of sixteen of the plays, was more influential than any of his works. He was impatient of Romantic excesses; and his annotations are often extremely valuable because his Johnsonian common sense was controlled by an immense learning. Another famous teacher, C. F. Tucker Brooke, edited a number of plays, but his *Essays on Shakespeare and other Elizabethans* (1948) do not do justice to his powers.

Scholarship and criticism would both suffer from a divorce, and numerous works of scholarship have affected the interpretation of Shakespeare. Leslie Hotson, for example, by his periodic discoveries has thrown new light on Shakespeare's methods of topical allusion. In *Shakespeare versus Shallow* (1931) he argued that Shallow and Slender were portraits of Justice Gardiner and his stepson, with whom Shakespeare had quarrelled, and thereby cast doubts on the old legend that Shakespeare had been a poacher. *I, William Shakespeare* (1937) contains an account of one of Shakespeare's executors and, by tracing links between the poet and the Virginia Company, Hotson fills in the background of *The Tempest*. His latest book, *Shakespeare's Sonnets Dated* (1949), seeks to prove that the sonnets were written by 1590, though not all readers have been convinced by his arguments. He is now grooming a new candidate for the role of 'Mr W. H.'

T. W. Baldwin, in the latest of his learned and voluminous works, also has designs on the orthodox chronology. By an examination of *Shakspere's Five-Act Structure* (1947) and a comparison of it with numerous commentaries on Terence's plays he argues plausibly that several of the plays were written before 1590. Dover Wilson's theories that many of the plays underwent one or more revisions would suit an early date for the commencement of Shakespeare's career, and it has even been argued that the *Ur-Hamlet* was written by Shakespeare himself. Other books by Baldwin, also demanding a leisured reader, argue that Shakespeare adopted a hanging in *The Comedy of Errors* and deal with the curricula of *Shakspere's Petty School* (1943) and the extent of his *Small Latine and Lesse Greeke* (1944). In the last of these Baldwin provides an immense number of parallels between the school text-books and Shakespeare's plays. To these books we may add Sister Miriam Joseph's admirable study of *Shakespeare's Use of the Arts of Language* (1947), Rosemond Tuve's *Elizabethan and Metaphysical Imagery* (1947), F. P. Wilson's *Shakespeare and the Diction of Common Life* (1941), Gladys Willcock's 'Shakespeare and Rhetoric', together with the relevant chapters in *Shakespeare's England* and *A Companion to Shakespeare Studies*. Between them these critics have effectually disposed of the idea that Shakespeare was uneducated and lacking in art. The man who pored over commentaries on Terence and eagerly perused new books on rhetoric as soon as they came out was a conscious artist; and if he read comparatively few books he displayed a really astonishing power of absorbing and using everything he read. This is also demonstrated by recent studies of the influence of several books on his work. G. C. Taylor examined his debt to Montaigne and proved, more convincingly than previous critics, that he picked up vocabulary, ideas, and phrases from Florio's translation. Another critic, Drayton Henderson, has less cautiously examined Florio's influence on *King Lear* (*Shakespeare Association Bulletin*, XLV (October 1939), 209–25). Alwin Thaler has shown that Sidney's *Apology* had been read and inwardly digested by Shakespeare, and there have been several articles and notes tracing the influence of *Arcadia* on *King Lear*. Edgar I. Fripp in one of the best of his essays discussed Shakespeare's knowledge of Ovid, both in the original and in Golding's translation. Richmond Noble has provided the best, but by no means an exhaustive, account of *Shakespeare's Knowledge of the Bible* (1935). (His earlier book on *Shakespeare's Use of Song* (1923) is also the best on its subject.) These books and a large number of articles have superseded such books as Churton Collins's *Studies in Shakespeare* (1903), in which he discussed the poet's knowledge of the classics. They are also preparing the way for a much-needed successor to Anders's pioneering work, *Shakespeare's Books* (1904). Another book that is badly needed is an authoritative and full-length account of Shakespeare's sources, and the use he made of them. M. W. MacCallum's work on *Shakespeare's Roman Plays* (1910) does contain a full discussion of Shakespeare's use of North's *Plutarch*, and his account may be supplemented by reference to Wyndham and Murry; but the book is so overloaded with detail that its impact is somewhat blunted. He does not read Shakespeare by flashes of lightning, but by the steady glow of an oil lamp; and we are left at the end wondering if after all our understanding of the plays has been widened, or whether we have merely acquired knowledge of incidentals. For Shakespeare's treatment of his other sources one has to go to introductions to individual plays and to articles scattered through the learned journals. In these there is often little attempt to explain why Shakespeare made the alterations he did. Perrett's elaborate discussion of *The Story of King Lear*, for example, establishes which versions of the story Shakespeare had read, but one has to supplement his account by reference to Greg, R. W. Chambers, McKeithan, Blunden and Pyle, and still be left with the feeling that there is a lot more to be said.

Allardyce Nicoll, though best known as a learned and indispensable historian of the drama and the stage, has written a book on the tragedies entitled *Studies in Shakespeare* (1927). He emphasizes that "a playhouse appreciation of the drama does not accord absolutely with the study appreciation of the same work"; but he rejects the realist school and claims that "character is interwoven with plot". His interpretations contain, along with much that is true, some questionable points: for example, that Hamlet had actually seduced Ophelia (cf. Madariaga), and that his indecision was partly due to his reliance on Horatio; that Desdemona, being unintelligent, was apt to lie herself out of difficulties; that Iago had not at first "the slightest thought of any tragic conclusion" to his scheme for making Othello jealous; that Othello is stupid, and given to romantic self-deception (cf. Leavis); that "to find an explanation for Lear's decisions [in the] first scene we need to know the subsequent development of the plot", for they are unintelligible by themselves; and that *King Lear* "is decidedly the least powerful of the four tragedies". It is possible to disagree with Nicoll on all these points and yet to recognize that his book is a serious attempt to cut through the jungle of commentary in order to see the plays freshly.

J. Dover Wilson's chief contribution to Shakespearian studies has been in the field of bibliography, and his critical work is largely an offshoot of his editorial labours. His *Essential Shakespeare* (1932) was written in a breathing space after he had helped to edit the Comedies; *What Happens in Hamlet* (1935) was an overflow from his edition of the play; and *The Fortunes of Falstaff* (1943) cleared his mind for the editing of *Henry IV*. With these books may be considered his introductions to five Histories and four Tragedies, his little book *Six Tragedies* and a lecture on *The Tempest*. Dover Wilson subscribes partly to the Romantic view of Shakespeare, the view that the tragedies and romances "reflect personal feeling and inner spiritual experience". This may in a broad sense be nearer the truth than Lee's views on the matter. Dover Wilson has also been influenced by the attitude which best finds expression in G. B. Harrison's *Shakespeare at Work*, in which the poet is conceived as a running commentator on the events of his time. The 'inessential' Shakespeare may have been grieved by the fall of Essex and the corruption of James I's Court—though *Macbeth* has been regarded as a compliment to the King—but it is difficult to believe that the tragic period can be accounted for by such things. One may doubt, too, whether Wordsworth, the great egoist, can throw much light on the poet Keats took as the supreme exemplar of Negative Capability.

It is interesting to compare the book on *Hamlet* with Granville-Barker's *Preface*. In one or two places Wilson is the victim of his own ingenuity: he is less convincing on the play-scene, for example, than the experienced producer, and perhaps on this scene Bethell is better than either. But Wilson's elaborate analysis of plot and character is masterly in its way. It may be true, as Knights has complained, that his "interest lies in the events and characters rather than in the poetry", and that "the labour that poetry demands is of a different order"; but Wilson's methods, though not the only ones, are perfectly legitimate. *The Fortunes of Falstaff* has the same merits and limitations. It is a useful reply to Morgann and Bradley on the subject of the rejection of Falstaff. Wilson goes back to Johnson who wrote before the character had been sentimentalized; he stresses the Morality element in the play; argues less effectively that Falstaff deteriorates; and makes a reasoned defence of Hal's character. He is not so good on the subject of Falstaff's cowardice, which exhibits merely a wonderfully developed instinct of self-preservation. He is uncharitable in his verdict on "the dreadful Doll, harridan and whore". And it may be argued that by concentrating on Falstaff Wilson inevitably neglects the interrelation of the rebellion scenes with the comic scenes, and he does not recognize that if Falstaff represents the World, the Flesh and the Devil, he is also a living criticism of the other world of 'policy'.

W. C. Curry's valuable book, *Shakespeare's Philosophical Patterns* (1937), contains an application of scholastic theories of demonology to *Macbeth*. Curry shows that a contemporary audience would have taken Lady Macbeth's invocation of the murdering ministers more literally than a modern audience, and that Shakespeare meant her to be possessed. He suggests that the Weird Sisters were neither norns nor witches, but demons who had assumed the form of witches. He argues that the storm that rages over Macbeth's castle is a manifestation of demonic power over the elements of nature, that his vision of the dagger is caused by demons, and that Banquo's ghost is also an infernal illusion. The book contains some excellent comments on the significance of Macbeth's reference to "Nature's germens". Whatever we may think of certain details of Curry's interpretation of the play, he has written a book that will be indispensable to future interpreters. The second part, however, on *The Tempest*, though it contains some useful information, deals rather with the incidentals than with the essentials of that play.

Ruth L. Anderson's *Elizabethan Psychology and Shakespeare* (1927), the first full-length study of a subject which had been treated earlier by Dowden and Hardin Craig, was followed three years later by Lily Campbell's *Shakespeare's Tragic Heroes*. These books certainly throw light on Shakespeare's characters, though both writers, by presenting a more or less coherent psychological theory, tend to misrepresent the climate of Shakespeare's age. The poet had certainly read Timothy Bright's *Treatise on Melancholy* and may have known other books of the kind, but it is surely unlikely that in his four greatest tragedies he was endeavouring to dramatize case-book histories. Hamlet was a 'melancholy' man, but few would agree that he could be adequately described in clinical terms. There is some truth in Louise C. Turner Forest's assertion (*PMLA*, LXI (September 1946), 672) that "such a substituting of learned case histories for interpretative and analytical dramatic criticism eventually destroys criticism itself".

The same kind of complaint might well be made against Ernest Jones's *Hamlet and Oedipus* (1949—expanded from an earlier article) and James Wertham's *Dark Legend* (1946). These psycho-analytical interpretations of the character of the hero are very ingenious, and Wertham, who found in *Hamlet* a clue to explain a case of matricide in New York, tells his story brilliantly. Neither book attempts to prove that Shakespeare deliberately saddled his hero with complexes discovered three hundred years later; but if Freud discovered certain truths about the human mind, it is not unreasonable to use these books as a second line of defence against the attacks of those critics who pretend that Shakespeare sacrificed character to situation and plot.[3]

REALISM AND CONVENTION

The increasing knowledge of the Elizabethan stage and its conventions exemplified by E. K. Chambers's massive volumes and by such writers as W. J. Lawrence and G. F. Reynolds, studies of *Shakespeare's Theatre* (edited by Muriel St C. Byrne, 1927) and similar books by A. H. Thorndike and J. Q. Adams, Charles Sisson's *Le goût public et le théâtre élisabéthain* (1922), A. C. Sprague's *Shakespeare and the Audience* (1935), and Alfred Harbage's *Shakespeare's Audience* (1941) inevitably affected the criticism of Shakespeare's plays. This can be seen by comparing G. P. Baker's *The Development of Shakespeare as a Dramatist* (1907), Brander Matthews's *Shakspere as a Playwright* (1913), Quiller-Couch's *Shakespeare's Workmanship* (1918), and even J. C. Squire's *Shakespeare as a Dramatist* (1935) with the books of Muriel Bradbrook and S. L. Bethell. Baker and Matthews treated Shakespeare, as Miss Bradbrook pointed out, "purely as a dramatist, and not as a dramatic poet"; and though Quiller-Couch can still be read with pleasure, one has to make allowances for his ignoring of the conventions of the stage for which Shakespeare constructed his plays. His introductions to the Comedies in the New Cambridge Shakespeare are desultory and often charming, but his description of Isabella's chastity as 'rancid', his attack on Bassanio as a mere fortune-hunter, and his tendency to call in a collaborator when he finds a passage or scene distasteful exemplify his weaknesses.

Meanwhile Edgar Elmer Stoll had been performing a very useful function: he had been making other critics think about the dramatic presentation of character. Beginning in 1907 he has written a long series of books attacking the orthodox view of Shakespeare's plays, and if they have not always been convincing their impact has been salutary. His early books were written soon after Bradley's masterpiece—*The Ghosts* (1907), *Shylock* (1911), *The Criminals* (1912), *Falstaff* (1914), *Othello* (1915) and *Hamlet* (1919)—and he was one of the first to focus attention on Shakespeare's lack of realism. Later volumes include *Shakespeare Studies* (1927), *Poets and Playwrights* (1930) and *Shakespeare and Other Masters* (1940). The most convenient statement of his position is to be found in *Art and Artifice in Shakespeare* (1933).

Stoll tries to show that the attempts made by previous critics to demonstrate the consistency of Shakespeare's characters have only led them into absurdity; that Shakespeare is a great illusionist who conjures us into temporarily believing impossibilities, and that he obtains some of his greatest effects from the contrast between the hero and his actions—between the noble Macbeth and his career of crime, between the noble Othello and his jealous mania; that we ought to consider the dramas as Elizabethan plays, obeying certain conventions, and not waste our time in trying to reconcile manifest inconsistencies which would not be noted in the heat of performance. In so far as Stoll has repeatedly pointed out that poetic dramas obtain their effects by methods other than those of realism, we may be grateful to him for his forty-five years of campaigning. He provides a useful antidote to Archer's *The Old Drama and the New*, in which poetry was treated as an excrescence. Stoll allows that Shakespeare's characters

more unmistakably than anyone else's, are, from the outset, given voices, accents, of their own—and not individual only, but beautiful—a fact which inveigles us, throughout the play, and even (witness the critics) afterwards, into accepting, not them only, but also the incredible things that they not infrequently do.

He regards it as a sign of Shakespeare's greatness as a dramatic poet that he "evades and hedges, he manœuvres and manipulates, he suppresses or obscures". There is some truth in this point of view; but to accept it wholly would be to shatter Shakespeare's reputation as the greatest of dramatists. Although we may agree with Bernard Shaw that "the score is more important than the libretto", great drama must in a very broad sense be true to life. We can have a staggering contrast between the doer and the deed provided that not only in the theatre but also in the study we are able to accept the play as an image of truth. In cold blood, particularly if we have tidy views about human nature, we may think it incredible that Macbeth should kill Duncan or Othello smother his wife. But great poets have this in common with the clearest gods: they

make them honours
Of men's impossibilities.

12

We accept, and not only in the heat of performance, that these events are true to human nature. Stoll found an opening for his attacks because of the inadequacy of nineteenth-century theories of psychology, and because of the 'realism' of late nineteenth-century drama. Without pretending that Shakespeare was confined by Elizabethan psychological theories, we may suggest that the Elizabethans and even eighteenth-century critics had no difficulty in believing in the behaviour of Shakespeare's characters; and even if we feel that J. I. M. Stewart was rash to bring in the new world of psychology to redress the balance of the old, he should at least give us pause if we are tempted to find irremediable inconsistencies in Shakespeare's characters. It may be added that if the characters were considered not from the point of view of psychology, but from that of theology, there would not have been so much beating about of brains.

We should beware of assuming that Shakespeare can be explained in terms of his contemporaries—to imagine, for example, that modern conceptions of Hamlet must be false because Shakespeare was fulfilling certain expectations, and because he was cabinned, cribbed and confined by his *donnée*. If Dekker's play about Orestes were to be discovered, future Stolls would doubtless assure us that Shakespeare was compelled to make his hero an unwilling avenger like his prototype. Shakespeare used the conventions of his time, but he used them for his own purposes. A convention like that of the 'calumniator believed' has a real relation to the facts of human nature, and even the marriages which round off *Measure for Measure* can be defended on other grounds than that of the satisfaction of the groundlings. There are impossibilities in Shakespeare's greatest plays, but they do not undermine the total impression of truth to life.

W. W. Lawrence's method in *Shakespeare's Problem Comedies* (1931) has something in common with Stoll's. He investigates the medieval elements surviving in the plays, and argues that when Shakespeare treats a traditional theme we should inquire first of all what it meant to an Elizabethan audience. He shows, for example, that the bed-trick used in *Measure for Measure* and *All's Well that Ends Well* is "hard to reconcile with the naturalness of the characters", and he declares that though the problem comedies seem real they contain "improbabilities and archaisms which must be judged in the light of early traditions and social usages". Most readers to-day would accept this view, which has the advantage of short-circuiting a good deal of unprofitable discussion on such things as Vincentio's irresponsibility and the alleged cynicism of *All's Well*. But although Lawrence recognizes that "when historical investigation has cleared the ground, aesthetic criticism must have the field in the last analysis", the reader may be tempted to feel that Lawrence sometimes implies that Shakespeare was the slave, rather than the master, of the conventions he employs. Middleton Murry's brilliant review of the book, reprinted in his *Shakespeare* (1935), provides a useful corrective.

Another book which stresses the survival of medieval elements in Shakespeare's plays is Willard Farnham's *The Medieval Heritage of Elizabethan Tragedy* (1936), who deals in the last chapter with Shakespeare's transformation of the reversal of fortune theme by attaining a "delicate balance between an overwhelming assault upon man's proud but imperfect moral security and a stimulating challenge to his faith in moral existence".

O. J. Campbell's two books, *Comicall Satyre* (1938) and *Shakespeare's Satire* (1943), may be considered here, as he deals with the relation of the satirical element in Shakespeare's plays to contemporary trends. He ascribes the popularity of satirical plays to the ecclesiastical ban placed on verse satires. In the course of his books he makes some interesting points, as when he suggests that Jacques was a satirical portrait of the satirists and shows that the Seven Ages of Man speech is "put in a context which neutralises its tone and contradicts all its assumptions", or when he discusses Shakespeare's 'humour' characters. But he is less convincing when he argues that Mercutio is a satirical commentator developed from the conventions of the lout's role, or when he defines *Coriolanus* as a tragical satire. His description of Troilus, in particular, as "an expert in sensuality, a sexual gourmet with the educated sensuality of an Italianate roué", exemplifies the pitfalls that lie in wait for the historical critic who judges Shakespeare by his contemporaries, and shuts his ears to the poetry. A rake would not have had his faith in the divine order destroyed by the infidelity of his mistress.

In E. M. W. Tillyard's four books—*Shakespeare's Last Plays* (1938), *The Elizabethan World Picture* (1943), *Shakespeare's History Plays* (1944) and *Shakespeare's Problem Plays* (1950)—the historical approach is subordinated to aesthetic criticism. The merit of the first of these books is that it provides an effective answer to Lytton Strachey, and interprets the plays of the final period in such a way as to bring out some of their essential characteristics. Tillyard argues that Shakespeare was dealing with two themes—the completion of the tragic pattern in reconciliation, and the juxtaposition of 'planes of reality'. The second of these books is an exposition of the common Elizabethan assumptions about the universe, shared of course by Shakespeare. It covers part of the same ground as Hardin Craig's brilliant survey of the Elizabethan mind, *The Enchanted Glass*, and Theodore Spencer's more speculative and wayward *Shakespeare and the Nature of Man* (1942). Spencer argues that the prevailing beliefs suffered three rude shocks in the lifetime of Shakespeare, from the impact of the discoveries of Copernicus, the political theory of Machiavelli, and the scepticism of Montaigne. Spencer has some excellent passages on the treatment of appearance and reality by Shakespeare; but some of his later chapters are disappointing after the stimulating exposition in the first half of the book.

Tillyard's third book is a comprehensive account of the Elizabethan attitude to history, and of Shakespeare's treatment of it. It contains, rather curiously, a chapter on *Macbeth*. Otherwise Tillyard discusses the English histories as two tetralogies, separated by *King John*. He has a striking defence of Prince Hal, even if it makes him out to be more interesting than he really is, and the book as a whole fills the gap caused by the comparative neglect of the Histories by most modern critics. Lily Campbell's *Shakespeare's Histories* (1947) covers much of the same ground; but though she makes some useful points about the influence of *The Mirror for Magistrates*, her book is more valuable for its scholarship than for its interpretative criticism.

Tillyard's book on the problem plays is less satisfying than his earlier criticism. Few will agree with his view that *Hamlet* lacks an important tragic ingredient, the "renewal consequent upon destruction". In his interesting chapter on *Troilus and Cressida* Tillyard makes too much of Hector's vices, because he is led astray by the sources; and though one may agree that it is not "an outburst of unrestrained bitterness against life", it is difficult to see why Shakespeare, had he been really bitter, "would have been glad to see Cressida making Troilus suffer". Tillyard is at his best on *All's Well that Ends Well*, a play on which few critics have had anything illuminating to say. He does not fully share the modern admiration for *Measure for Measure*, and he complains that the second half of the play (after III, i, 151) is on a lower level, both poetically and dramatically, than the first half. It may be argued, however, that the last scene of the play, regarded by Tillyard as a failure, is one of the most moving scenes in the canon. It contains comparatively little detachable poetry, it is true, but the effect of the action itself is poetical in the highest degree.

With Levin L. Schücking we have the historical approach in its purest and simplest form. He is mainly concerned with the survival of primitive technique in Shakespeare's plays, and his criticism, unlike Stoll's, is entirely negative. In *Character Problems in Shakespeare's Plays* (1919, translated 1922) he argues that Shakespeare was fettered by his plots; that the mixture of tragedy and comedy often destroys the illusion; that "one might as well to-day interrupt the performance by reading the latest edition of the evening papers to the audience", as insert the Porter's speech in *Macbeth*; that the multitudinous scenes in *Antony and Cleopatra* exhibit a primitive technique; and that such scenes as the blinding of Gloucester show that Shakespeare unwisely imitated atrocities from earlier dramas. Schücking believes that the Cleopatra with immortal longings is a totally different character from the strumpet of the early scenes; that Lear in his madness does not acquire wisdom by the purgation of suffering—he merely conforms to the melancholic type; and, indeed, that Shakespeare frequently sacrificed character to the demands of the plot. Characters frequently explain themselves to the audience in a way that is unnatural; villains announce their villainy, whereas in real life they would either think of themselves as good fellows or else offer excuses for their conduct; Miranda, a child of nature, talks self-consciously about her chastity; and the device Shakespeare employs to emphasize Cordelia's goodness has the effect for the modern reader of making her sound complacent.

There is certainly some truth in Schücking's theory of 'direct self-explanation', and it has the merit of explaining away certain difficulties, such as Prince Hal's first soliloquy. But many of his examples of 'primitive' technique can be interpreted in other ways. Certainly Shakespeare was unrealistic in his presentation of character, but he was hardly ever in the last resort untrue to life; and we can see from the cavalier way in which he altered his plots to suit his poetic conception (e.g. *King Lear*) that he was not bound by them in the way that Schücking suggests. It is only fair to say that in his later books, *The Meaning of Hamlet* (1937) and *Shakespeare und der Tragödienstil seiner Zeit* (1947), and in his British Academy lecture (1938) Schücking seems to recognize that Shakespeare transformed the conventions he inherited; but he still fails to realize the positive and liberating merits of the dramatic conventions which were developed by the greater dramatists of the time.

Muriel C. Bradbrook has written two books which betray the influence of Stoll and Schücking, but she has a surer critical instinct than either of her predecessors. Although she points out that

writers of appreciative criticism who neglect the historic approach are liable to blunder on questions of tone; to mistake conventions for faults, to rationalise an illogical custom of the theatre, or to miss the point of a device:

she is nevertheless aware that

the proof and test of Shakespeare's genius lie precisely in that he hardly ever bowed to a single exigency, or utilised a single stage device without making it an integral part of the play; so that of both necessities and conveniences he makes virtues.

In *Elizabethan Stage Conditions* she tried to cover too much ground, but she adapted Stoll for her own purposes and extracted the truth that lies imbedded in Schücking's too rigid formulations.

Her second book, *Themes and Conventions of Elizabethan Tragedy*, is indispensable to an under-standing of Shakespeare and his contemporaries. *The School of Night* contains an interesting chapter on *Love's Labour's Lost*, which should be read in conjunction with Frances Yates's *Study* of the play. Both critics throw a good deal of light on topical allusions in the play, even though the existence of an actual School of Night depends on a dubious reading. Miss Bradbrook's later essay on *Measure for Measure* (*Review of English Studies*, XVII (October 1941), 385–99) treats it as a morality play.

Alfred Harbage's *As They Liked It* (1947) contains some useful criticism of the historical approach, but he displays an excessive tolerance when he suggests that a critic may see almost anything he likes in Shakespeare. His main theme, which takes us back to Moulton and Bridges, though Harbage wears his rue with a difference, is the morality of Shakespeare's plays. He shows that the poet was primarily an entertainer; that he provided morality, but no moralizing; that he keeps to the highroad which leads us back to where we were—the normal moral views of mankind; and that he gives "homely truth a wonderful, a beautiful investiture". We may doubt whether much can be learnt from the percentages Harbage gives of the good and bad people in the plays.

S. L. Bethell's *Shakespeare and the Popular Dramatic Tradition* (1944) shows the influence of Schücking and Bradbrook in its treatment of conventions, but his book contains an interesting analysis of the psychology of the popular audience, with illustrations drawn from the cinema as well as from Elizabethan drama. He argues that an audience possesses multi-consciousness, so that it can react to a speech or scene in several different ways at once, and so that a dramatist can fluctuate easily between conventionalism and naturalism. This theory enables Bethell to put forward a valuable defence of anachronisms and topical allusions, and to argue that Shakespeare used allegory and symbolism in his character-presentation. Much of what Bethell has to say is excellent, but in a few places readers may think that he tends to impose his own theological views on Shakespeare, even though one is prepared to admit that Shakespeare was nearer in his views to the modern High Churchman than to the modern agnostic. It may also be doubted whether an Elizabethan audience was continually conscious, during a performance of a play, that the actors were only pretending. When Cleopatra expresses her fear that the comedians will boy her greatness in the posture of a whore the reference to acting was not inserted to shatter the illusion, but rather to reinforce it; and it may be doubted whether the passage implies (as Bethell suggests) a 'critically detached' audience. Bethell's study of *The Winter's Tale* (1947) applies his theories to a single play; once again he has many true things to say, together with a number of remarks which are liable to arouse the reader's scepticism.

At the end of the period under review there have been signs of a reaction towards Bradley. J. I. M. Stewart, whose *Character and Motive in Shakespeare* (1949) has already been referred to, has written in this book the best defence of Shakespeare from the attacks of the 'realists'. He analyses with wit and perspicuity the work of three critics we have discussed here—Bridges, Stoll and Schücking—and though he admits that Bradley's work cannot continue to stand without qualification in face of such attacks, he claims by the help of psycho-analysis that Shakespeare had more insight into "the obscurer regions of man's being" than had been suspected. In other words, he believes that the apparent inconsistencies in Shakespeare's characters give them a psychological realism they would not otherwise have had, and that, on the other hand, "in poetic drama substantial human truth may be conveyed by means other than those of an entire psychological realism". He suggests, too, that the convention of the 'calumniator believed' may witness to

some central human disposition by which these are prompted and sustained....A convention, like a superstition, may represent a significant perception gone fossilised or inert. And to reanimate a convention, to strip it of sophistication so that its essence is again near the surface and working, is perhaps part of the instinct of the original artist.

Stewart's book has at times a Johnsonian common sense, at other times a practised ingenuity which sets the reader on his guard. His researches into morbid psychology are likely to lead to a counter-attack by Stoll; but it is only fair to say that he does not pretend to diagnose Shakespeare's characters; he merely uses text-book figures as warnings against the assumption that apparent inconsistency is untrue to life.

This section may fittingly conclude with a discussion of Harley Granville-Barker's work. As producer, actor and dramatist he had three valuable qualifications for the writing of his *Prefaces*, which developed out of his editing of the *Players Shakespeare*. The five series published between 1927 and 1947 contained studies of ten plays, but he also wrote one or two others which were never expanded or reprinted. Apart from these he wrote a lecture 'From *Henry V* to *Hamlet*', describing Shakespeare's transition from experiment to maturity, a volume *On Dramatic Method*, and an essay in *A Companion to Shakespeare Studies* which he edited with G. B. Harrison.

Granville-Barker's aim was to find the best method of presenting Shakespeare on the modern stage, with due regard to the technique and conventions of the Elizabethan stage, but also to the subtlest interpretations of Bradley and other critics, in order to advise a modern producer on the staging of the plays and on the acting of the parts. On the whole he succeeds brilliantly, and the improvement in stage productions of Shakespeare since 1910 is largely due to him. We may differ from him occasionally in the interpretation of certain scenes and characters, in his division of the play into two or three parts—instead of acts—and in his advice about cutting, but he provides the sort of detailed commentary most useful to the actor and producer. Not only would producers learn to avoid numerous mistakes by a study of these *Prefaces*, but most readers would derive an enhanced appreciation of Shakespeare's stage-craft.

He is at his best where Shakespeare is at his, as, for example, in his defence of the stage-worthiness of the storm scenes in *King Lear*, in his appreciation of the construction of *Antony and Cleopatra*, in his detailed analysis of Iago's temptation of Othello, and in much of the *Hamlet* preface, where he crosses swords with Dover Wilson. He is less successful in his treatment of *Love's Labour's Lost* and *Cymbeline*; he misses the charm of the one, and speaks of the other as the work of a wearied artist in collaboration, apparently, with another dramatist. These verdicts suggest that although Granville-Barker appreciated the main characteristics of Shakespeare's craftsmanship he did not understand that there is something to be said for the deliberate artificiality of the verse of the early plays and for the equally deliberate, though very different, conventionalism of *Cymbeline* and *The Winter's Tale*. It is true, of course, that in some ways Shakespeare was more 'realistic' in his greatest period. Here Granville-Barker was unduly influenced by the prevalent fashion of the modern theatre which has suicidally mislearnt the lesson of the poet, Ibsen. Bernard Shaw, indeed, doubted whether Granville-Barker was an ideal producer of Shakespeare—or of Shaw—because he was more at home with realistic plays. It may be a symptom of this that the first volume of *Prefaces* was dedicated to William Archer who had cheerfully assumed that modern dramatists were superior to the Elizabethans because they were more naturalistic, and who believed that poetry was an ornament of poetic drama, not its essence. Granville-Barker, it is true, displays a loving understanding of the music of the verse; he recognizes how necessary it is to speak the verse superbly; he has some fine remarks on the verse of *Coriolanus*; he even realizes the importance of the imagery; but he gives very little help to the actor who wishes to steer a course through the complexities and ambiguities of Shakespeare's mature style, and his treatment of character is trammelled by an unconscious preference for 'realism'. Yet if Granville-Barker's *Prefaces* might have been improved by the incorporation of the ideas of some of the critics we have been discussing, they are likely to remain unsurpassed in their kind; and, it may be added, they will always provide what may be a necessary antidote to the excesses of symbolic criticism.

IMAGERY, SYMBOLISM, AND THE LIBERTY OF INTERPRETING

The year 1930 was a decisive one in Shakespearian criticism, as it saw the publication of the first systematic studies of his imagery and symbolism. There had, indeed, been a pioneer work by Walter Whiter published in 1794 under the deceptive title of *A Specimen of a Commentary*; but this made little stir, and the second edition, prepared by the author, has had to wait 150 years for publication.[4] Dowden had some interesting remarks on the prevalence of blood in *Macbeth*, and Bradley referred to the animal imagery in *King Lear*. More recently E. E. Kellett discussed concealed puns and iterative images, not knowing that Whiter had forestalled him, in an essay in *Suggestions* (1923), and George Rylands touched on the subject in *Words and Poetry* (1928), a book devoted to the development of Shakespeare's style. Una Ellis-Fermor, in her pamphlet on *Some Recent Research in Shakespeare's Imagery* (1937), mentions several other pioneers in this field: T. Hilding Svartengren's *Intensifying Similes in English* (1918), Henry W. Wells's *Poetic Imagery* (1924), Stephen J. Brown's *The World of Imagery* (1927) and Elizabeth Holmes's *Aspects of Elizabethan Imagery* (1929). Miss Ellis-Fermor herself has attempted to produce a synthesis of the work of such critics as Spurgeon, Clemen and Knight in the pamphlet mentioned, in her inaugural lecture (1947) and in a chapter in *The Frontiers of Drama* (1945). Another chapter in the same book, on *Troilus and Cressida*, and one in *Jacobean Drama* (1936) on Shakespeare's final period show her using the new criticism for her own ends.

In 1930 appeared a group of interesting books: F. C. Kolbe's *Shakespeare's Way*, William Empson's *Seven Types of Ambiguity*, Caroline Spurgeon's *Leading Motives in the Imagery of Shakespeare's Tragedies* and the first of G. Wilson Knight's books. Of the four Kolbe is the most mechanical and therefore the least valuable. His book is not concerned with images, but rather with the iteration of individual words. He estimates, for example, that in *Macbeth* 'blood', 'sleep' and 'night' occur 70–100 times each, and that the opposition of 'sin' and 'grace' occurs no less than 400 times. Such mathematical methods are not likely to do more than confirm the idea of the play that is generally held. But occasionally Kolbe is illuminating. The fact that 'counterfeit' or its equivalent is used 120 times in *Much Ado about Nothing* really throws light on the play, and reveals a connexion between the two plots which might not otherwise have been recognized.

Empson draws many of his illustrations from Shakespeare's plays and sonnets, and he has since written on the dog symbolism in *Timon of Athens*, on the reiteration of 'honest' in *Othello*, and brilliantly on the Fool in *King Lear*—an essay which may be compared with Enid Welsford's chapter in *The Fool*. Empson is ingenious and subtle, though he sometimes seems to forget that Shakespeare was, on one level, a popular playwright. He sometimes increases our appreciation of the 'texture' and complexity of Shakespeare's poetry, even though there may be a danger of missing the whole by a microscopic attention to detail. Another book which may be mentioned in this connexion is Edith Sitwell's *Notebook on William Shakespeare* (1948). This is partly concerned with 'texture' in a rather different sense—the manipulation of vowels and consonants to achieve particular sound-effects—but the book contains some eccentric as well as some profound observations on most of the plays.

Caroline Spurgeon followed up two pamphlets with a major work on the subject, the fruit of ten years' research. It was entitled *Shakespeare's Imagery and What it Tells us* (1935). Previous work on imagery has been selective and subjective; Miss Spurgeon made an heroic effort to be objective and inclusive. She not only tabulated all Shakespeare's images, but also a representative selection of those of the major Elizabethan and Jacobean dramatists. She sought to show that the subjects from which the images are drawn provide a clue to the 'furniture' of the poet's mind, "the channels of his thought, the qualities of things, the objects and incidents he observes and remembers, and perhaps most significant of all, those which he does not observe and remember". She shows that "each writer has a certain range of images which are characteristic of him". The validity of this method of studying imagery has been questioned by Rosemond Tuve in *Elizabethan and Metaphysical Imagery* (1947); and certainly the evidence that Spurgeon educed about Shakespeare the man tells us little we had not already assumed without her help. Her suggestions, moreover, that Shakespeare must have been agile because he admired agility, and apt to blush easily because he often noted this peculiarity, are not likely to win general acceptance. More valuable is the analysis of image-clusters, as of the famous flatterers-dogs-sweets one, noted by Whiter years before. The presence of such a cluster in a doubtful play would go far to proving Shakespeare's authorship; but it was left to Edward A. Armstrong to investigate, in *Shakespeare's Imagination* (1946), a substantial number of these clusters, all connected with birds. As Armstrong is himself an ornithologist it makes one suspect that there are dozens of other clusters waiting to be discovered by experts in other fields.

Caroline Spurgeon's most valuable discovery is that of the presence of what she calls iterative imagery in all Shakespeare's mature work, the presence, that is, of a characteristic image, or series of images, repeated many times, such as the kitchen and sickness imagery of *Troilus and Cressida* and the ill-fitting garments in *Macbeth*. These iterative images can be used to reveal what was Shakespeare's conception, conscious or unconscious, of his own plays, though there is plenty of room for disagreement about the actual interpretation of the images so tabulated. There is, for example, disagreement about the interpretation of the sickness imagery in *Hamlet*, and Cleanth Brooks in *The Well Wrought Urn* (1947, English edition, 1949) interprets the *Macbeth* imagery in a different way from Caroline Spurgeon. Reference may also be made to the examination of the time theme in the same play by Middleton Murry (in his *Shakespeare*) and by Stephen Spender in *Penguin New Writing*, No. 3. Caroline Spurgeon's comprehensive classification, which deliberately excludes aesthetic evaluation, was a necessary first step; but it must be recognized that a casual and conventional simile will probably be less revealing than an original and striking metaphor. It was pointed out some years ago (*Penguin New Writing*, No. 28, pp. 114–15) that by confining herself to one or two dominating images Miss Spurgeon was apt to over-simplify the plays. Not unless the imagery is studied in relation to other factors—plot, character, symbolism, iteration of words—are we likely to reach a satisfactory conception of a play. Wilson Knight, though less 'scientific' than Miss Spurgeon, has the great merit of not abstracting the imagery from the totality of the play, and there have been several attempts by recent critics to provide a detailed analysis of the imagery of individual plays, including Richard Altick's excellent essay on *Richard II* (*PMLA*, 1947) and R. B. Heilman's more ambitious book on *King Lear* which is discussed below.

These criticisms of Caroline Spurgeon's work are not intended to minimize the great value of what she accomplished, and it was a loss to Shakespearian scholarship that she did not live to complete her projected volumes. One thing that her method cannot do is to provide a short cut to the understanding of Shakespeare, and it is to be feared that, if in the hands of good critics the study of imagery will prove fruitful and illuminating, in the hands of critics not endowed by nature with tact and understanding it will merely become a new method of boring the reader and leading him away from the play as a poetic and dramatic experience.

Wolfgang Clemen's *Shakespeares Bilder, ihre Entwicklung und ihre Funktionen im dramatischen Werk* (1936) is a study of imagery from a rather different angle. He insists that Shakespeare's images are dramatic in intention, and attempts

to interpret the development of this particular aspect of his art in terms of the whole development of the poet and, from the different use of images in successive periods of his creative work, to show how the style and methods of expression grew, developed and changed.[5]

He shows how in Shakespeare's first period the imagery is inorganic and ornamental, how in the second period meaning and metaphor were fused so that the inmost thoughts of the characters and Shakespeare's deepest insights came to be formulated in imagery, and how in the final period metaphors were expanded into plots. Clemen shows also that character is differentiated by means of imagery, a subject on which Caroline Spurgeon also touched. Unlike her, he distinguishes between essential and inessential imagery, and this means (as Miss Ellis-Fermor points out) that his book is more subjective than that of his predecessor. He is not concerned with the subject-matter of the imagery, but with its quality and functions, and its relationship to its setting. Each image is spoken at a given moment, in a particular situation and by a particular character; so that "each image is like a cell in the organisation of the play and is united to it in many ways". This is a valuable book, and an English edition of it is shortly to appear.

The interpretative criticism of G. Wilson Knight has aroused violent antipathies ever since it began to appear some twenty years ago, but it has also had a direct or indirect influence on other critics, including some of the best. Knight himself has expressed indebtedness to Colin Still's interpretation of *The Tempest*, entitled *Shakespeare's Mystery Play* (1921), which interprets that play in esoteric and allegorical terms, and also to the early work of J. Middleton Murry. Murry's essays on Shakespeare in *Countries of the Mind* and *Discoveries*, together with his two books on Keats, had made one hope that he would produce the best Romantic criticism of our generation, but his *Shakespeare* (1935) turned out to be something of a disappointment. It is a badly planned book, consisting of a series of essays of very unequal merit, so that one obtains comments on individual plays rather than a comprehensive view of Shakespeare as a whole. Those parts of the book which discuss Shakespeare's character, and particularly the embarrassing epilogue, are infected with sentimentality. Yet his main thesis, developed from Keats's dictum that Shakespeare possessed "negative capability", is on the right lines, and he has an interesting expansion of Keats's and Bradley's notion that only Hamlet, of all Shakespeare's characters, could have written the plays. Some of the chapters could hardly be bettered. There is, for example, a fine defence of *The Merchant of Venice* against Quiller-Couch's strictures; there are excellent chapters on the problem comedies, *Macbeth* and *Antony and Cleopatra*. Scattered through the other chapters are magnificent passages, such as the ones on the significance of Desdemona's handkerchief, and on the verse of the final plays. Murry's weaker side can be seen in his refusal to discuss *Troilus and Cressida* and in his remarks on *King Lear*. He believes, in spite of Keats, that this play is inferior to *Coriolanus*. He claims that *Coriolanus* is warm and human, *King Lear* cold and inhuman, an 'artefact' in which the imagination is strained and the verse spasmodic, and yet unwholesome and obsessed—perhaps, he suggests, Shakespeare's "deliberate prophylactic against his own incoherence". Murry's view on *Coriolanus* may be affected by his previous rehabilitation of Virgilia by ingenious textual improvements, but we must assume that there is some inhibition that prevents him from appreciating *King Lear*. Perhaps he recognizes the terror of the play and, believing with Keats that Shakespeare led a life of allegory, his works being the comments on it, he finds it intolerable to suppose that *King Lear* and *Timon of Athens* were reflexions of the poet's own experience. Murry elsewhere confesses that he once averted his eyes from the Crucifixion, and so he concludes that *King Lear* was manufactured rather than experienced. Yet Murry, especially before he became a political philosopher, was often a critic of penetrating, if intermittent, insight; and the best chapters of this book, together with his essays in *Countries of the Mind* on North's translation of Plutarch and on metaphor only make one regret that he has never concentrated his powers to produce a really great book on Shakespeare.

Knight, then, derived a few hints from Murry's early work, and though he has sometimes been regarded as an iconoclast, an upsetter of the Bradley tradition, he tells us in the enlarged edition of *The Wheel of Fire* (1949) that he first defined his own aims as "the application to Shakespeare's work in general of the methods applied by Bradley to certain outstanding plays"; and he hopes that his "own labours will be regarded as a natural development within the classic tradition of Shakespearian study". It is true that his interpretations place less emphasis on character than Bradley did, and more on 'symbolic overtone' and atmosphere; but his essays *are* concerned with character within the framework of the plays, as one might expect from his experience as actor and producer and his volume devoted to *Principles of Shakespeare Production*.

The Wheel of Fire appeared originally in 1930, with an introduction by T. S. Eliot, and was followed by three other substantial volumes on Shakespeare: *The Imperial Theme, The Shakespearian Tempest* and *The Crown of Life* (1947). In a preliminary essay Knight deprecates the maxim that a work of art should be criticized according to the artist's intentions or explained by reference to the sources; he claims, that is, the full liberty of interpretation outlined by Abercrombie, with all the dangers implied in it. He attacks an unduly ethical criticism of character which is apt, as with *Antony and Cleopatra*, to conflict with poetic appreciation.

Then he lays down four main principles of interpretation: first, that we should "regard each play as a visionary unit bound to obey none but its own self-imposed laws"; secondly, that we should be prepared "to relate any given incident or speech either to the time sequence of story or the peculiar atmosphere, intellectual or imaginative, which binds the play"; thirdly, "we should analyse the use and meaning of direct poetic symbolism"; and fourthly, we should relate each play to its place in the significant sequence of the plays written between 1599 and 1611. A distinction must be drawn between Knight's method, which has been fruitful, and his particular applications of the method, which are not always satisfying. Some have doubted whether the Elizabethans, and even Shakespeare himself, would have understood these four principles; but even if this could be proved, Knight would argue that it did not follow that the analysis of poetic symbolism was an illegitimate method of interpretation, for a poetic conception might be unconsciously expressed in terms of symbols. Knight at least demonstrates that Shakespeare, whether consciously or unconsciously, used tempests and music as symbols of discord and concord, hatred and love.

Perhaps the strongest argument for the validity of Knight's methods is the fact that he has genuinely increased our understanding of certain plays which had baffled critics who had approached them by earlier methods. After his essays on *Timon of Athens* and *Troilus and Cressida* no serious critic is likely to write off those plays as failures, even though they may not agree with Knight's own interpretation. He has done more than anyone else to justify the methods employed by Shakespeare in the plays of the final period, and the 'transcendental humanism' he discovers in *Antony and Cleopatra* would seem to be closer to Shakespeare's conception than 'the world ill lost' of Henry Morley and Quiller-Couch. Perhaps the best example of Knight's method in *The Wheel of Fire* is the essay on *Measure for Measure*. It has been treated as a cynical and unpleasant play; the happy ending has been regarded as an example of the way Shakespeare the popular playwright made concessions to the groundlings; the Duke has been blamed for his irresponsible conduct; and the pardoning of Angelo has been variously lamented. Knight by interpreting the play by means of the Gospels and by treating it as a dramatic parable has, though he was unwittingly following in the footsteps of Pater, immeasurably increased our understanding of it. He published his interpretation before those of R. W. Chambers, Muriel Bradbrook, Middleton Murry, J. C. Maxwell, Roy Battenhouse, Elizabeth Pope and Reimer, who have all stressed the Christian element in the play. Knight deserves the credit for being first in the field, even if we have to qualify his harsh verdict on Isabella by reference to Chambers and Maxwell. This verdict may be explained by Knight's belief that the Elizabethans were less competent than ourselves to understand Shakespeare and by his conviction that both religion and philosophy should be subsumed under poetic wisdom.

Another example of Knight's positive qualities is afforded by his chapter on *The Winter's Tale* in *The Crown of Life*, which brings out the poetic unity of the play and contains a satisfying defence of the 'resurrection' of Hermione. On the other hand, as I have mentioned elsewhere, Knight's interpretation of *Hamlet*—even as it is qualified in the second edition of *The Wheel of Fire*—does not altogether correspond with the impression we get of the play from reading or performance, and it is difficult to agree with his accounts of Macbeth's development, especially the brief one given in *Christ and Nietzsche* (1948).

There are certain obstacles to the enjoyment of Knight's books. His originality sometimes turns to eccentricity; he is not always alive to aesthetic values, and one has the feeling that he might praise a minor poet above his deserts if only he manipulated symbols with reasonable competence; he claims the right to find meanings in the plays which could hardly have occurred to the poet; and though he formally allows the possibility of other kinds of criticism he believes in the subordination of scholarship to interpretation. Scholars for their part have often regarded his books with suspicion, and we get the urbane Charlton expressing his irritation with those who regard Shakespeare's men and women "as plastic symbols in an arabesque of esoteric imagery", though this phrase is surely a palpable distortion of Knight's methods and intentions.

L. C. Knights belongs partly to the School of Knight, though he is less prolific, less original, and more critical. In 'How many Children had Lady Macbeth?' (1933), reprinted with other essays in *Explorations* (1946), he attacks Bradley's method of concentrating on the characters of Shakespeare's plays. He remarks that

to stress in the conventional ways character or plot or any of the other abstractions that can be made, is to impoverish the total response....Losing sight of the *whole* dramatic pattern of each play, we inhibit the development of that full complex response that makes our experience of a Shakespeare play so very much more than an appreciation of 'character'.

Knights argues that "we start with so many lines of verse on a printed page", and that we have to unravel ambiguities, give full consideration to the imagery, and "allow full weight to each word, exploring its 'tentacular roots'". There is no doubt much truth in this, though to start with words on a printed page rather than with scenes performed on a stage is not without dangers. Knights's own critique on *Macbeth* is an admirable analysis of the play, owing something, as he freely admits, to Wilson Knight's early books. He shows the function and value of certain scenes that have been regarded as spurious or dull, and he corrects Bradley's mistake of supposing that because Macbeth continues to utter great poetry he is never entirely ruined. In a later essay, 'Prince Hamlet', Knights complains that many readers identify themselves with the hero, and so obtain "an indulgence for some of [their] most cherished weaknesses". They fail to realize that Hamlet is neurotic and immature, that he desires "to escape from the complexities of adult living", and perhaps that he has not been entirely 'objectified' by the poet. This essay is a useful corrective to the sentimentalists, but it seems rather to ignore the unlucky situation in which Hamlet found himself, one which might well make cowards of us all. An essay on the Sonnets (1934), also included in *Explorations*, is admirable. His 'Notes on Comedy' in *Determinations* are mainly concerned with Falstaff's dramatic function.

It will have been observed, perhaps, that Knights has also been influenced by Empson, Eliot and Leavis. Eliot, the most reputable modern critic, has published little on Shakespeare, and that little is not on the level of his best work. His main concern has been to establish the difference between realistic drama and poetic drama, and to stress the element of ritual in all serious dramatic writing. In certain respects he links up with Robertson and Stoll rather than with the critics discussed in this section, yet he appeared in the guise of introducer of both Knight and Bethell. His brief essay on *Hamlet*, in which he speaks of the play as an 'undoubted failure', no longer represents his views; and it may be retorted that even if the play is "full of some stuff that the writer could not drag to light, contemplate, or manipulate into art", some of the greatest works of art have skeletons in their cupboards. The essay is perhaps worth preserving for its use of the term 'objective correlative'. The essays on 'Shakespeare and the Stoicism of Seneca' and 'Seneca in Elizabethan Translation' open up several lines of inquiry. It is surprising that Cunliffe's pioneer work on *The Influence of Seneca* has never been properly followed up, though Hardin Craig has a valuable essay entitled 'The Shackling of Accidents' (*Philological Quarterly*, XIX (January 1940), 1–19); meanwhile Eliot has tried, as he dryly remarks, "to disinfect the Senecan Shakespeare before he appears", though not all will agree with his interpretation of Othello's last speech as 'Bovaryism' or self-deception, even though Eliot has found support from F. R. Leavis (*Scrutiny*, December 1937). Eliot's other essays, including those on Elizabethan dramatists, contain some shrewd comments on Shakespeare and on the nature of poetic drama. He has done much by his own practice as a poet as well as by his essays to reawaken interest in Elizabethan drama, and on a more mature level than that which obtained in the nineteenth century under the influence of Lamb's *Specimens* and Swinburne's eulogies, for Eliot stressed the fact that poetic passages must not be detached from their context.

Leavis has himself written little about Shakespeare, though his method of detailed analysis in *How to Teach Reading* and elsewhere has been followed by several of the contributors to *Scrutiny*. Of these may be mentioned James Smith (*As You Like It* and *Much Ado*), J. C. Maxwell (*Timon*), F. C. Tinkler (*Cymbeline* and *Winter's Tale*), A. A. Stephenson (*Cymbeline*) and D. A. Traversi, who has written studies of six plays (*Coriolanus, Troilus and Cressida, Tempest, Henry IV, Measure for Measure* and *Winter's Tale*) in addition to his *Approach to Shakespeare* (1938). Traversi is perhaps too sanguine in his belief that his method, which is that of his fellow-Scrutineers, of starting with the *word*, enables the critic to correct his own partiality. But although no critical method guarantees immunity from error there is no doubt that this particular method has produced, in the right hands, some good criticism.

Roy Walker owes something to Knight and something to Murry, though his own books have plenty of originality. He has written detailed studies of two of Shakespeare's tragedies. *The Time is out of joint* (1948) is partly a development of Max Plowman's theory that *Hamlet* is a study of "moral man in an immoral society", and Walker argues that only in his weaker moments did Hamlet "conceive his duty to be no more than the murder of his uncle", and that in the last act of the play he resolved the dilemma with which he was confronted—inaction or violence. We have met the 'pacifist' Hamlet before, but Walker faces the difficulties more squarely than those who have previously held the view, and he does not turn a blind eye to other aspects of the play. Even those who do not find the book wholly convincing, if only because there was nothing to prevent Shakespeare from making the theme more explicit, must admit, with *The Malcontent* and *Measure for Measure* in mind, that we should be rash to assume that Shakespeare could not have been concerned with the ethics of vengeance. It is more satisfying, at least, than the studies of Clutton-Brock, Santayana, Madariaga and C. S. Lewis. Walker's companion study, *The Time is Free* (1949), depicts Macbeth as immoral man in a moral society, and there is hardly a scene in the play which he does not illuminate by his commentary. Occasionally he is wilful and eccentric, as when he suggests that Hecate was intended to be a sort of projection of Lady Macbeth; but his defence of the authenticity of the opening scenes, his demonstration of numerous Biblical echoes, and his brilliant analysis of Angus's speech in the third scene of the play are only a few of the points which will come to be generally accepted as necessary to the complete understanding of the play.

Two recent books on *King Lear* may fitly close this section. John F. Danby's *Shakespeare's Doctrine of Nature* (1949) is an interesting book on the two doctrines of nature which, he argues, were dramatized by Shakespeare in the play—the orthodox view of Hooker and Bacon, which is held by the good characters in the play, and what was to be the Hobbesian assumption that man is governed entirely by appetite and self-interest, which is held by the villains. Danby holds clearly defined religious and political views; as I share them, I may not be a good judge of the extent to which he sometimes forces the evidence to fit in with his theories. Some readers will feel that he over-stresses the allegorical element in the play, but there are few who will not have their appreciation heightened by a fine chapter on the Fool, and indeed by many other passages which reveal genuine insight.

R. B. Heilman's *This Great Stage* (1948) is also valuable. It is a long and detailed inquiry into the imagery and structure of *King Lear*. The author discusses all the closely linked themes of the play as they are expressed in images and recurrences—those linked with the idea that Gloucester stumbled when he saw, those concerned with clothes and nakedness, the animal in man, reason in madness, madness in reason, and several more. The distinction of Heilman's book, which I believe has been undervalued by several reviewers, lies in its sanity, its comprehensiveness, and its integration of several kinds of Shakespearian criticism.

Conclusion

There has been a great advance in Shakespearian scholarship during the past fifty years, and this has been reflected, if not always sufficiently, in the criticism of the period. The yearly flood of Shakespeariana submerges all but the strongest swimmers and makes it increasingly difficult to see Shakespeare steadily, and see him whole. The interpretative critics rarely satisfy the scholars, and the scholars are sometimes regarded by the critics as dealers in the inessential— though, of course, scholars have made welcome incursions into the field of criticism.

It is rather surprising that so much remains to be done. There is, for example, no comprehensive book on Shakespeare's treatment of sources, no recent and satisfactory account of what Shakespeare owed to his immediate predecessors, and no good books on such outstanding contemporaries as Chapman and Middleton. We may hope that these gaps will be filled during the next few years. But perhaps the most useful direction which Shakespeare criticism could take during the next generation is towards a synthesis of existing methods. The study of character, plot, imagery, symbolism, stage conventions and language, though all legitimate methods, would gain enormously by being used together. This is a consummation devoutly to be wished, but unlikely to be achieved.

NOTES

1. Recent French criticism is discussed by Henri Fluchère in *Shakespeare Survey*, 2. There is a brief account of contemporary Russian criticism in Mikhail Morozov's *Shakespeare on the Soviet Stage* (1947).

2. The story of the disturbance of this orthodoxy is brilliantly told by F. P. Wilson in *Studies in Retrospect* (1945).

3. The numerous articles on the authenticity of certain scenes in *Sir Thomas More* are considered by R. C. Bald in *Shakespeare Survey*, 2.

4. It is now being edited by G. A. Over.

5. Translated by U. Ellis-Fermor in *Some Recent Research*.

MOTIVATION IN SHAKESPEARE'S
CHOICE OF MATERIALS

BY

HARDIN CRAIG

The field of study which I propose for consideration has to do with Shakespeare's plots in two aspects, the general and the detailed. When he utters the familiar lines in *A Midsummer Night's Dream*,

> And as imagination bodies forth
> The forms of things unknown, the poet's pen
> Turns them to shapes and gives to airy nothing
> A local habitation and a name,

he gives a perfect description of the most fundamental operation of the human mind. As the possessor of one of the greatest minds on record, he is at the same time describing his own transcendent skill.

There is usually to be discovered in Shakespeare's plays a form or pattern, sometimes easily identified, sometimes not; sometimes apparently consciously developed, sometimes seemingly almost accidental. These are "the forms of things unknown". The power of determining forms, that is, of regarding as irrelevant all attending circumstances except a certain conceptual form that controls the complex of events, is the most characteristic mental trait of mankind, and in the recognition of significant form in any configuration presented to experience Shakespeare excelled. This operation is psychologically equivalent to the formation of concepts, and we may go further and say that, as soon as the concept is formed, the imagination takes it up, completes it, often amplifies it, gives it its environment, and makes of it a conception special to the mind of the thinker; let us say gives it "a local habitation and a name". There are thus two processes involved in the building up of a fully formed conception, namely, the abstractive ability which sees and grasps a central form and a later mental operation in which imagination adds to this concept the subsidiary details which complete the picture or the play.

There is no reason to think that these two operations were successive with Shakespeare or consciously discriminated. Indeed, the genesis of his plays no doubt presents a wide series of special circumstances. It may be that his interest in any particular subject was first aroused by some relatively minor feature of the plot, and there is, of course, no way of telling how it was; but, on the other hand, there is no doubt that the greatness of the greatest literature resides very largely in the treatment in detail of a central thought or concept. Let it be remembered that the artist does not invent the forms of things but discovers them as the scientist discovers facts and laws.

Let me illustrate this by a conjectural account, not without some plausibility, of Shakespeare's experience in the writing of *Measure for Measure*. He had read Whetstone's *Promos and Cassandra*, or, more probably, the tale on which it is based, and learned that Cassandra, who is represented as a faithful and virtuous woman, yielded to the base demands of Promos and sacrificed her honour in order to save her brother's life. Shakespeare, celebrated for his faith in the integrity of women, fresh from the depiction of Desdemona in *Othello*, and perhaps even then engaged in the delineation of Cordelia in *King Lear*, said to himself, "Cassandra would never have sacrificed her honour". So enraptured was he with his idea that he proceeded to represent what would actually happen if his heroine was a faithful and virtuous woman. With this concept in mind he proceeded to write for two acts and a part of one scene on the very highest level of his ability. At this point he found himself involved as a dramatist in serious difficulties and one can see evidence of his perplexity. Having to his own satisfaction rescued his heroine, how was he to save her brother's life, punish her would-be seducer, and, since this was to be a comedy, provide everybody with a matrimonial union at the end? Shakespeare in comedy never lets an eligible bachelor or a lonely maid escape. He bethought himself of the device of the bed trick he had used in *All's Well That Ends Well* and shamelessly used it over again. It served the purpose very well, but how did the Duke know about Mariana? His knowledge of Angelo's past behaviour and therefore of his base character is certainly a surprising thing for him now to know and does not agree at all with the high opinion which the Duke seems to have entertained about Angelo in the first act. Perhaps Shakespeare's major interest in the subject was exhausted. At any rate, he never wrote so well in the play again. He engages himself with a lot of not very original or successful satirical low comedy, and at the end, as a sort of confession of weakness, he resorts to theatrical intrigue, and ends the play with the usual pairing off of lovers, even marrying off Isabella to the Duke without, so to speak, asking her consent, since she is at least unexpectedly silent.

Shakespeare inherited from his sources many stories whose significance lies in their unity. They had already been selected and told because of their embodiment of some striking concept. The story of Antony and Cleopatra, for example, had rested for ages on the concept of an empire lost through the sin of lust. The story of Romeo and Juliet came to Shakespeare complete in its members; the pattern is the tragic conflict between age with its prudence and prejudice and youth with its impetuosity, so that it was and had been impossible to tell that story badly from Xenophon of Ephesus to Shakespeare. The story of Marlowe's *Dr Faustus* is also of this naturally unified sort. Plutarch was a master in the production of significant unity, and the English chronicles by the time they reached Holinshed had been, so to speak, well abstracted. They had been reworked along the lines of classical historiography, and most of the stories of English kings, at the hands of Polydore Vergil, Sir Thomas More, the authors of *The Mirror for Magistrates*, and others, had come to present certain moral abstractions. A good many of Shakespeare's subjects were, so to speak, pre-digested, but it is hardly necessary to add that he was not dependent, as *Othello* shows, on such pre-workings of his plots.

The Renaissance inherited a belief that human behaviour is characterized by universality and that a particular line of conduct repeats itself in pattern. Historical records were thus looked upon as mirrors in which men might see reflexions of themselves as individuals and of the states and societies around them. Such books as John Barclay's *The Mirrour of Mindes*, Thomas Wright's *The Passions of the Minde in Generall*, and Pierre de la Primaudaye's *The French Academie* differentiated the people of various nations, classified the passions, the described types of conduct. The doctrine of elements and humours, fundamental to the physiology and psychology of the time, provided a 'scientific' basis for these stereotyped treatises, and similitudes, such as those found in the explanations of the microcosm and the macrocosm, perpetuated modes of expression and modes of thought.[1] The learning of the past, acquired in grammar school, was put to use in writing without thought of plagiarism. Indeed, the whole theory and practice of composition was based on the teaching of the art of copiousness or amplification of already existent themes with already existent matter. Repetition of thought and imagery is inseparable from the concept of the universality of man, and the idea is not false. Men are still similar organisms that mirror, by and large, pretty much the same environment, and the similarities of men are still far greater than their differences. Shakespeare did not reject this fundamental idea of his age, and his greatness consists largely in the perfection with which he expresses the concept of the universality of man. As to the literary method which his indoctrination in school and the custom of his age forced upon him, that too is not out of line with the creation of great literature and great art. It is interesting to note that Poe acknowledges the virtue of Shakespeare's practice[2] when he says "to originate is carefully, patiently, and understandingly to combine".

This method of operation seems to have been taken for granted by Sidney and by Shakespeare himself, and neither has any suggestion that stories may be invented by poets, although they both have something to say about the improvement or betterment of nature at the poet's hands. They both proceed on the basis of an established body of material. In Sidney's *The Defence of Poesie*, the poet and the historian are, as regards their subject-matter, on exactly the same basis. What distinguishes them are certain liberties allowed to the poet. He says:

So, then, the best of the historian is subject to the poet; for, whatsoever action or faction, whatsoever counsel, policy, or war stratagem the historian is bound to recite, that may the poet, if he list, with his imitation make his own, beautifying it both for further teaching and more delighting, as it please him; having all, from Dante his heaven to his hell, under the authority of his pen.

To the Poet in *Timon of Athens* the poet's material is nature, and nature is plastic:

> My free drift
> Halts not particularly, but moves itself
> In a wide sea of wax; no levell'd malice
> Infects one comma in the course I hold,
> But flies an eagle-flight, bold, and forth on,
> Leaving no tract behind. (I, i, 45–50)

Certainly, in any case, there is little outright invention of plots and incidents in Elizabethan literature, whether drama or fiction. This is borne out by the notorious ransacking of the writings of the past and present by Elizabethan authors and confirmed by the long-continued practice of source-hunting by generations of scholars. As subjects for their plays Elizabethan dramatists hunted all over the world of literature. Nothing was safe from them. They found events and situations in the Bible, in folk-lore, in popular literature, and in local happenings. A favourite hunting ground was the Italian and French short story, itself an aggregate of historical or local event and of popular and traditional matters of all sorts. English dramatists used Plutarch, Livy, Virgil, Ovid, and casual history, story and mythology from other sources; particularly, they used the history and traditions of their own country as embodied in the chronicles.

Source-hunting practised industriously in the eighteenth, nineteenth, and twentieth centuries was and is a sound instinct and a natural and fruitful approach to the study of Elizabethan literature.

The trouble has been that those engaged in *Quellenuntersuchungen* have not known why they did it or have not known what to do with sources after they are found. Accounts of sources have been tucked away in the pages of learned journals and special studies, whence they have been available for mention, and for very little else, by editors of the works of Elizabethan authors. But the instinct was sound, because sources tend to furnish basal concepts. The age was *one* to a degree we can scarcely comprehend. To read one author is in some sense to read them all. Sources have an added importance in the age, because Elizabethan authors seem to have been unaware that incident could be invented, manufactured out of whole cloth or even the raw materials of whole cloth. This dependence on sources is true, even if it is only roughly true, and one can at least say that Elizabethan dramatists had no habit of inventing plots and apparently very slight tendency to invent incidents. Instead of inventing what they needed, they sought for it widely, and it may be said without derogation that from the point of view of plot-construction an Elizabethan play is built like a mosaic with varying skill and ingenuity in putting the parts together. In some instances the parts are collected from wide areas. In others, as in Shakespeare's history plays and in his plays derived from Plutarch, the immediate source itself was so well filled out that most of the necessary parts were close at hand. We shall have to do with the methods and principles apparently employed by Shakespeare in filling in his plots and fitting together various constituent elements. It is to be presumed that in most instances these filling-in operations were controlled by patterns.

When the necessary parts had been found, Elizabethan dramatists were set free. They were then in the region of amplification or copy, to the practice of which they had been trained in school. Amplification was their challenge, the test of their literary ability, and they met the challenge so well that there are few limits to their ingenuity. It is a remarkable fact that there are almost no plot elements in Shakespeare's plays for which some source, analogue or suggestion has not been found. The same is true of Greene, Lyly, Marlowe, Dekker, Heywood, Webster, Middleton, Jonson himself, and, so far as I know, of most of the rest. So true is this that when some incident or character for which no source has been found exists, one bears it in mind for years in the belief that somewhere a source or originating suggestion will be unearthed. There may yet be found an original for Malvolio in *Twelfth Night*, and I myself have at last found at least a suggestion for the sinful liaison between Edmund and the wicked daughters of Lear in *King Lear*.

A good deal of erroneous criticism of Elizabethan drama has come from the fact that this same invention of plots is in our time considered a primary characteristic of originality. Modern writers of fiction and drama are not, however, so wholly new as perhaps they think they are, since a limited body of themes and situations are in common currency in contemporary as well as in Elizabethan fiction and drama. Perhaps the Elizabethans, who supported their originality by means of a wide search, were the more varied of the two. It is, at any rate, an error to belittle Shakespeare's genius on the ground that he did not supply from some vague reservoir of general human experience such incidents as he might need to complete his patterns, but actually sought out and borrowed from definite places such incidents as he might need. In *Cymbeline*, for example, Shakespeare needed to get in princely fashion Guiderius and Arviragus, the lost sons of the King, back into the main action of the play, and he found the perfect means of doing this as far afield as Holinshed's *Chronicle of Scotland*, in which it is related of a Scottish husbandman named Haie how he and his sons, observing the dangerous approach of the Danish army, placed themselves in a sunken roadway and stayed the advance of the enemy; as Shakespeare puts it (v, iii, 52):

A narrow lane, an old man, and two boys.

Shakespeare's originality seems to have consisted in the selection of great significant patterns, in the discovery of incidents, in unequalled ingenuity in fitting parts together so that they reinforced one another, and in masterly skill in realistic amplification. It did not consist for some reason in the exercise of the facile modern ability to invent incidents.

Perhaps this apparent limitation of operation may be accounted for, in part at least, on the ground that to the Renaissance a basis of truth was always to be preferred to a basis of fiction. Authors liked to think that they were recording actual truth, and true stories were commended as such on title-pages. All authors seemed to feel secure when they were dealing with something that had actually happened. Truth was sufficiently strange and carried with it a greater weight of importance than fiction. Perhaps, indeed very probably, the very idea of outright invention had not occurred to them, had not been discovered.

This attitude of the acceptance only of that which already existed was in line with the philosophy of the age, which was pre-Baconian and pre-Cartesian. The mind of the age went backward toward a lost perfection and not forward toward unknown and unexploited novelty. The age believed in exploration in the hope of the discovery of the already existent. Everything that had been still existed for the guidance of humanity, and man must exert himself to find it; there was strictly nothing new under the sun. One would not apply this principle too strictly, for people were much as they are now, but one might use it safely to describe a tendency. It merely says that literary methods were governed by the same system of thought as were scientific methods.

Out of this discussion comes the idea that the significance of the pattern is a first consideration in the study of Shakespeare's work as a dramatist. One might say for this occasion that a pattern or design is something simpler and of wider general significance than is a plot. For example, the pattern of a morality play of the full-scope kind presents a central figure, symbolic of humanity, called Mankind or Humanum Genus, born with an ultimately irresistible compulsion to sin. This figure is tempted by error in the person of Satan (operating as Mundus, Caro et Diabolus, the Seven Deadly Sins, or a variety of Vitia) to leave the path of righteousness and follow a course or career of wickedness at the end of which he is convicted of sin and becomes a manifest candidate for damnation. He is, however, saved in the only possible way by the intercession of Christ, the Blessed Virgin Mary, or some kindly saint and is taken without merit of his own into the bosom of God. This simple pattern cannot disappear. It is seen in its pure form in *Dr Faustus* and *Macbeth*, except that in neither play does the element of intercession appear. The former has, however, so many morality features that it may certainly be regarded as a transitional document. All great literature subsists in some measure because of its bearing on man's salvation, and universality of scope with the appearance or absence of special application and situations serves as a sort of criterion. There are many such generalized works from *Pilgrim's Progress* to *The Egoist*. There is no attempt here to connect such works in a chain of conscious imitation, but only to claim that such works are recurrent. To this form of literature so conceived that a hero stands in some sense for all mankind, since his adventures and reactions are of the most general sort, *Macbeth* belongs. *Odyssey, Aeneid, Prometheus, Oedipus, Job,* and many of the greatest works of literature, modern as well as ancient, are also here. To do evil is to wander from the true way, to enter into a career of error and sin, to encounter some sort of retribution or punishment, and to end unhappily. Such seems to be the common judgement of humanity, and it matters not whether the force inciting to evil and ending in calamity is thought of as fate, the displeasure of the gods, or voluntary action under delusion or rebellion.

The oldest and as yet the best explanation of why men do this is that they are deluded, so that they mistake evil for good. There is a mystery about temptation and sin, as there is about love and other powerful human motives, and the oldest symbolization of that mystery is Satan and his angels—the devil, the evil one, imps, witches, and malign spirits—and it is to that conception that morality plays belong. The central figure, which represented mankind in the broadest possible way, passed, consciously or unconsciously, into romantic tragedy. *Macbeth* is such a case, and in such tragedies we necessarily find the two forms of thought described above, a concept and a conception or, we might say, a primary pattern and a completed drama. The story of Macbeth supplies what might be called the morality pattern. Shakespeare got it from the chronicles of Duncan and Macbeth in Holinshed's *Chronicle of Scotland*. There he got the figure of a great warrior, a loyal subject, and a man of normal human kindness. He is deluded by the emissaries of Satan, as truly as was Everyman, and entered upon and pursued a career of crime until he was overtaken and destroyed by the righteous judgement he had provoked.

But the Macbeth of the chronicles kills his king as an open rebel, and this was insufficient for Shakespeare's enlarged conception. In his dramatic treatment he demanded more particular motivations. Banquo belonged to the story of Macbeth and there were other parts supplied from it, but mainly Shakespeare resorted for amplification to the chronicle of King Duff. In that he found the story of Donwald, a man whom King Duff never suspected, who murdered King Duff in the castle of Forres. This deepens Macbeth's guilt, since in his own story he had been an open rebel against King Duncan, but the story of Donwald amplified the plot in another way. Having, with the aid of his wife, drugged the two chamberlains who lay with the King, Donwald, although he greatly abhorred the deed and did it only at the instigation of his wife, induced four of his servants to cut the King's throat. When morning came, he slew the chamberlains and cleared himself of the crime by his power and authority, though not without being suspected by certain noblemen because of his over-diligence. Thus from the chronicle of King Duff came Lady Macbeth and all that pertains to her. Shakespeare also laid many parts of his brilliant and spirited source under contribution. The voice of sleeplessness comes from the chronicle of King Kenneth, and it was only last year that a pupil of mine, A. L. Crabb, found in Holinshed a source for the pageant of the kings which was needed to form a connexion between the descendants of Banquo and King James I.

In the morality pattern of *Macbeth*, which has been amplified but not changed, we see the aberration of a hero, under delusion of the powers of evil, pursue a career of crime and wickedness, violent to the last degree and continued until such time as his course of evil was arrested. It is still the faith of men that such careers will eventually be arrested, and this faith was ardently held by Shakespeare and his age. Macbeth stands at the end the same man he was at the beginning, but weakened by his sins and confronted by outraged man acting as the punitive agent of God.

It will be recalled that he had always feared this recoil of human justice, but he is none the less a sinner in the hands of an angry God. His situation is not different from that of Mankind, or Everyman, or Humanum Genus. He is overthrown by an enemy his sins have created. Another way of saying this is that he is in the clutches of a tragic fate. Macduff, laden with wrongs and burning with the fire of righteous revenge, is the hand of fate, or God, or immutable justice. There is even in Macbeth a peripeteia not always recognized by critics. I said that Macbeth stands at the end the same man he was at the beginning. His state is weakened, but he sees what has happened to him and utters the perfect definition of evil, which is delusion:

> And be these juggling fiends no more believed,
> That palter with us in a double sense;
> That keep the word of promise to our ear,
> And break it to our hope.   (v, viii, 19–22)

Macbeth's last act is to resort to his word, and he dies as a man.

I have advanced a theory of Shakespeare's use of bits of truth which, under the guidance of significant concepts, he fitted together into significant and convincing wholes. Perhaps the clearest illustration I can give of this is to be drawn from *King Lear*. The old play which Shakespeare used as a source, *The True Chronicle History of King Leir, and his three Daughters, Gonorill, Ragan and Cordella*, is not a tragedy. It never threatens to be, and it is not tragic in tone or outcome. It contains villainy, and two wicked daughters plot the murder of their father, but they are easily thwarted. There are no deaths in the play. It has been customary to say that the very logic of Lear's errors, sufferings and disasters caused Shakespeare to give the drama of *King Lear* a tragic ending. I do not pretend to know how Shakespeare felt about it, and I do not deny the perfection of his tragic genius in writing and concluding the play as he did, and yet I have another and a different account of the matter to offer. There are certain circumstances which reveal in my judgement a more original movement of his thought and provide naturalistic reasons for his handling the story of Lear as he did.

The old *King Leir* was apparently a Queen's Company play which for some unexplained reason Shakespeare seems to have known very well indeed. One would like to think that Shakespeare had acted in it, since not only the Second Murderer in *Richard III*, but other bits in other plays seem to echo the old *King Leir*. It seems doubtful, however, whether he had the play actually at hand when he wrote *King Lear*. From the point of view of the old play the story is imperfectly retold by Shakespeare, and new invention takes the place of good and naturalistic devices in the old play. For one thing, Shakespeare, without apparent cause, inverts the roles of Cornwall and Albany (called Cambria in *King Leir*); likewise he gives to Goneril some acts and qualities which belong to Ragan in the old play and to Regan certain features which belong to Gonorill. These circumstances and some others seem to indicate that, although he knew the old play well, he worked on it from memory.

The True Chronicle History of King Leir is a rather bright and cheerful play. It furnished events for Shakespeare's *King Lear*, but it did not furnish tone, atmosphere, the deeper significances and the tragic concept. These came from the story of the "Paphlagonian unkinde King, and his kinde sonne" as narrated in the tenth chapter of the second book of Sidney's *Arcadia*. The story of the Paphlagonian king is tragic, that of the old King Leir is not. The concept or pattern of

Sidney's story is the tragic consequences of filial ingratitude. That concept is taken over from the *Arcadia* and applied to the Lear story. It is natural to conclude that the genesis of the tragedy of *King Lear* is to be found in the story of the blind king of Paphlagonia; that is, that the tragic possibilities of filial ingratitude came from the reading of *Arcadia* and not from familiarity with the old *King Leir*. Sidney furnishes active cruelty, filial ingratitude in a dreadful form, base deceit and dark intrigue. It furnishes the theme of hunted fugitives, exposure to storm, a cave of refuge (which may be the hovel), blindness, danger, destitution, and, more than all, the deepest possible reflexion on tragic folly and the worthlessness of miserable life. To be sure, there is in the old play the attempted murder of Leir and Perillus by the Messenger, but it is a poor thing compared even with Oswald's attempt on the life of Gloucester. Finally, in Sidney the prototype of Gloucester dies. In the case of *King Lear*, Shakespeare through the influence of *Arcadia* becomes bound by the conventions of tragedy just as in the writing of *Measure for Measure* he had been bound by the conventions of comedy.

Perhaps the greatest contribution of *Arcadia* to *King Lear* is the element of sinful and dangerous intrigue. From the fifteenth chapter of the second book of *Arcadia*, which treats of the story of Plangus, come by plain suggestion the machinations by which Edmund undermines and uproots Edgar.[3] It is by means similar to those used by Edmund against Edgar that the corrupt stepmother achieves the downfall and banishment of Plangus. From that story also comes the suggestion for the disagreeably appropriate liaison between Edmund and the wicked daughters of King Lear.

It was natural and yet a stroke of genius that made Shakespeare combine two stories so different in their tone and yet so closely parallel in their course as that of King Leir and the blind king of Paphlagonia. He knitted these stories together with a naturalness which will always be amazing, but his general task may be described as that of permeating the Lear story with the tragic tone and temper of the Gloucester story. The tragedy as tragedy is to be found in the tale from *Arcadia*. Shakespeare retains from the old play the sweetness of Cordelia and the faithfulness of Kent (Perillus). The stoutness in the character of the aged Lear is yet to be accounted for, since the Leir of the old play is merely pathetic. Again, few parts of *King Lear* seem to be invented outright. There is the figure of the Fool, a traditional part provided no doubt for Robert Armin, the trial by combat, no very difficult thing to invent, and the patriotic change from British defeat to British victory. When, however, one talks about this glibly as an indication of Shakespeare's own patriotic feeling, one should remember that Shakespeare needed it as a means of entangling Lear and Cordelia in the mesh of tragedy. In other words, the British victory serves Shakespeare as a device for the carrying out of his tragic purpose.

I have endeavoured to apply to Shakespeare's choice of materials a fundamental principle of the psychology of art and have illustrated Shakespeare's practice from some of his plays. Behind what I have said lies a consideration of still greater importance. Shakespeare's sources are worth studying because they have significance, value, meaning; Shakespeare chose them for that reason. This statement finds its place in the most promising philosophy of art in our age. To the definitions of the logic of Aristotle and of modern science this philosophy has added the idea of value. Symbolic logic is not content with denotation and connotation only, but insists on a third definitive element which is significance or value. This philosophy promises to change our attitude toward art by uniting it to life, and it offers a broad and adequate epistemology for the acceptance of symbolic truth. It carries with it an extension of our conception of man; as, for example, that man is known by his actions and not by any analytical formulae; in other words, that man is an organism whose function is living. It thus comes about that Shakespeare's sources are usually formulations of function. The fact that these sources have been neglected or disdained is not a matter of any importance whatever, since much of the work so far done in the interpretation of Shakespeare needs to be rendered more comprehensive and more adequate.

NOTES

1. See Ruth Anderson Maxwell, 'The Mirror Concept and its relation to the Drama of the Renaissance', *N.W. Missouri State Teachers College Studies*, III (1939), no. 1, and an as yet unpublished paper 'Ideation in Renaissance Plays depicting Ambition and Tyranny'.

2. 'Peter Snook', *Complete Works*, ed. James A. Harrison (1902), XIV, 73.

3. See D. M. McKeithan, '*King Lear* and Sidney's *Arcadia*', *Studies in English*, Austin, Texas, no. 14 (1934), pp. 45–9.

THE SOURCES OF *MACBETH*

BY

M. C. BRADBROOK

A very broad definition of 'sources' must be my excuse for considering so familiar a topic as the origins of *Macbeth*. In this, the most concentrated of the tragedies, a particularly wide diversity of material was fused into unity. "In the quick forge and working-house of thought", Shakespeare wrought at white heat. The material to be considered falls into three classes. First, the Scottish and English Chronicles supplied the facts, and one important scene; secondly, various works on witchcraft and demonology, including those of King James, gave some material for the witches' scenes (but here the interest lies rather in Shakespeare's innovations than in his borrowings); thirdly, earlier works by Shakespeare himself present in a simpler form some of the ingredients of this play, and an examination of what might be called the internal sources elucidates its inward structure. The repetitions, echoes and restatements which are to be detected in Shakespeare offer more than mere opportunity for pedantic correlation; they are alternative statements, varied embodiments of those deep-seated and permanent impulses which underlie all his work and make it, in spite of its variety, a vast and comprehensive whole—a single structure, though of Gothic design.

In reading through Holinshed's voluminous Scottish Chronicles, Shakespeare would come, about a third of the way through, upon the story of Duncan, the eighty-fourth king according to that account, and the narrative with which we are all familiar. The chronicle gives a brief and bald summary of reign after reign, describing the same round of violence, murder, rebellion and general turbulence. It is as monotonous as the series of apocryphal portraits of these early kings to be seen in Holyrood Palace; and the power of its monotony is considerable. The picture of a strange, bleak, haunted world emerges, where savage beings fulfil the passionate cycle of their dreadful lives as if under enchanted compulsion.[1] But why, in reading through these legendary stories, did Shakespeare stop where he did?

The story of Duncan and Macbeth glorified the ancestors of King James, both the ancient house of Macalpine, and in Banquo, an imaginary figure invented by Hector Boece during the fifteenth century, the later Stewart line. It also introduced the weird sisters, whose prophecies might be adapted to foretell the happy future rule of King James himself, and who were at the same time akin to the North Berwick witches whose practices against him had provided one of the most celebrated witch-trials of the age. Moreover, Malcolm Canmore, husband of the English princess Margaret and initiator of many new customs, stood at the beginning of one new age in Scottish history, as James, heir to the united crowns of Scotland and England, stood at the beginning of another. A royal command performance was clearly in view from the very inception of the play.

In the Chronicle, the history of Macbeth is briefly told, but Shakespeare shaped it both by expansion and compression. He crammed into a single act of war the rebellion of Macdonwald, two Danish invasions and the revolt of Cawdor—which happened only *after* the prophecy in Holinshed. The whole account of how Duncan was murdered he took from elsewhere, the murder of King Duff; though Macbeth's stratagem to send into the Danish camp supplies of drugged food and surprise them "so amazed that they were unable to make any defence" might have suggested the drugging of the grooms. In the Chronicle, Macbeth slew Duncan in open revolt, and no indications of remorse are given either before or after the event. The long reign of Macbeth Shakespeare shortens into a few weeks; the wizard who prophesied to Macbeth about Birnam Wood merges with the weird sisters; Macbeth's death takes place before Dunsinane, and not at the end of an inglorious flight. In sum, the debt to the Chronicle is of the slightest; so bald a narrative gave Shakespeare the merest skeleton of a plot. There is, however, one scene, that between Malcolm and Macduff in England, which is reported in very great detail. Indeed, it is out of all focus in the Chronicle and occupies almost as much space as the whole of the rest of the reign. This scene represents Shakespeare's greatest debt to Holinshed; clearly it took his eye, and here perhaps is the germ of how he first conceived the play.

Malcolm's self-accusations are much more convincing to the present age than they were to the nineteenth century, when this scene was generally disliked. It was usual to cut it for stage performance. Yet an exile trying to evade the trap of his totalitarian enemy might plausibly test the reactions of his promised supporters. In a world still full of displaced persons and *agents provocateurs*, this scene can be harrowing. In Holinshed, the whole incident is weakened by the fact that both Malcolm and Macduff know of the murder of Macduff's family before the dialogue begins, so that it is hardly conceivable that Macduff could at this time be Macbeth's agent. Shakespeare, on the other hand, makes his leaving of the defenceless 'wife and child' a reasonable cause of suspicion to the young prince. Macduff does not answer Malcolm's query on this point. It is the silence of a man embittered and mature, deeply mortified by such incomprehension of the depths of sacrifice for which his loyalty prepared him.

Here again the modern reader may add his personal endorsement. In 1942 I had the honour to meet in London one of the highest officers of the French Navy, who had escaped from France after the German occupation to fight from this country. He too left his wife and child exposed to the retaliation of the enemy. In those days no one asked him why.

In Holinshed, Malcolm accuses himself of licentiousness, avarice and promise-breaking, and it is only the last which drives Macduff to renounce him. Promise-keeping is so essential to the ruler that although as all treatises on government declared—and particularly King James's[2]—it is the bounden duty of the subject to conceal the ill deeds of rulers and not even to let his *thoughts* harbour any treasonable reproof of them, yet this particular crime is indefensible. Holinshed makes the rather subtle point that while Malcolm is diffident about his other crimes, he seems to expect Macduff to conceal the last. Shakespeare omits the irony, but he was engaged in adding to the list of crimes, mentioning especially contentiousness, which, as Dover Wilson points out,[3] would be particularly obnoxious to the pacifist James. Malcolm's final speech constitutes almost a definition by contraries of the perfect ruler.

Such ingenious dissimulation would appear to the royal auditor a proof of his wisdom, more striking that it was precocious—and the more likely to foreshadow that of his illustrious descendant. Might not James also remember those ten painful months following the Ruthven Raid in 1582, when as a boy of eighteen he had to practise dissimulation with the gang who kidnapped him and forced him to govern in accordance with their faction? "Better bairns greet nor bearded men", exclaimed Lord Ruthven, when James at his first capture burst into tears.

The King never forgot, and years later he contrived Lord Ruthven's death should pay for it. Such memories might well have recurred and given to the scene of Malcolm's exile a deep personal significance.

The ruler was always allowed to practise extraordinary stratagems in view of his extra responsibilities, as the Duke of Vienna did in *Measure for Measure*. Malcolm was showing himself fit to rule—cleverer than his father, who knew no art to find the mind's construction in the face, and did not probe below a fair appearance.

In his recent book on Shakespeare,[4] Hardin Craig has classed *Macbeth* among the political tragedies, and there is no doubt that it was more than a personal tragedy which happened to be about princes. The natures of an ill-governed and a well-governed kingdom are contrasted throughout the latter half of the play. Here Shakespeare moved away from the Chronicle, and relied partly on other works, including those of King James, and partly on those views which had formed in his own mind during the writing of his English histories.

The relation between the King and the body politic is a sympathetic one. When the King is sick or disordered, the land is disordered too. First we are given the picture of a happy kingdom, in which Duncan and his thanes support and respect each other. Duncan plants honours, and labours to make them full of growing. His subjects return to him all the bounties with which he nourishes them, in duty and service. In her welcome Lady Macbeth falsely strikes this note of devotion, which Duncan repays with an old man's gallant politeness.

After his coronation, Macbeth tries vainly at his feast to recreate the atmosphere of close-knit amity. But "honour, love, obedience, troops of friends" he must not look to have. His thanes look forward to the time when they may "do faithful homage, and receive free honours", but the Scotland they inhabit is disordered, sick, a distracted body swollen with evil humours. This picture of the distracted kingdom is familiar from the plays of *Richard II*, *Henry IV* and *Richard III*, where it is described at more length. Even Macbeth sees that his land is diseased (v, iii). He himself is haunted with the sleeplessness that tormented the usurper Bolingbroke, and to read the opening of the third act of *Henry IV Part II* is like listening to an overture to *Macbeth*:

> O sleep, O gentle sleep,
> Nature's soft nurse, how have I frighted thee,
> That thou no more wilt weigh my eye-lids down,
> And steep my senses in forgetfulness?...
> Then you perceive the body of our kingdom,
> How foul it is; what rank diseases grow,
> And with what danger, near the heart of it? (III, i, 6–9, 38–40)

Malcolm is "the medicine of the sickly weal", the 'sovereign flower' who comes with the blessing and aid of the saintly Edward. The reference in IV, i to the Confessor's sacred powers of healing was an especial compliment to James who prided himself on the inherited gift of 'the healing benediction'; but it was also necessary as a counterweight to the picture of Macbeth's unholy rule; as such, Shakespeare took it from the English Chronicle and inserted it in his main political scene.

Further, into Macduff's reproaches of the supposedly vicious Malcolm, Shakespeare inserts an account of the forbears from whom he has degenerated; his father Duncan was "a most sainted king" and his mother one who "Oftener upon her knees, than on her feet, died every day she lived". This is Shakespeare's Duncan, not Holinshed's; while of Malcolm's mother nothing is known. Shakespeare has borrowed the saintliness from the description of Malcolm's wife, the English princess, St Margaret, who transmitted the blood of the Saxon line to the Scottish royal house, and whose little chapel still stands within the walls of Edinburgh Castle. It was she and Malcolm himself who rivalled each other in pious practices and holy living. But by putting this picture a generation earlier, Shakespeare has brought into the play yet another contrast with Macbeth and his fiend-like queen, whose land is described in terms of the plague:

> where nothing
> But who knows nothing, is once seen to smile:
> Where sighs, and groans, and shrieks that rend the air
> Are made, not mark'd: where violent sorrow seems
> A modern ecstasy: the dead man's knell,
> Is there scarce ask'd for who, and good men's lives
> Expire before the flowers in their caps,
> Dying, or ere they sicken.   (IV, iii, 166–73)

As rightful heir Malcolm alone has the power to depose an anointed king, usurper though he be; but the conquest is almost unopposed. "The time is free." An immense feeling of relief surges up as Macduff appears on the battlements with these words. Malcolm, encompassed with his kingdom's pearl,[5] proceeds to inaugurate a new era by bestowing new honours. He thus fulfils his father's words that "signs of nobleness, like stars shall shine on all deservers". He also introduces the principle of feudal monarchy, with hereditary succession, and tenancy of the crown, which in fact Malcolm Canmore did institute in Scotland, following the unsuccessful attempts of his great-grandfather and grandfather, Kenneth II and Malcolm II.[6]

This particular theme, however, Shakespeare does not emphasize, and for good reason. The ancient succession of Scotland had been by tanistry, that is, the monarchy was elective within a small group of kinsmen, the descendants of Macalpine. In consequence, the king was almost as a matter of course assassinated by his successor, who chose the moment most favourable to himself to 'mak siccar' an inheritance that could never be regarded as assured. In spite of earlier attempts to make it hereditary, elective monarchy still persisted; by tanist law Macbeth had as good a claim as Duncan, and his wife a rather better one. By nominating Malcolm as his heir, the historic Duncan committed a provocative act which Macbeth might not unreasonably resent, and in Holinshed his real notions of murder are formed only at this point. Shakespeare did not wish Macbeth to have any such excuse for his deed. It must be unprovoked to give the full measure of pity and terror. Therefore by suppressing the conflict between tanistry and the hereditary principle, he was bound to slur over the full nature of Malcolm Canmore's innovations.[7]

On the contrary, the principle of hereditary succession is firmly emphasized by the prominence given to Banquo and his descendants, and in the cauldron scene Shakespeare has gratified the family pride of his royal patron by a pageant of his ancestors. Henry Paul has recently pointed out[8] that the Stewart line presented the striking picture of nine successive sovereigns in *lineal* descent the one from the other. This direct lineal descent of the crown was a matter of pride to

James, who referred to it in his speeches to Parliament and in his writings. Shakespeare's interest in genealogy had been amply shown in his English histories. Edward's seven sons, seven branches growing from one root, are recalled to mind by the family tree which has Banquo as its root—he so describes himself.

Banquo was a purely imaginary character, inserted into the Chronicle by Hector Boece to provide a proper ancestry for the Stewarts. Fleance's escape to Wales and his marriage with a Welsh princess 'explained' why the Stewarts did in fact come from the Welsh borders. But after 1603 the original expansion of the weird sisters' prophecy, whereby Banquo was hailed as father to a line of kings, was expanded still further, so that they also prophesied that his descendants should unite the kingdoms of England and Scotland. In the pageant of the three sybils given at St John's College, Oxford, in 1605, James and his family were greeted in this fashion, and moreover an endless progeny was promised him.[9] The show of the eight kings was an apotheosis of the Stewart line, and must have been staged with great grandeur. To a Jacobean audience it symbolized all the stability and order which they hoped from a settled succession. A family which had produced nine kings in lineal descent offered a fair hope of escape from those dynastic difficulties which Elizabeth's reign had made familiar. The eight phantoms are all "too like the spirit of Banquo". They are physical replicas of him, but in the last Henry Paul would see the person of Mary Queen of Scots, the eighth Stewart to wear the crown. At all events this scene would have a very powerful topical significance.

These two scenes, then, the cauldron scene and the scene in England, are the *political* high-lights of the play. They are the scenes in which Shakespeare relied most heavily on his immediate sources—those he would start from. And they are the two scenes which would most particularly appeal to King James. They are also the least tragic in tone. One is spectacular, and the other, although, as I have said, it is much more poignant to the present age than to the previous one, is still in rather a different manner from the rest of the play. What have the theoretically well-justified dissimulations of this canny young man, this perfect looking-glass for princes, to do with the agonized visions of Inverness and Dunsinane? How do they fit one who has a father murdered as well as revenges to execute on the tyrant who popped in between the election and his hopes? Malcolm is own brother to that other canny young man, Harry Monmouth, who is likewise justified by all the text-books on government, including *Basilikon Doron*; but we are not moved. He is impersonal. The man is lost in the ruler. He may be *Vox Dei*; it means that he is merely *vox*.

Because of the close relation to source-material, the impersonal subject and the specific appeal to royal interest, it seems to me that these two scenes are probably the earliest to be written. I do not believe that Shakespeare, or any original writer, starts inevitably with Act I and ends with Act v. Nor do I think that, once submerged in his tragedy and well away from his sources, he would suddenly curb himself in mid-career and begin to treat these cooler matters. At the same time these scenes are too well articulated with the main plot to be additions, though small additions may have been made to them. The cauldron scene and the English scene are both in a quite laudatory, or at least a quite neutral sense, superficial. They belong to the top layer of the play.

The character of Lady Macbeth owes nothing to the Chronicle; it has been suggested that Shakespeare might have seen the MS. of William Stewart's *Buik of the Chroniclis of Scotland*, a metrical and expanded translation of Boece finished in 1535 which contains a few very crude hints on the behaviour of Donwald's wife during the murder of King Duff.[10] The resemblances seem to me negligible and unconvincing.

But a passage from the *Description of Scotland* which is prefixed to Holinshed's Chronicle and which to my knowledge has not hitherto been noted seems to be relevant. It is from chapter XIII:

…each woman would take intolerable pains to bring up and nourish her own children. They thought them furthermore not to be kindly fostered, except they were so well nourished after their births with the milk of their breasts as they were before they were born with the blood of their own bellies: nay, they feared lest they should degenerate and grow out of kind, except they gave them suck themselves, and eschewed strange milk, therefore in labour and painfulness they were equal [i.e. with the fighting men]….In these days also the women of our country were of no less courage than the men, for all stout maids and wives (if they were not with child) marched as well into the field as did the men, and so soon as the army did set forward, they slew the first living creature that they found, in whose blood they not only bathed their swords, but also tasted thereof with their mouths, with no less religion and assurance conceived, than if they had already been sure of some notable and fortunate victory.[11]

The intimate relation between tenderness and barbarity, suckling and bloodshed in this passage seems to me to give the fundamental character of Lady Macbeth as it is embodied in the most frightful of her speeches, that in which she invokes the spirits of murder to suck her breasts, and that in which she finally goads Macbeth:

> I have given suck, and know
> How tender 'tis to love the babe that milks me,
> I would, while it was smiling in my face,
> Have pluck'd my nipple from his boneless gums,
> And dash'd the brains out, had I so sworn
> As you have done to this.   (I, vii, 54–9)

Lady Macbeth is siren as well as fury. The tenderness of Macbeth for her is reciprocated; they are indeed one flesh. There are a number of parallels between her part and that of Webster's *White Divel*[12] which suggest that her seduction of Macbeth should not be too far removed from Vittoria's seduction of Brachiano in the manner of its playing. When Macbeth comes out of the death chamber she says two words: 'My husband?' The usual form of address is 'My thane' or 'My lord', but in this supreme moment she uses the more intimate, and for an Elizabethan the more unusual form.

The double crime of treason and murder is also deadly sin. In 1604 William Willymat, the translator of *Basilikon Doron* under the title of *A Prince's Looking-Glass*, followed it with an original work, *A Loyal Subject's Looking-Glass*, in which he described the prime causes of rebellion as pride, ambition and envy. All three animate Macbeth. "Pride can in no wise brook to be at command, and to submit himself willingly…to the obedience of magistrates, rulers and governors…be they never so well worthy of their place." Macbeth cannot brook 'the boy Malcolm', who has only been saved from captivity by the sergeant, should be nominated heir. Almost his last words are:

> I will not yield
> To kiss the ground before young Malcolm's feet.

The stripling—he should be of an age with his cousin, young Siward—provokes his pride; the Weird Sisters have stirred up ambition, always thought of as evil; and his very hunger for golden opinions makes him envy imperial dignity and the graces of kingship which he discerns in Duncan, and which he so vainly tries to reproduce. By the end of the play, Macbeth is accused of the other deadly sins also (IV, iii, 55–7)—in fact he is equated with the devil:

> Not in the legions
> Of horrid hell, can come a devil more damn'd
> In evils, to top Macbeth.

He is 'this fiend of Scotland', a 'hell-kite' and a 'hell-hound'.

In its treatment of the supernatural, the play shows the same subtle blending of a variety of material which is seen in the political theme; and it was again especially calculated to interest James, hero of *Newes from Scotland* and author of *Daemonologie*.

There was no real scepticism about witches. *Macbeth* comes at the end of a decade when the convictions for witchcraft in the Middlesex circuit reached their highest point. New statutes had been passed in 1604 reinforcing those of 1580, which made the consulting and feeding of spirits, the use of dead bodies as charms, and even unsuccessful efforts to harm by enchantment into indictable offences.[13]

It is rather surprising that before *Macbeth*, witches had appeared on the stage only in such harmless forms as Mother Bombie or the Wise Woman of Hogsdon. *Faustus* had been the only great tragedy to be based on the supernatural. The magician is a magnificent and powerful figure, a man of intellect. He enters into a formal pact with the devil and consciously chooses damnation; in return for the sale of his soul he obtains supernatural powers (*Daemonologie*, book I, chapter VI). Henceforth, though still free to repent, the devil coaxes and bullies him out of such wishes. The equal poise of Heaven and Hell that characterized the moralities is not maintained; the scales are weighed for Hell, dramatically speaking. The emissaries of Hell are more active, numerous and powerful than the emissaries of Heaven. The sinner, however, is led to will and choose his own damnation. He is never *possessed*.

Macbeth was the first play to introduce to the stage in a serious manner the rites and practices of contemporary witchcraft. The witch differed sharply from the magician, as King James observed (*Daemonologie*, book I, chapter III). William West of the Inner Temple thus distinguishes them in his *Symbolaeographie* (1594):

Soothsaying Wizards. Of this kind…be all those…which divine and foretell things to come and raise up evil spirits by certain superstitious and conceived forms of words. And unto such questions as be demanded of them do answer by voice, or else set before their eyes in glass, crystal stones, or rings, the pictures or images of things sought for.

[Witches]...shake the air with lightnings and thunder, to cause hail and tempests, to remove green corn or trees to an other place, to be carried of her familiar which hath taken upon him the deceitful shape of a goat, swine, or calf etc. into some mountain....And sometimes to fly upon a staff or fork, or some other instrument....[14]

Whilst Dee or Forman consorted with kings and princes, the witch was generally a poor, solitary, ignorant old woman. King James points out that magicians were learned and sought public glory; witches were unlearned and sought revenge. They blighted man and crops, were ugly and bearded, and went accompanied by a familiar. The more lurid practices of the continental sabbat are not recorded of English witches; though in *Daemonologie* and in the record of the North Berwick case, elaborate rituals are described, blasphemous as well as mischievous.

Shakespeare's play, though the first to deal with this topic seriously, was quickly followed by others. *Sophonisba* (1606) and *The Divil's Charter* (1607) were succeeded by a number of Chapman's plays introducing spirits, and in 1615 by Middleton's *Witch*, a song from which was incorporated in *Macbeth*. Jonson's *Masque of Queens*, with its celebrated antimasque of hags, was produced in 1609. As in *A Midsummer Night's Dream*, and later in *The Tempest*, Shakespeare created a new kind of supernatural drama and one which was very widely and generally imitated.

In all these plays, however, witches are used for spectacular and intermittent effects, and the marvellous elbows out the sinister. Marston and Jonson drew largely on classical sources. Hecate, in *The Witch*, is used to supply love charms and is surrounded by familiars but her influence is not decisive. Barnabe Barnes in *The Divil's Charter* is mainly indebted to *Faustus*, but the crimes of Alexander Borgia and Lucretia occasionally parallel those of Macbeth and Lady Macbeth, and the conjuring scene especially seems modelled on the cauldron scene, whilst Alexander is cheated by a riddle at the end, in much the same way as Macbeth.

In *Macbeth* Shakespeare combines many different traditions, so that the Weird Sisters, or Three Destinies of Holinshed become assimilated with the North Berwick coven in their malevolent rites, yet they also acquire something of the magician's power to raise and command spirits and to foretell the future. Shakespeare's witches, like those of North Berwick, appear capable of flying "through the fog and filthy air". They are able to sail in a sieve, to assume animal forms, and control the weather. All this Agnes Sampson and her coven claimed to do in their attempts to destroy the ship carrying King James from Denmark.[15] But Shakespeare's hags also have marks of the English witch—their beards, their animal familiars and their acts of petty revenge against the sailor and his wife. These were the things charged against many a poor old woman at the sessions. Their gift of prophecy expressed in riddles—the riddling form of words is not found in Holinshed—links them with such characters as Mother Bombie, or Erestus, the "white bear of England's wood" in *The Old Wives' Tale*. Incidentally, Rosalind, in the last act of *As You Like It*, makes her promises to the lovers in the riddling form proper to the Magician which she professes herself to be:

I will marry you, if ever I marry woman, and I'll be married tomorrow: I will satisfy you, if ever I satisfied man, and you shall be married tomorrow. I will content you, if what pleases you contents you, and you shall be married tomorrow. (v, ii, 122–6)

The prophecies of the witches about Birnam Wood and the man not born of woman are sprigs of folklore which also recall the earlier comedies; for instance, Erestus's prophecy that Eumenides is to be released from enchantment by a dead man.[16]

On the other hand, they have powers superior to those of common witches. Bishop John Leslie called them devils disguised as women (*De Origine, Moribus et Rebus Gestis Scotorum*, Rome, 1578). They can vanish instantly like bubbles, which suggests a demonic power assuming and discarding human shape. They have no trace of any fear of or subjection to higher demonic forces; though the spirits raised in the cauldron scene are called 'our masters', yet the witches conjure them up and speak to them with authority, such authority as belongs to the magician like Faustus, the friar in *Bussy d'Ambois* and Owen Glendower. Macbeth, who sells his eternal jewel to the common enemy of man, is himself in Faustus's position, but he makes no formal compact, nor is he given any supernatural powers. He is tempted by rousing of his own worse instincts and led to natural crimes; but, on the other hand, he never renounces God and his baptism, as both witches and magicians were compelled to do. After the murder of Duncan there is no possibility of his going back. He has crossed the invisible boundary which cuts him off from his kind. His hand is against every man. He is no longer a member of the human community, and finally he sinks to the level of a hunted rogue animal.

Yet although Macbeth's career recalls a descent into hell, it is not presented openly as a descent into hell. In the end he finds himself deceived in the witches, as the witch or magician was so often deceived by the devil.[17] "Be these juggling fiends no more believ'd", he cries. In murdering Duncan, he committed mortal sin—the sin against the Holy Ghost as James called it in *Daemonologie* (book I, chapter II)—that is, he consciously and deliberately did that which he knew to be evil, and which he detested even as he did it. The act brings the punishment which he foresaw, he loses this clear sight, wades in blood so far that he is blinded and becomes in the end insensible even to the death of his wife.[18] But the overt theological issue is never bluntly put. Hence H. B. Charlton can deny any religious significance to *Macbeth*, while W. C. Curry, Helen Gardner and Hardin Craig, not to mention Roy Walker,[19] see the play as "essentially medieval and Christian". The Prince of Darkness is present only through the acts of his emissaries, but they, while in many ways recalling the realistic witch, are "creatures of another sort". I would not be prepared to say whether they are human or not; they are more recognizable as human in act I than in the later scenes, where they replace Holinshed's 'wizard', and have something of the devil's power of deceit.

Lady Macbeth's relation with the dark powers is more mysterious. Women were thought far more susceptible to demons than men, and were far more frequently accused of evil practices. King James put the proportion as high as twenty women to one man (*Daemonologie*, book II, chapter V). In her invocation to the spirits "that tend on mortal thoughts" Lady Macbeth offers them her breasts to be sucked and invites them to take possession of her body; this was as much as any witch could do by way of self-dedication. Professor Curry considers the sleep-walking scene to be evidence of possession, and if she did lay "self and violent hands" upon herself, Lady Macbeth committed the final act of Despair.

Neither Macbeth nor his wife has any defences. Though his conscience at first speaks clearly, he has no Good Angel as Faustus has. Banquo may pray to the merciful powers to restrain his cursed thoughts, Malcolm and Macduff appeal to Heaven, old Siward commit his dead son to the soldiery of God, but Macbeth lives in an amoral world of old wives' tales and riddles— except for that one vision of the pleading angels with their trumpet tongues, and heaven's cherubim horsed upon the sightless couriers of the air, which recalls Faustus's vision of Christ's blood streaming in the firmament.

The portents which accompany the death of Duncan, and foreshadow that of Banquo, are such as on the stage always appeared with the death of princes. The strange screams in the air and the horses that ate each other are developed from hints in Holinshed, but they are distinguished from other portents by the tone and colour of the language in which they are described. The thick darkness which hangs over the sky, the raven, owl and cricket's note are much less distinct than the fiery warriors who fought above the clouds in *Julius Caesar*. It is the thick night, the fog and filthy air, the smoke of hell which create the peculiar horror of this play, and the omens are chosen to accord. How quickly it rolls down on the sunlit battlements where the martlet flits, as a Scotch mist will roll from a mountain! Just as the witches are more horrible because we do not know what they are—it would be a relief to meet Mephistopheles—so the whole treatment of the supernatural in *Macbeth* is characterized by a potent and delicately controlled imprecision. Hell is murky. The creatures of *Macbeth*, like the ghost in *Hamlet*, are not susceptible of any one theoretical explanation, religious or natural.

Yet in the end justice, whether God's or Nature's, prevails. There is no direct intervention, but in the final vengeance the ingredients of the poisoned chalice are commended to the sinner's own lips. (This happens literally in *The Divil's Charter*, where Borgia is poisoned with his own wine: it also happens, of course, in *Hamlet*.) Macbeth, who had begun as Bellona's bridegroom, ends in the same role as Macdonwald, his head hacked off and put on a pole. (Did Macdonwald's head appear in the early scenes? According to Holinshed it was cut off.) The early description of Macbeth in battle which is given by the sergeant seems to me indubitably Shakespeare's. By the violence of it we are made unforgettably aware that bloodshed of itself is familiar to Macbeth—that his trade is hand-to-hand fighting. The physical side of Duncan's murder can cause him no qualms at all. Lady Macbeth, on the other hand, is not quite Holinshed's Valkyrie; perhaps she had not smelt blood before, and though she goes through the scene unflinchingly, she is haunted by the physical atrocity of it. To Macbeth, we may believe that the dastardly act of stabbing a sleeping old man was as instinctively repugnant as stabbing a kneeling man in the back was to Hamlet: "Look on't again, I dare not", he cries—he, who had unseamed men from the nave to the chaps.

It is here that we approach the deepest levels of the play and that we must leave external sources and seek within Shakespeare's own earlier work the foreshadowing of the terror and the pity which we feel. In the speeches of Macbeth, especially his five great speeches,[20] lies the heart of the mystery. They embody the experience which fundamentally gives rise to the play; and there are no sub-plots, no digressions to modify it.

Macbeth acts, according to Bradley, under a horrible compulsion; Dover Wilson imagines him following the air-drawn dagger in "a horrible smiling trance". The murder fascinates him as damnation fascinates Faustus. It is the inevitable, the irrevocable deed, after which he too dies in some sense:

Had I but died an hour before this chance,
I had liv'd a blessed time: for from this instant,
There's nothing serious in mortality:
All is but toys: renown and grace is dead,
The wine of life is drawn.... (II, iii, 40–53)[21]

A period of intense and almost delirious anticipation is followed by complete collapse. There is one earlier picture of an "expense of spirit in a waste of shame", one earlier picture of conscious guilt calling in night and the creatures of night for aid, one act of physical violence followed by as swift a repentance, one equally dishonourable breach of hospitality and trust. It is the one to which Macbeth himself refers;

Now o'er the one half-world
Nature seems dead, and wicked dreams abuse
The curtain'd sleep: witchcraft celebrates
Pale Hecate's offerings: and wither'd murder,
Alarum'd by his sentinel, the wolf,
Whose howl's his watch, thus with his stealthy pace,
With Tarquin's ravishing strides, towards his design
Moves like a ghost. (II, i, 49–56)[22]

What is to be learnt by turning back to the sententious *Rape of Lucrece*, with its emblematic description of the heroine, its lengthy complaints and testament, its studied ornament and its formal indictment of Night, Time and Opportunity? Here, I think, are the emotional components (as distinct from the narrative components) of *Macbeth* lying separate, isolated, and more crudely and simply expressed. Tarquin's feelings before the deed, and Lucrece's feelings after it, are identical with the central core of feeling in *Macbeth*.

Night, Opportunity and a deceitful appearance are accessories to the deed. In her lament, Lucrece indicts these three. An atmosphere of tragic gloom and murk is diffused in the description of Tarquin's rising and stalking through the darkened house towards his victim. Like Macbeth, he tries to pray in the very act of entering her chamber and is startled to find that he cannot do it. There is a remote likeness to the physical horror of Duncan's corpse in the sight of Lucrece's body at the end, so ghastly inert in its great pool of blood

Who like a late sack'd island vastly stood
Bare and unpeopled, in this fearful flood. (1740–1)

But it is, above all, in the opening soliloquies of Tarquin that the likeness is apparent. Tarquin foresees the emptiness of his satisfaction, which Macbeth does not fully understand till after the deed; but the comment with which Tarquin's inward debate is introduced might serve as prologue to the later story.

Those that much covet are with gain so fond,
That what they have not, that which they possess
They scatter and unloose it from their bond,
And so by hoping more they have but less,
Or gaining more, the profit of excess
Is but to surfeit, and such griefs sustain,
That they prove bankrupt in this poor-rich gain.

The aim of all is but to nurse the life,
With honour, wealth, and ease in waning age;
And in this aim there is such thwarting strife,
That one for all, or all for one we gage:
As life for honour, in fell battles rage,
   Honour for wealth, and oft that wealth doth cost
   The death of all, and altogether lost.

So that in venturing ill, we leave to be
The things we are, for that which we expect,
And this ambitious foul infirmity,
In having much torments us with defect
Of that we have: so then we do neglect
   The thing we have, and all for want of wit,
   Make something nothing, by augmenting it.   (134–54)

In his protracted debate with himself, Tarquin points out the shame to his family, his blood and his posterity, the transient nature of the gain (and here Macbeth echoes him):

Who buys a minute's mirth to wail a week?
Or sells eternity to get a toy?   (213–14)

He dreads the vengeance of Collatine even while he recognizes the ties of kinship and hospitality which bind them:

But as he is my kinsman, my dear friend,
The shame and fault finds no excuse nor end.   (237–8)

Finally he rejects the counsel of reason in words which anticipate Lady Macbeth's "tis the eye of child-hood, That fears a painted devil":

Who fears a sentence or an old man's saw,
Shall by a painted cloth be kept in awe.   (244–5)

The crime which Tarquin commits, even more clearly, though not more truly, than Macbeth's, destroys the natural ties between him and the rest of the community. It is a sort of suicide. Both Macbeth and he commit a violence upon themselves from which they cannot recover. Examples have been known in the modern world where acts of sufficient violence will destroy the personality of the perpetrator; and even periods of acute nervous strain and danger, such as those to which combatants were subjected, will issue in nervous prostration and a feeling of complete emptiness of being. It is this identity between violence and self-violence (though in *The Rape of Lucrece*, the effects of the crime are given in the soliloquies of the victim) which a comparison of the two works reinforces as the central idea, the germ of the play. Macbeth's real victim is himself. Both *The Rape of Lucrece* and *Macbeth* reflect with very different degrees of skill a deep-seated and permanent experience; and the difference serves only to emphasize the unity of Shakespeare's art, the modifying and shaping power which his work as a whole seems to exert upon each of its parts. I think it is not fancy to say that *Macbeth* is the greater for being demonstrably by the hand that wrote *Othello*, or even the hand that wrote *Lucrece*; since the likeness which is discernible within such variety is proof that the play was written from the very depths of his mind and heart, and together with the multiplicity of sources which have furnished the subject of this paper, it gives a measure of the power, the intellectual and spiritual strength and pressure required, to weld them into one.

NOTES

1. The atmospheric strength of the chronicle is noted by Dover Wilson in the New Cambridge edition of *Macbeth* (Cambridge, 1947), p. xii. He quotes the earlier edition of Sir Herbert Grierson and J. C. Smith at this point in support of the Celtic atmosphere of the story. In a paper read at Cambridge in November 1950, Mrs N. K. Chadwick suggested that the earliest chronicle, Wyntoun's, incorporates material from lost Celtic sagas on Macbeth, particularly in the parts relating to the supernatural. She bases this on changes in the style, indicating a Celtic original. There is an independent Norse saga of Macbeth.

2. *Basilikon Doron*, and *The true lawe of free monarchies* (Edinburgh, 1597, 1598).

3. *Ed. cit.* pp. xxxi–xxxii.

4. Hardin Craig, *An Interpretation of Shakespeare* (New York, 1948).

5. Henry Paul points out in his article, 'The Imperial Theme in *Macbeth*' (*Adams Memorial Studies*, ed. J. G. McManaway and others, Washington, 1948, pp. 253–68), that the *pearls* set in the base of an imperial diadem represented the several dependent fiefs (*loc. cit.* p. 264). What follows in my text is indebted to this valuable article.

6. St Margaret, Malcolm's wife, and a strong influence in the shaping of his policy, obtained from the Pope the privilege that Scottish kings should be anointed (i.e. hallowed) at their coronation.

7. It is melancholy to note that Donalbain returned from Ireland to the Isles and (after Malcolm's death) slew his nephew, David, but was in turn succeeded by another of Malcolm's sons. With this one interval, the line of Malcolm Canmore retained the throne.

8. *Loc. cit.* p. 258.

9. It has been much disputed whether Shakespeare knew this pageant or not. Henry Paul thinks he did.

10. See Dover Wilson, *ed. cit.* p. xvii, for a summary of the material.

11. *The Description of Scotland*, chapter XIII (translated from the Latin of Hector Boethius by William Harison, and prefixed to Holinshed's *Historie of Scotland*, 1577). As in the other quotations the spelling has been modernized.

12. Vittoria's "Terrify babes, my Lord, with painted devils" and the words of Flamineo about her, "If woman do breed man, She ought to teach him manhood", recall respectively "tis the eye of child-hood That fears a painted devil" and "Bring forth men-children only". The figure of the great lady, great in wickedness, was popular on the Jacobean stage. Lucrezia Borgia in *The Divil's Charter* also recalls Lady Macbeth in her laments and swoon over the husband she has slain, her invocation of the furies and her careful concealment of the murder by staging a mock suicide.

13. C. H. L. Ewen, *Witch Hunting and Witch Trials* (London, 1929), pp. 19–21, 31. I am indebted for this reference and for much general information on the subject of demonology to Mrs Florence Trefethan.

14. Quoted Ewen, *op. cit.* p. 23.

15. See *Newes from Scotland*, 1591 (reprinted with King James's *Daemonologie* in the Bodley Head Quartos, London, 1924).

16. *The Old Wives' Tale* (*The Works of George Peele*, ed. A. H. Bullen, vol. 1, p. 323).

17. In the words of King James (*Daemonologie*, book I, chapter v)—which seem to be recalled by Banquo in I, iii—the devil tries "to make himself so to be trusted in these little things, that he may have the better commodity thereafter, to deceive in the end with a trick once for all; I mean the everlasting perdition of their soul and body". Cf. the deception of Alexander Borgia, unmasked at the end of *The Divil's Charter*.

18. This insensibility is contrasted with the Christian stoicism of Macduff and old Siward, who endure their bereavements courageously, not barbarously.

19. H. B. Charlton, *Shakespearian Tragedy* (Cambridge, 1948); W. C. Curry, *Shakespeare's Philosophical Patterns* (Baton Rouge, 1937); Helen Gardner, 'Milton and the Tragedy of Damnation' in *English Studies*, 1948, ed. F. P. Wilson (London, 1948); Hardin Craig, 'Motivation in Shakespeare's Choice of Materials', *supra* pp. 31–2; Roy Walker, *The Time is Free* (London, 1949).

20. *Macbeth*, I, vii, 1–28; II, i, 31–64; III, ii, 13–26, 46–53; v, iii, 40–53; v, v, 17–28.

21. Cf. the line below, from *Lucrece*: "Who...sells eternity to get a toy?" and the lassitude of Cleopatra at Antony's death:

> The odds is gone,
> And there is nothing left remarkable
> Beneath the visiting moon.   (IV, xv, 66–8)

22. It may be noted that this atmosphere is recalled again in Iachimo's speech over the sleeping Imogen: night, 'our *Tarquin*' with his stealthy tread, the crickets' cry (*Cymbeline*, II, ii, 11–14).

SHAKESPEARE AND THE 'ORDINARY' WORD

BY

D. S. BLAND

I

Analysing Shakespeare's development as a poet, George Rylands has said: "He was first an Elizabethan poet and it is of this stuff [i.e. the sonnets of Petrarch, the Pléiade, Lyly, etc.] that Elizabethan poetry was made." That is undeniably the case; but Rylands goes on to say:

In the two following passages there is hardly a distinguishing mark. Both are Elizabethan:

> At last the golden Oriental gate
> Of greatest heaven gan to open fair,
> And Phoebus fresh as a bridegroom to his mate
> Came dancing forth shaking his golden hair.

> See how the morning opes her golden gates,
> And takes her farewell of the glorious sun,
> How well resembles it the prime of youth
> Trimmed like a younker prancing to his love.

The first is Spenser, the second the young Shakespeare; and although Shakespeare is a little freer in movement and cannot resist transforming Phoebus Apollo into an Elizabethan gallant, the idiom is the same.[1]

It is true that the rhetorical texture (of a neo–classic, decorative kind) of the two passages is the same.[2] There are, however, and in spite of the striking verbal parallels, more distinguishing marks than Rylands perhaps had space to enumerate. In the first place, Spenser would appear to be more conscious that he is addressing a cultivated audience. His poetry, therefore, is deliberately reminiscent and sophisticated in a way which Shakespeare largely abandoned when he turned to the theatre.[3] Further, the passage from Spenser is a description of what (within the context of the poem) we are meant to take as a natural scene which the bridegroom image is intended to emphasize, whereas it is the first two lines of the passage from Shakespeare that are the decorative image, a parallel intended to reinforce the picture of "the prime of youth". The dawn-lover relationship, that is to say, plays opposite roles in these two passages. This tying down of his image to aspects of reality, however decorative the image may be in itself, is a characteristic of Shakespeare's style which has often been commented on. There is another, however, which the passages already quoted serve to bring out, and which has not, perhaps, attracted the attention it deserves. To my mind, the most obvious distinguishing mark between these two passages is the use of the word 'younker'. For Rylands the use of this word amounts to "transforming Phoebus Apollo into an Elizabethan gallant", but is this all that can be said about it? The word strikes the eye and the ear with more force than any other word in these two passages and, in conjunction with 'prancing', gives a liveliness to Shakespeare's lines that is lacking in the passage from Spenser, producing an effect similar to that produced by the introduction of a slang word or phrase into the later prose of Henry James (a prose as mannered in its texture as the poetry of Spenser). This impression is reinforced if we compare the use of 'younker' here with that in the *Dialogue in Verse* ascribed to Marlowe:

> Fie, lusty younker, what do you here,
>   Not dancing on the green to-day?
> For Pierce, the farmer's son, I fear,
>   Is like to carry your wench away.

Within *this* context, a conversation carried on by rustics in an unsophisticated ballad rhythm, 'younker' seems perfectly at home, and does not impinge on the attention with the force of Shakespeare's usage.

The point I wish to make by this somewhat extended examination of eight lines of not very distinguished Elizabethan verse is this: that for all Shakespeare's indebtedness to the influences that shaped him into an undeniably Elizabethan poet (and in *Henry VI* his prentice days are scarcely behind him), he had, as a natural part of his poetic rhetoric, a fondness for the 'ordinary' word and an ability to put it to effective use that is outside the usual canons of Elizabethan prosody. His poetic speech derives strength from common speech to a degree that far surpasses anything that, say, Wordsworth tried to do, for all his professed aims in that direction. But more than this (for the ability to make words do what he wants them to do is the mark of any true poet), the use of the ordinary word is a characteristic that set Shakespeare apart from his contemporaries very early in his career. Hence, at this early stage, the uncomfortable juxtaposition of 'younker' and the more conventional 'golden gates'. Part of this bias comes, as F. P. Wilson has reminded us, from the nature of his medium, but not all:

The conditions of Shakespeare's art as a dramatist did not permit him to stray far from popular idiom, but even if they had his mind was of a cast that would still have found the material upon which it worked mainly in the diction of common life.[4]

Although Elizabethan English was a language still to a large extent in a state of flux, the conception of a 'standard' speech was on the way to being established by the time Shakespeare became a dramatist.[5] Most important for the poet was the idea of a proscribed language, a vocabulary which he should *not* use. Over and above the emerging standard language, that is to say, a language which was mainly that of London and the Court, there was a poetic speech which grew by deliberate choice and rejection, and which was (among other influences) fostered by the study of the Classics, the Pléiade and *Euphues*. It is from this formative influence that Shakespeare plays truant, not only in his lifelong habit of making up words to suit his purpose as he goes along and in his ridicule of verbal fashions, but in his use of the ordinary, the colloquial word. He is seen doing it in his use of 'younker' in the passage already quoted from the third part of *Henry VI*. But leaving this disputed trilogy on one side, for fear that the passage is not by Shakespeare at all, and moving to the safer ground of *Richard III*, we still find this early use of the ordinary but vivid word:

> God take King Edward to his mercy,
> And leave the world for me to *bustle* in,   (I, i, 150–1)

an image made all the more vivid by the suggested contrast with the reality of Richard's awkward gait. Another example occurs in the third scene of the same act:

> Because I cannot flatter and speak fair,
> Smile in men's faces, smooth, deceive and *cog*,
> *Duck* with French nods and apish courtesy,
> I must be held a rancorous enemy. (I, iii, 47–50)

Nor is this distinguishing mark absent from the early, conventional comedies, which is where we should least expect it. Proteus uses the exact and expressive word when he says:

> Thus have I shunned the fire for fear of burning,
> And *drenched* me in the sea. (*Two Gentlemen*, I, iii, 78–9)

There is no place in Shakespeare's work where this characteristic turn of words is missing, and when he comes to the full use of his mature poetic style, it is with an increased and increasing boldness in the use of such words. How brightly, for example, the epithet lights up Pandarus in these lines:

> I cannot come to Cressid but by Pandar,
> And he's as *tetchy* to be woo'd to woo,
> As she is stubborn, chaste, against all suit. (*Troilus*, I, i, 98–100)

And how expressive of Antony's dotage is his scornful '*dungy* earth'—of which he himself is the triple pillar! This characteristic has often been noted, but usually only when critics are speaking of Shakespeare's Elizabethanisms; his use of double epithets, for instance, as in 'exsufflicate and blown surmises' and the parallel habit of linking a Romance word with a Saxon, as in:

> To lie in cold obstruction and to rot,

or when indicating his use of dialect. My point, however, is that the use of the ordinary but vivid word, apart from these compound uses and dialect borrowings, was an important element in Shakespeare's make-up as a poet, independent of and unaffected by the accidents of fashion, time and place; not a conscious reaction against the conventions of the day, but his natural and ever-present way of speech. It was with him at the beginning of his career:

> These blue-veined violets whereon we lean
> Never can *blab*, nor know not what we mean. (*Venus and Adonis*, 125–6)

It remained with him throughout his poetic life, reaching its noblest use in *Antony and Cleopatra*, perhaps, and is still present in the *Tempest*:

> You *cram* these words into my ears. (II, i, 106)

It is a verbal habit subject to none of the fluctuations which other traits of his style underwent in his search for an instrument fit for his purpose.

II

One of the greatest effects in poetry is produced by using familiar words in an unfamiliar way, though not necessarily in an unfamiliar order. This is the corollary to Shakespeare's use of the single vivid word. There is more of a woman's charm in

> Age cannot wither her nor custom stale
> Her infinite variety,

than in a thousand Elizabethan sonnets. Yet, with the possible exception of 'infinite' in such a context, there is not one word here which is not taken from "the language really spoken by men". Familiar though the words are, however, they are poetry because of the way in which they are used. There are no loose ends. 'Age' fits into 'wither', 'custom' into 'stale', the two nouns pair off with the verbs and stand in contrast to 'variety'. The whole is close-knit, concentrated, distilled, and yet there is nothing unusual about the words, their order is familiar. It is this turn of thought and vocabulary which (among other things) gives universality to Shakespeare's poetry, and it is when he is thus free of Elizabethanisms that he is 'for all time', so that we can say of him what C. S. Lewis has said of Chaucer:

Often a single line…seems to contain within itself the germ of the whole tradition of high poetical language in England. It is not so much poetical, as 'English poetry' itself—or what Englishmen most most easily recognize as poetry….[6]

Discussing the difficulties of interpretation caused by changes in the language since Shakespeare's day, Johnson wrote in his *Proposals*:

If Shakespeare has difficulties above other writers, it is to be imputed to the nature of his work, which required the use of the common colloquial language, and consequently admitted many phrases allusive, elliptical and proverbial, such as we speak and hear every hour without observing them; and of which, being now familiar, we do not suspect that they can ever grow uncouth, or that, being now obvious, they can ever seem remote.

This is shrewdly observed, both as a generalization and of Shakespeare in particular. At the same time, it is a paradox of Shakespeare's style that he often achieves *universality* of speech by the use of words current in the common language of his own day. It cannot be said of Shakespeare's poetry, with any close approximation to the truth, what W. MacNeile Dixon says of poetry in general: "In poetry…you discern…not only a peculiar aloofness from life's daily routine, but a singular language."[7] It is true some of the time, but not continually, and, on balance, it is not true of the bulk of Shakespeare's work, for the reason noted by Johnson. Nor is it true, I think, in relation to his reputation. It is not the voice of the whirlwind in a phrase like "the multitudinous seas incarnadine" that takes the breath away and causes us to put Shakespeare in a class apart, but the still, small voice of "Pray you, undo this button".

But though Shakespeare uses words which are current in the common speech of his day, they are words which are vividly descriptive of his subject, words which are often, as nearly as possible, 'the thing itself'. When Octavius says that Antony *frets*

> That Lepidus of the triumvirate
> Should be deposed,   (III, vi, 27–9)

we can *see* Antony, sunk in dotage, his imperiousness become mere peevishness. The word 'frets' does not only describe; it creates.

We may note in passing, however, that Johnson is not always as shrewd as he shows himself to be in the quotation made above. His most remarkable failure of perspicacity, in the well-known *Rambler* discussion of Lady Macbeth's 'blanket of the dark' speech (which he errs in attributing to Macbeth), is a passage most apposite to the present inquiry:

> Come, thick night,
> And pall thee in the dunnest smoke of hell,
> That my keen knife see not the wound it makes,
> Nor heav'n peep through the blanket of the dark,
> To cry, Hold! Hold!
>
> (I, v, 51–5)

Apart from the subtle interplay of vowels, in which 'peep' plays its part, and of consonants, particularly *k* and *l*, to which 'blanket' contributes, the whole passage is marked by simplicity of vocabulary, which, by its very ordinariness—as though only the most elemental ideas can find expression—serves to emphasize the hysteria underlying Lady Macbeth's tautness of mind and will. Johnson could "scarce check his risibility" at the thought of "the avengers of guilt peeping through a blanket". We are more likely to smile at Johnson's paraphrase of the passage: "Macbeth proceeds to wish that the inspection of heaven may be intercepted, and that he may, in the involutions of infernal darkness, escape the eye of providence."

III

Two qualities are to be observed in the ordinary but vivid words which have been quoted so far. Without any deliberate choice being made, they have consisted almost entirely of active verbs: *bustle, cog, duck, drench, blab, cram, fret, peep,* as against *younker, tetchy, dungy* and *blanket.* This, however, is what we should expect, since the more work that can be thrown on to the verb, the more effective is the sentence likely to be. As Quiller-Couch has said (in referring to Basic English, but with larger implications):

the verb is the very nerve of the sentence; and for preference the active verb. Nouns and adjectives are but dead haulage, prepositions and conjunctions inert couplings, until the verb (*verbum*, the 'Word') comes along, supplies the motive power, starts and keeps the whole train going....In matters of intellectual or emotional persuasion the verb takes charge, insomuch that, as a rough general rule for judging of a writer's style whether it be forcible or feeble one may usefully note if by instinct or habit he uses active transitive verbs in preference to laying them on their passive backs and tying his nouns and particles together with little auxiliary 'is's' and 'was's'.[8]

From any such test Shakespeare would emerge successfully.

Secondly, we may note that these ordinary words are vivid in their contexts because, even when they are not specifically used as metaphors, as in the case of *cram*, they have a pictorial quality that brings them very close to metaphor nevertheless.

It scarcely requires saying, of course, that this sort of word-counting is an operation which the poet himself does not perform. It is a post-mortem act by the critic. (Though post-mortem is not the right metaphor. The death of the passage usually occurs *after* the critic has done his worst in this way.) What Shakespeare did with his vocabulary he did through his instinct as a poet, or more accurately, through his instinct as a dramatist. For this ability to use the ordinary word vividly is one of his chief attributes as a dramatic poet. The oblivion, in terms of the theatre, which has fallen on *Sejanus*, for example, shows what can happen when this element of ordinariness is lacking in a dramatic poet. It is the aridity of the language, as well as the subject-matter and the construction of the play, which sets *Sejanus* among the Elizabethan plays which are rarely, if ever, performed. And this use of the ordinary but vivid word is one reason why even in Shakespeare's early plays, with all their youthful and self-conscious tricks of style, we recognize the true dramatic accent. Such a speech as Berowne's upon love, beginning

> And I—
> Forsooth, in love! I that have been Love's whip,
> A very beadle to a humorous sigh,
>
> > (*Love's Labour's Lost*, III, i, 175–7)

is in notable contrast to the deliberately formal speeches of the first scene of the play. It marks the invasion of reality into the earlier fantasy and attitudinizing, and the language reflects this change in the dramatic situation. It is true that compared with, say, the indigenous metaphors of Antony's

> > The hearts
> That spanieled me at heels, to whom I gave
> Their wishes, do discandy, melt their sweets
> On blossoming Caesar, and this pine is barked
> That overtopped them all,
> > > > > > > > > > > > (IV, xii, 20–4)

Berowne's speech can be seen to be still mannered. Each image is limited to a single line, and though there are clusters of images they do not grow out of one another as they do in Antony's speech. It is true also that the mannered quality of the earlier speeches is essential to the dramatic situation, and that in spite of being written in stanzas they are conceived as speeches and not as something to be read. All the same, Berowne's speech has more gesture and dramatic movement than these. There is a freshness of imagery, drawn from Shakespeare's personal observation ("a night-watch constable") and a humour ("with two pitch balls stuck in her face for eyes") which is lacking in the earlier speeches, and for which we would look in vain in Shakespeare's predecessors.

Shakespeare, then, discovered early in his career that the decorative writing which he had employed in *Venus and Adonis* would not work in poetic drama. Dramatic verse, to be effective, must move; it needs activating as much as plot and character, and Shakespeare makes no exceptions to this rule, even where (as his stage frequently required) he is building up a scenic effect:

> This castle hath a pleasant seat; the air
> *Nimbly* and sweetly recommends itself
> Unto our gentle senses.
> > > > > > > > (*Macbeth*, I, vi, 1–3)

And this is a lesson which later poetic drama seems gradually to have forgotten, partly, no doubt, because much of it was written by men who were poets first and dramatists only second, if at all, who wrote blank verse, not because it was a vital poetic form, as it was to Shakespeare, but because its 'poetic' associations helped to cover poverty of material and a lack of a true dramatic sense. Part of this activating quality in Shakespeare's dramatic verse comes, as I have tried to show, from his effective use of words which, by the standards of Elizabethan poetry, are colloquialisms or even slang, but which, in the contexts in which Shakespeare uses them, are vivid and arresting; and this element in his verse was not something he acquired by experience but something that was inherent in his style from the first.

NOTES

1. Essay on 'Shakespeare the Poet' in *A Companion to Shakespeare Studies*, ed. Harley Granville-Barker and G. B. Harrison (1934), p. 94.

2. The root of this sun-bridegroom image would appear to be in Psalm xix, verses 4 and 5: "In them hath he set a tabernacle for the sun, which is as a bridegroom coming out of his chamber."

3. A useful analysis of the different types of Elizabethan writer, in which Spenser figures as the example of the well-connected poet and Shakespeare as the commercially successful one, will be found in 'The Poets on Fortune's Hill: Literature and Society, 1580–1610', John F. Danby, *The Cambridge Journal*, II, no. 4, pp. 195–211.

4. *Shakespeare and the Diction of Common Life*, F. P. Wilson (1941), p. 5. The present essay explores a corner of the question which this lecture leaves untouched.

5. See 'Shakespeare and Elizabethan English', G. D. Willcock, in *A Companion to Shakespeare Studies*, pp. 117–36.

6. *The Allegory of Love* (1936), p. 201.

7. *An Apology for the Arts* (1944), p. 23.

8. 'On Basic English: A Challenge to Innovators', *Times Literary Supplement*, 30 September 1944.

E

MALONE AND THE UPSTART CROW[1]

BY

J. DOVER WILSON

The Three Parts of *Henry VI*, unquestionably written before the beginning of March 1592, as I hope to show on a later occasion, are, if Shakespeare's, probably the earliest productions we have from his pen. But are they his? And if so, are they his entirely? Their inclusion in the First Folio shows that Heminges and Condell considered him to be, at least in part, responsible for them all. On the other hand, it is impossible to deny their unequal quality; poor scenes and pedestrian or over-pretentious verse being interspersed with scenes and verse which all but extreme disintegrators accept as authentic Shakespeare. In 1790 Malone offered an explanation of this state of affairs which satisfied most students until twenty years ago. The trilogy, he argued, was originally composed by two or more of Shakespeare's immediate predecessors (he suspected Greene and Peele) and was afterwards rehandled and in part rewritten by him. These views he set forth in *A Dissertation on the Three Parts of Henry VI*, which, apart from Farmer's *Essay on the Learning of Shakespeare*, 1767, was the earliest and most elaborate treatise yet written on a single point of Shakespearian scholarship and was pronounced on its appearance by no less distinguished a scholar than Porson to be "one of the most convincing pieces of criticism he had ever met with".[2] That it no longer convinces is due to the disproof of a proposition which held a conspicuous place in the thesis. It was not, however, the original ground of Malone's conviction or even the main support of his argument; and, though its demolition seems in the eyes of many to leave the *Dissertation* in ruins, if we examine the theory closely we shall, I think, find the foundations unimpaired, and the lines of the main structure still unbroken.

To understand how Malone came to hold these views it is necessary to go back a little. For he was not the first to hold them. Writing on *Henry VI* in 1734, Theobald had remarked that

...though there are several master-strokes in these three plays, which incontestably betray the work-manship of Shakespeare; yet I am almost doubtful, whether they were entirely of his writing. And unless they were wrote by him very early, I should rather imagine them to have been brought to him as a director of the stage; and so have received some finishing beauties at his hand. An accurate observer will easily see, the diction of them is more obsolete, and the numbers more mean and prosaical, than in the generality of his genuine compositions.[3]

This careful and diffident expression of opinion was caught up, like much else of Theobald's, by the crude and arrogant Bishop Warburton thirteen years later, and reappears in his edition as a dogmatic statement that *Henry VI* was "certainly not Shakespeare's". And this in turn attracted the eye of Dr Johnson, ever on the look-out for examples of literary coxcombry, who lumped the two editors together, and without, I fear, troubling to pay due attention to what 'poor Tib' had written, pitched upon a word or two in the second sentence just quoted, and dismissed the contention with a dogmatism as sweeping as the bishop's: "In these plays no such marks of spuriousness are found. The diction, the versification, and the figures are Shakespeare's."[4] A year later Tyrwhitt discovered the now famous allusion to Shakespeare as an upstart crow in

56

A Groatsworth of Wit by Robert Greene, who by parodying a line in *3 Henry VI* seemed to point to that play as his. Thus the verdict of the Great Cham was apparently confirmed by a contemporary witness, and held the field for the next twenty-two years.

Even Malone himself was convinced, for he raises no question of Shakespeare's authorship in the first draft of his *Attempt to Ascertain the Order of Shakespeare's Plays* published in 1778, where he also refers to Tyrwhitt's discovery and evidently takes it as corroborative evidence. One person, however, remained sceptical, Richard Farmer;[5] and it has been suggested that but for him Malone would never have come to question Johnson's conclusions.[6] The change in Malone's views which took place between 1778 and 1790 is, however, to be set down to a different cause. What moved him was what had moved Theobald before him, the experience of editing most of the other plays. For he begins the *Dissertation* by stating that he had long believed all three parts to be Shakespeare's, until "a more minute investigation of the subject, into which I have been led by the revision of all our author's works...convinced me that...my conclusion was too hastily drawn". Furthermore, the grounds of his conversion are set forth in the second paragraph, as follows:

What at present I have chiefly in view is to account for the visible *inequality* in these pieces; many traits of Shakespeare being clearly discernible in them, while the inferior parts are not merely unequal to the rest (from which no certain conclusion can be drawn), but of quite a different complexion from the inferior parts of our author's undoubted performances.[7]

These words, it will be observed, restate Theobald's position, but in a form at once more discriminating and less diffident, while they are also clearly intended as a reply to Johnson, whom immediately after Malone goes on to challenge on the score of "diction, versification and the figures".

But opinion on such things was a matter of taste, and on matters of taste Johnson's verdict was at that date well-nigh final. Malone therefore cast round for evidence of an objective kind, and found (he thought) more than enough to prove his case in the very passage from Greene which Tyrwhitt had cited as proving Johnson's, but which Malone now claimed as 'the chief hinge' of his own argument.[8] For while of course the allusion to a line from *3 Henry VI*[9] in an attack upon 'Shake-scene' left nothing to be said in favour of Warburton's absolute denial of Shakespeare's authorship, it did not touch Theobald's thesis of a Shakespearian revision of other men's plays. On the contrary, Malone contended, it corroborated it completely, since Greene's sneer about the "vpstart Crow, beautified with our feathers" was obviously meant to be a charge of appropriation; in other words, Greene was accusing Shakespeare of stealing and adapting plays upon *Henry VI* by himself and his friends.

Had Malone stopped there modern scholarship might not perhaps have followed a will o' the wisp for the past twenty years. But, as was inevitable in the state of knowledge at that time, Greene's words suggested a further step in the argument. Side by side with the Folio texts of *2* and *3 Henry VI* we have the patently inferior versions printed in 1594 and 1595 as two quartos, bearing the titles of *The First Part of the Contention* and *The True Tragedy of Richard Duke of York*. Before Johnson, editors had regarded these as Shakespeare's first drafts of the later texts. But Johnson pointed out that productions "so apparently imperfect and mutilated" could hardly be of this nature; and he was therefore "inclined to believe them copies taken [down] by some auditor" present at two or more performances, and afterwards sent to the printer.[10] It was a shrewd guess, which tallies closely with what is now considered the true explanation. Moreover, like Johnson's contention as regards the authorship of the good texts, it seemed to be confirmed immediately afterwards by the discovery of contemporary evidence, this time of one of Thomas Heywood's references to his own plays coming into print in a corrupt and mangled state because they had been "copied only by the ear".[11] Here again, however, Malone was ready with what appeared a complete answer, since he was easily able to demonstrate that "no fraudulent copyist or shorthand writer" could possibly have produced the quarto texts as they stand.[12]

The argument of the *Dissertation* seemed impregnable and became part of the orthodox Shakespearian creed for 140 years. Questioned from time to time,[13] it was not seriously challenged until Greg and others some thirty years ago began to explore the character of 'bad' Elizabethan dramatic texts. Malone had put Johnson's explanation of the *Contention* quartos out of court on the matter of the only agency then contemplated as likely to produce spurious editions of plays. But from about 1910 onwards it came more and more to be accepted that Heywood's references to stenographers had led criticism astray, that the pirate player or traitor actor was the nigger we might look to find behind most of the piles of rubbish which Pollard first labelled 'bad quartos'; in short that the explanation Johnson had offered for the 'bad quartos' of *2* and *3 Henry VI* would after all fit a large class of printed Elizabethan plays, if one substituted actor in performance for auditor at performance as the agent responsible. The relevance of all this to the *Henry VI* problem was not perceived at once. In 1924 and 1926, however, Peter Alexander (working on previous suggestions of J. S. Smart) and Edmund Chambers independently began applying to it the principles Greg had worked out elsewhere.[14] And Alexander's brilliant little book on *Shakespeare's 'Henry VI' and 'Richard III'*, published in 1929, proved without question that Malone had been wrong on that point. But Alexander did not stop there; he went on to attack the argument at its 'chief hinge'. So far, he claimed, were Greene's words from being a charge of plagiarism, they were merely one of his periodical grumbles at the acting quality, aggravated by the realization that the quality had thrown up a dramatist from its own ranks who was now a serious rival to better scholars than himself. Alexander's book appeared with Pollard's blessing in the form of an introduction; Edmund Chambers, as I said, had independently reached identical conclusions both on the *Contention* quartos and on the meaning of Greene's words;[15] and Greg and McKerrow subscribed to these conclusions shortly afterwards. Thus Alexander found all the four leading Shakespearian scholars of the day in agreement with his main theses, an agreement which Greg has since reaffirmed in his important book on *The Editorial Problem in Shakespeare* (1942).[16]

The two principal props of Malone's *Dissertation* seemed to have collapsed, and the crash was hailed as a turning-point in our whole conception of Shakespeare's apprentice years. "We must in fact start afresh," proclaimed Alfred Pollard;[17] and I thought so too for eighteen years. Yet as my first enthusiasm began to cool a little, one or two doubts crossed my mind. Was the demonstration after all as complete as Greg and others claimed? As a matter of logic, even if Malone was wrong about the Bad Quartos and the Upstart Crow, it did not *necessarily* follow that he was wrong about the mixed authorship of the authentic texts; and when I looked at the *Dissertation* I found to my surprise that he had originally come to that conclusion on quite other grounds. Then, too, most scholars are agreed that Shakespeare spent at least part of his early years revising or rewriting the plays of other men. *King John* is based upon *A Troublesome Reign*, and Chambers himself admits the presence of a second or third hand in *1 Henry VI*, *Titus* and *The Taming of the Shrew*, though he prefers the word 'collaboration' to 'revision' in describing Shakespeare's part. But what troubled me most of all were two contemporary references to Greene's attack on Shakespeare, both of which, as I read them, speak of it as an accusation of literary theft, while one of them implies that others took it in that sense also. Yet none of Malone's critics, to my bewilderment, seemed to attach any significance to these references.[18] And so, being at the time much occupied with other matters, I recorded my doubts on the point in a little book called *The Essential Shakespeare* published three years after Alexander's and then put the whole matter out of my head. But when I took up *Henry VI* about thirty months ago and re-read it after many years, years the leisure of which had been spent in the minute examination line by line of some twenty-two other plays of Shakespeare, I discovered that my response was almost exactly that of Theobald and Malone. Like them I was immediately struck by an extraordinary inequality of style and temper in all three parts: while I constantly came upon passages, now long, now brief, in which I recognized the unmistakable impress of the master's hand, side by side with these were inferior scenes and speeches which I could not possibly regard as his, since, to quote Malone's careful words again, they were "not merely unequal to the rest (from which no certain conclusion can be drawn), but of quite a different complexion from the inferior parts of our author's undoubted performances". And finding myself unable to escape those impressions, my doubts of seventeen years before recurred to my mind. Malone had gone astray over the Bad Quartos; but did not his 'chief hinge' still hold? Might not we moderns have overlooked something in Greene's words about the Upstart Crow and the contemporary comments upon them which Malone and those who agreed with him in the eighteenth century had seen?

Anyone who knows anything of Shakespeare must know the passages in Greene's *Groatsworth of Wit* and Chettle's *Kind-Heart's Dream* almost by heart. Yet if what follows is to be clear I must quote them once again, with apologies to the reader for thus thrashing over old straw. Writing shortly before his death in squalid poverty on 3 September 1592, Greene addresses three of his fellow-dramatists, two of them being clearly identifiable as Peele and Marlowe and the third being probably Nashe, in the following terms:

Base minded men all three of you, if by my miserie you be not warnd: for vnto none of you (like mee) sought those burres [the players] to cleaue: those Puppets (I meane) that spake from our mouths, those Anticks garnisht in our colours. Is it not strange, that I, to whom they all haue beene beholding: is it not like that you, to whome they all haue been beholding, shall (were yee in that case as I am now) bee both at once of them forsaken? Yes trust them not: for there is an vpstart Crow, beautified with our feathers, that with his *Tygers hart wrapt in a Players hyde*, supposes he is as well able to bombast out a blanke verse as the best of you: and beeing an absolute *Iohannes fac totum*, is in his owne conceit the onely Shake-scene in a countrey.[19]

In "his *Tygers hart wrapt in a Players hyde*", Greene is of course making use of the line

O tiger's heart wrapt in a woman's hide!—

which occurs in York's dying curse upon Margaret of Anjou in *3 Henry VI* (I, iv, 137), and Tyrwhitt held that the allusion would be pointless if the original were not the work of the

Johannes Factotum whom the dying Greene was abusing. But the crux of the passage lies in the description of the person attacked as an "vpstart Crow, beautified with our feathers". What did Greene precisely mean by that? Nothing more, reply Alexander, Chambers and Greg, than that this new rival to him and his fellow-scholars was one of the ignorant players who had left him to die in poverty. They insist that the phrase is simply a variation upon "puppets that spake from our mouths, antics garnished in our colours" earlier in the passage, and that it had for some time been more or less of a cliché with Greene and Nashe in speaking of the acting profession.[20] It all sounds most reasonable and indeed obvious. Yet we can be certain that this was not the sense which readers of Greene's pamphlet in 1592 and 1593 put upon his words.

Of the two contemporary comments on them, the earlier and more interesting comes from Henry Chettle, at this time a master printer, who in a preface to his *Kind-Heart's Dream* published in December 1592, three months after Greene's death, admits that he had seen the *Groatsworth of Wit* through the press, states that Greene's letter "written to diuers play-makers" was "offensiuely by one or two of them taken", and then continues as follows:

With neither of them that take offence was I acquainted, and with one of them I care not if I neuer be: The other, whome at that time I did not so much spare, as since I wish I had, for that as I haue moderated the heate of liuing writers, and might have vsde my owne discretion (especially in such a case) the Author beeing dead, that I did not, I am as sory as if the originall fault had beene my fault, because my selfe haue seene his demeanor no lesse ciuill than he exelent in the qualitie he professes: Besides, diuers of worship haue reported his vprightnes of dealing, which argues his honesty, and his facetious grace in writting, that aprooues his Art.

Finally, while admitting that he had 'stroke out' of Greene's letter some charge against the former "of them that take offence" because "had it beene true, yet to publish it, was intollerable", he went on to deny that he had added anything of his own; "for I protest it was all Greenes, not mine nor Maister Nashes, as some vniustly haue affirmed".[21]

The two persons who took offence have been, I think almost universally, identified as Marlowe and Shakespeare. "This implies", Chambers notes,

some looseness in Chettle's language,[22] since Greene's letter was obviously not written to Shakespeare. But there is nothing in the letter as we have it which could be offensive to any play-maker except Marlowe, who is spoken of as an atheist and Machiavellian, and Shakespeare, who is openly attacked. The others, presumably Peele and Nashe, 'young Iuuenall, that byting Satyrist, that lastlie with mee together writ a Comedie', are handled in a more friendly spirit.[23]

It is true that just about this time (autumn 1592) Nashe seems to have first found patrons 'of worship', viz. the Careys, and to have become acquainted with Chettle, so that part of what the latter says (as we now assume) about Shakespeare might apply to him.[24] But, in addition to the points Chambers makes, it is to be noted that immediately after the apology just quoted Chettle goes on to exonerate Nashe by name from having a hand in Greene's pamphlet, and in so doing clearly has him in mind as a different person from the unnamed man of 'civil demeanour' mentioned before. Furthermore, this man is, he tells us, "exelent in the qualitie he professes", words that almost certainly imply an actor, which Shakespeare was and Nashe was not. We need not hesitate, I think, to assume that Chettle's 'exelent' player and Greene's 'vpstart Crow' are the same individual.

This being so, the bilious outburst of the one and the frank apology of the other give us our first glimpse of Shakespeare as a person; and almost our last, since we have nothing later about him so vividly focused. They are therefore biographically of capital importance; and it is worth while holding up the argument for a moment to consider them in this aspect, more especially as the full significance of Chettle's apology has never yet been properly appreciated. What Greene says shows us Shakespeare's standing in the theatrical world and the opinion held of him by the literary circles of London in 1592. Evidently he sees him as a portent, able to write blank verse as good as, if not better than, that of any other dramatist, a serious rival therefore to the old 'university' gang, Marlowe included, and withal an astonishing Johannes Factotum ("a would-be universal genius" or "one who meddles with everything"[25]), i.e. confidently ready to turn his hand to any and every form of dramatic work going. This is no beginner or prentice hand, as many modern critics suppose Shakespeare to have been at this stage, though the word 'vpstart' may suggest that Greene had only recently come to realize the brilliance of the newly risen star.[26] And what Chettle says reveals something of the man's spirit and of Marlowe's also. For note, no corresponding apology is offered to the latter, though Greene had called him an atheist without qualification, a serious, indeed a criminal, charge in those days. On the contrary, Chettle informs his readers that he had suppressed a worse charge which it would have been 'intollerable' to publish; thus virtually restoring the previous excision, for all men might now guess what the charge had been. Further, it is pretty obvious that the two dramatists had made their protests in very different fashion. Chettle's statement that he was not acquainted with Marlowe, and "I care not if I never be", together with the words later in the passage ("him I would wish to use me no worse than I deserve"), suggests the receipt of an angry and threatening message. The reference to Shakespeare's 'civil demeanour', on the other hand, and the genuine regret which breathes from the whole apology, point to a personal call from one who parts friends after expostulating politely but firmly. It is clear too, I think, that the caller either brought with him, or was followed up by, a weighty testimonial to his character from 'divers of worship', which we may legitimately translate as several noblemen interested in defending the slandered poet.

And this brings me back to my argument. Why should men of rank in that age of rigid class distinction go out of their way to make representations to an obscure printer on behalf of a player-poet? Such things are not done without good cause and a definite end in view, and Chettle's words themselves strongly suggest that the extraction of a complete and public apology was what was aimed at, possibly even peremptorily required. But an apology for what? What was the nature of the charge which had moved these gentry of worship to intervene in defence of their protégé? Here Chettle is plain enough. They have assured him, he tells us, and we may guess have bidden him assure the world at large, that Shakespeare is both an excellent dramatic poet and an honourable man. Moreover, these two assurances were, we need not hesitate to assume, directly related to the attack made upon him. Greene's sneers about 'bombast' and "an absolute *Iohannes fac totum*" are, for example, countered by the testimony to a "facetious grace in writing", that is to say, a polished and witty poetic and dramatic style. But why drag in that pointed reference to 'honesty' and 'uprightness of dealing'? One does not publicly certify a friend is no thief unless someone else has previously asserted the contrary as publicly. Yet if, as Alexander and those who follow him maintain, "an vpstart Crow, beautified with our feathers" simply means that Shakespeare was an actor who had the impudence to write plays, then the certificate of honesty is entirely irrelevant, not to say maladroit. If, on the other hand, the said description, as Malone interpreted it, was intended to insinuate in no uncertain terms that Shakespeare had appropriated and rehandled plays by Greene himself and one or more of the three fellow-scholars he was addressing (*3 Henry VI* being pointed at as an example of the plunder), then the certificate would be pertinent indeed. Can there be any real doubt that Shakespeare's defenders and Chettle who printed their defence understood Greene's attack in the same way as Malone?

Some modern critics object that Shakespeare was an unknown poet in 1592 and therefore unlikely to have been asked to revise plays by the best dramatists at that date in London.[27] Surely, as I have already suggested, there is nothing in this. In the first place, we cannot infer anything about Shakespeare's reputation with the acting profession before Greene's attack for the simple reason that we possess no information on the point whatever; he is unknown to *us* before 1592, but he was then twenty-eight years old, and what he was doing earlier is to-day anybody's guess. In the second place we *can* infer from what Greene says that Shakespeare had become by that date a leading dramatist, as good as, if not better than, the best of the old school. Thirdly, the solicitude of 'divers of worship' for his reputation shows he was already famous enough to be able to count upon the support of persons of social standing. And lastly, if Middleton was allowed as most critics believe to rehandle and revise *Macbeth*, a play written at the height of Shakespeare's powers and contemporary fame, we need not surely be surprised to find this "absolute *Iohannes fac totum*" rehandling and revising Greene or Peele or both in 1592.

Others may ask, if that was the extent of his guilt, why all this pother about it? Why, on the one hand, was Greene so angry? And why, on the other, did Shakespeare put his influential friends to the trouble of witnessing in his favour? Whoever wrote the plays had sold them to Shakespeare's company, which had every right to adapt and improve them, from the acting point of view, in any way they saw fit. If a jaundiced rival wished to interpret such a perfectly normal procedure of the playhouse as plagiarism, he was only making himself ridiculous in the eyes of all who knew the facts. Besides, he was dead. Yet it is not difficult to supply reasons for Shakespeare's disquietude. While the company and their player-dramatist were no doubt entirely within their rights, the rewriting of large portions of plays purchased from others was scarcely a 'normal procedure'. Had it ever been done before on such a scale? Further, the publication of *A Groatsworth of Wit* must have created a considerable stir. In the first place, Greene was a writer of many pamphlets and tales, a famous dramatist and probably also a well-known figure in the streets and taverns of London, while, as a contemporary puts it, his writings "priuiledged on euery post", made his name familiar "vnto infinite numbers of people" who did not know him by sight.[28] And in the second, before the *Groatsworth* appeared, the squalid circumstances of his death, together with many details of his no less disreputable manner of life, had been exhibited to public gaze in another pamphlet by his enemy Gabriel Harvey, and this provoked Nashe to take up the cudgels, and so started the most notorious and long-continued flyting of that period. Yet Greene, for all his shady past, had done public service by exposing the coney-catching crew, and had died according to his own account a deeply repentant man.[29] We need not doubt therefore that a large number of godly and respectable people paid attention to his words. "Truth sits upon the lips of dying men." Knowing nothing of what went on behind the scenes of the playhouse, readers would gather that this fellow Shakespeare was in the habit of stealing other men's plays, was little better in fact than that notorious atheist Marlowe, whom the penitent had also denounced with his dying breath. Lastly, as some would note, whatever his grand friends said about his honesty in general, neither he nor they had been able actually to deny the particular charge Greene brought against him. And that some of the mud he slung at Shakespeare stuck, and was still sticking sixteen months later, is evident from the second comment on the business that has survived in print. This occurs in a little book of verses by a defender of Greene, entitled *Greene's Funerals*, published in February 1594 and attributed on its title-page to R. B., Gent., who writes punningly as follows:[30]

> Greene, is the pleasing Obiect of an eie:
> Greene, pleasde the eies of all that lookt vppon him.
> Greene, is the ground of euerie Painters die:
> Greene, gaue the ground, to all that wrote vpon him.
> Nay more the men, that so Eclipst his fame:
> Purloynde his Plumes, can they deny the same?

have often asked myself why Greene harboured so much evident hatred for a man whom Chettle found of civil demeanour and all the world later agreed to speak of as 'gentle'. That Shakespeare rewrote his plays and made, as he evidently realized, a much better job of them, no doubt angered him. But to call that stealing was of course ridiculous; and it is difficult to believe the charge could have been seriously entertained for a moment, or that it was put forward with any other purpose than to injure his rival in the eyes of the general public. Surely there was something else behind. According to a writer in the late April of 1592, Greene had sold his *Orlando Furioso* to two different acting companies in succession, and after the fraud was discovered had excused himself on the ground "that there was no more faith to be held with players than with them that valued faith at the price of a feather", for they were "men that measured honesty by profit and that regarded their authors not by desert but by necessity of time".[31] We do not know, but is it not likely, that this piece of sharp practice proved the final cause of Greene's ruin? It is highly improbable he found any company to employ him as a writer of plays afterwards, while it is of being 'forsaken' by the players that he complains on his death-bed. We do not know either whether Shakespeare had anything to do with discovering the practice or with the boycott which almost certainly followed. But of one thing we can be sure: a man who has himself been convicted of dishonesty is likely to take a peculiar pleasure in bringing the same charge against one of his judges, no matter how much he has to trump it up for the purpose.

And may there not have been something more still, some act of unkindness or one that Greene interpreted as such? The burden of his complaint is that the players first lived on him and his plays and then left him to die without succour; and he seems to point at Shakespeare as the most callous of them all. For that surely is the true meaning of the misquoted line from *3 Henry VI*. Tyrwhitt took "his *Tygers hart wrapt in a Players hyde*" to be a parody of Shakespearian rant, and Smart and Alexander follow him up by insisting that the "use of 'his' indicates that the victim is being condemned out of his own mouth".[32] They may be right. But the words bear a more pointed interpretation not incompatible with theirs. For if, as is unquestioned, the 'player's hide' is Shakespeare's, the 'tiger's heart' must be his as well. The quotation amounts, in short, to a charge of cruelty. And in making this use of a line spoken by Richard of York, was not Greene suggesting a parallel between their fates? Like Richard he spoke as a dying man; like Richard, his last act was to fling words of scorn and hatred in the face of his persecutors; like Richard he was bitterly conscious all the while that the crown, which was his by right, must descend to one of them.

> Yea, even my foes will shed fast-falling tears,
> And say, "Alas! it was a piteous deed!"
> There, take the crown, and with the crown my curse,
> And in thy need such comfort come to thee
> As now I reap at thy too cruel hand![33]

As he read Greene's reference to his 'tiger's heart' and heard that the dead poet had, at his own request, been crowned with a garland of bay, did not those lines spring to the mind of the man who wrote them? What was it Shakespeare did, or left undone, to bring Greene's curse upon him? Something perhaps connected with the boycott suggested above, or possibly just a failure to respond to a last appeal for help, an appeal which may have miscarried. We shall never know. But if, so far from being tiger-hearted, he was the 'gentle' Shakespeare other contemporaries found him and his plays seem to attest, then, however unjust the charge of cruelty may have been, would not the bitter words of this poet "in his misery dead" have filled him with pity and remorse? We can be sure, I think, that the taunt of "tiger's heart wrapped in a player's hide" touched Shakespeare much nearer in September 1592 than any talk of an Upstart Crow.[34]

But to-day, now Shakespeare has become a central fact in the history of our literature, it is the latter that matters, at any rate to us historians. And I have yet one more reply to those who, at this stage of the argument, may still believe Malone to have been wrong. How do you know, they will say, that Chettle, the "divers of worship", and R. B. were not all mistaken in their reading of Greene's words, a reading which though, as Alfred Pollard remarked, making "attractively good sense", need not have been intended by Greene himself for a moment? And I shall be reminded again that the image of the crow decked out in the feathers of other birds was a stock jibe both of Greene and of Nashe when speaking of the actors by whom they lived and whom they affected to despise. Let me begin by reminding them in turn that it was a favourite trick of these two writers to distort a well-known fable, proverb or allusion in order not only to make it fit the object of their attack, but to draw the reader's attention to the fact that they *were* attacking somebody. Nashe's famous reference to "the kidde in Aesop", brilliantly expounded by Østerberg, is a case in point.[35] Or take the following, in which Greene represents Cicero thus rebuking Roscius:

Why *Roscius*, art thou proud with *Esops* crow, being pranct with the glorie of others feathers? of thy selfe thou canst say nothing, and if the Cobler hath taught thee to say Ave Caesar, disdain not thy tutor because thou pratest in a Kings chamber.[36]

This combines two stories from Macrobius, one about a crow taught by a cobbler to cry 'Ave Caesar' and the other about Roscius, both widely current in renaissance literature,[37] but neither saying anything about a crow "pranct in others feathers", which is dragged in by Greene to make the reference to actors more insulting. Where then did he get this crow from? Aesop, he tells us. But 'Esops crow' might mean simply the 'crow in the fable', just as Nashe's 'kidde in Aesop' really meant the kid in Spenser. And there were many versions of 'Aesop' about in that age, though the oldest, the Aesop of Phaedrus, was not actually available until 1596.[38] The fable of the crow and the feathers, however, goes back to a source older than Phaedrus or Babrius and one more familiar to readers in Shakespeare's day than any 'Aesop'. I refer to the third of Horace's *Epistles*, which seems to have been overlooked by all those discussing Greene's attack in recent times.

The epistle in question, addressed to Julius Florus, conveys, after Horace's allusive fashion, good advice to certain of his young literary friends, not unmingled with touches of kindly satire. He inquires anxiously, for example, whether Titius is curbing his muse or letting himself go, to storm and swell [39] in the pompous style of tragic drama,

An tragica desaevit et ampullatur in arte.

And he then goes on to warn Celsus not to pilfer from other writers any longer, lest those he has robbed should return one day to claim their feathers, when like the crow (*cornicula*) stripped of its stolen splendour (*furtivis nudata coloribus*), he would become a laughing-stock.[40] The *Epistles* were so well known that Nashe, whose classical learning was mostly second-hand, quotes from them twenty times or more.[41] And this particular passage seems to have been especially well known. For instance, Sir John Harington jestingly complains that his scandalous *Metamorphosis of Ajax*, 1596, had been condemned, not on account of its impropriety but because it was so full of loans from other writers that it resembled "Horace's crow decked with many feathers".[42] But the best proof of the universal currency of Horace's version of the crow fable is to be seen in the way it is reflected in renaissance Aesopian collections. Thus in *Æsopi Phrygis Fabulae*, printed at Basle in 1541, the fable in question (p. 243) is headed 'De cornicula et caeteris avibus', that is to say, it substitutes Horace's contemptuous diminutive 'cornicula' for 'cornix' or 'graculus'. Even more to the point, the popular collection of *Fabellae Aesopicae* made by Camerarius expressly for school use, and with a preface by Melanchthon, actually quotes Horace in the fable which runs as follows:

De Cornice superbiente aliarum avium pennis. Cornicula collectas pennas de reliquis avibus sibi commodaverat, & superba varietate illa, reliquas omnes prae se aviculas contemnebat. Tum forte hirundo notata sua penna, advolans illam aufert, quo facto & reliquae postea aves quaeq(ue) suam ademere cornici: ita illa risum movit omnibus, *furtivis nudata coloribus*, ut ait Horatius. Significat fabula, commendicatam speciem neq(ue) diu durare, & perlevi momento dissolvi.[43]

Horace's crow and Aesop's were so closely associated in readers' minds in Shakespeare's day as to be practically identical; and the crow in other birds' feathers was closely associated with the idea of literary theft in the mind of anyone who knew anything of the classics and of many who did not. It was just because it carried this flavour of dishonest appropriation that Greene was so fond of employing the image in his periodical girding against the players who, he complained, flourished and waxed rich on the products of their starving authors. Byron's famous *mot*,

"Now Barabbas was a publisher", gives utterance to the same cry of the heart. And when, as in the outburst against Shakespeare before us, the person attacked was dramatist as well as player, no reader could fail to interpret "beautified with our feathers" as a direct accusation of theft. Finally, any lingering doubt whether Greene himself had the pilfering crow of Horace in mind [44] should be dispelled when his words are laid side by side with those of the third Epistle, and it is perceived that not only does 'with our feathers' tally with *furtivis coloribus*, but 'bombast out' and the parody of a line of rant from *3 Henry VI* are clearly inspired by *tragica desaevit et ampullatur in arte*. In a word Robert Greene, Master of Arts, is warning his 'learned' fellow-dramatists that this Johannes Factotum the players have discovered among themselves is a Celsus and a Titius in one.[45]

In this paper I have dared to challenge the considered opinion of the five Elizabethan scholars whose learning and judgement I value above those of most others. Two of them, alas for all of us, are now beyond the reach of controversy, while a third seems like Cephalus in *The Republic* to have left the endless discussion which we call Shakespearian scholarship to younger disputants. But the remaining defendants are, as Suffolk says of two opponents in *2 Henry VI*, 'no simple men'. Indeed, when I recollect how that pard-like spirit, my friend Peter Alexander, pursued me down the arches of the years all for the sake of a comma or two in *Hamlet*,[46] I tremble to think what his response may be to a challenge that aims so near his heart as this one does. And all the world knows in what peril they stand who venture to differ from W. W. Greg. Yet I have crossed swords with him before now; and, as some of my readers may have learnt, danger is an element I live in. Besides, it is also dangerous to differ from Edmond Malone, even when one is founder and acting president of the Malone Society. On Malone's interpretation of the Upstart Crow passage Greg comments thus severely:

When we examine this interpretation closely we may well wonder how it came to be put forward, and still more how it came to be an article of faith among Shakespearian scholars.[47]

He might have wondered less had he examined the interpretation more closely still. For though Malone does not mention Horace, he alludes to the third Epistle by quoting the words *furtivis coloribus*,[48] and evidently expected the reference to be understood and accepted as a piece of corroborative evidence, as no doubt it was by eighteenth-century readers, many of whom knew their Horace by heart. It is even possible that had we of the twentieth century kept our Horace in repair, Malone's main position would never have been called in question. Not that I claim to be any better than others, for it was only when I began tracking Greene's crow back to its classical origins that I myself came to recognize the source of Malone's quotation.

NOTES

1. Apart from slight alterations and one or two additions, this article was read at Oxford on 14 October 1949, as the first of four Chichele lectures on 'Shakespeare and the Wars of the Roses'.
2. Boswell's edition of Malone's *Shakespeare* (1821), XVIII, 597.
3. *Ibid.* p. 3.
4. Johnson's *Shakespeare* (1765), V, 224–5. See Boswell's *Life* (ed. Birkbeck Hill) I, 329 for Johnson on 'poor Tib' whom he considered "a man of heavy diligence, with very slender powers"; holding that the Bishop would

"make two-and-fifty Theobalds, cut into slices". Aldis Wright and his fellow editor wrote a century later: "From this judgment, whether they be compared as critics or editors, we emphatically dissent." Indeed, they find "Theobald, as an editor...incomparably superior to his predecessors and to his immediate successor Warburton, although the latter had the advantage of working on his materials" (*Cambridge Shakespeare* (1863), I, xxxiv*n*, and xxxii).

5. See the reference to *Henry VI* in his 'Essay on the Learning of Shakespeare' (Nichol Smith, *Eighteenth Century Essays on Shakespeare*, p. 212).

6. Peter Alexander, *Shakespeare's 'Henry VI' and 'Richard III'*, pp. 122 ff. Cf. Boswell's *Malone*, XVIII, 565, 570.

7. Boswell's *Malone*, XVIII, 557.

8. *Ibid.* p. 570.

9. See p. 62 above for Malone's interpretation of this point.

10. Boswell's *Malone*, XVIII, 549.

11. *Ibid.* p. 550 (top).

12. *Ibid.* p. 578.

13. See F. P. Wilson, 'Shakespeare and the "New Bibliography"' in *Studies in Retrospect* (Bibliographical Society, 1945), p. 115.

14. See articles by Alexander in *Times Literary Supplement*, 9 October and 13 November 1924, and a paper read on 6 December 1926 by Chambers and reported in *Proceedings of the Oxford Bibliographical Society*. Smart's notes, posthumously published in 1928 as *Shakespeare: Truth and Tradition*, present the case against Malone in outline.

15. *William Shakespeare*, I, 216–18.

16. See p. 53 of that book.

17. Alexander, *Shakespeare's 'Henry VI' and 'Richard III'*, p. 7.

18. Alexander does not even refer to them; and though Pollard quotes R. B.'s lines he gives them as an instance of a contemporary being deceived like Malone by a misinterpretation which, he admits, makes "attractively good sense" (Alexander, *op. cit.* p. 14).

19. Quoted from Chambers, *William Shakespeare*, II, 188.

20. See Alexander, *op. cit.* pp. 43 ff.; Chambers, *William Shakespeare*, I, 217–18, and above, pp. 64 ff.

21. *Kind-Heart's Dream*, ed. G. B. Harrison (1923), pp. 6–7.

22. A looseness, one may note, in keeping with the style of the rest of the Preface.

23. *William Shakespeare*, I, 59.

24. I owe this point to Richard David, together with a reference to an article on 'A mistaken allusion to Shakespeare' by Staunton in *The Athenaeum* for 7 February 1874, who is the only writer I know to think Chettle is here apologizing to Nashe. See Richard Simpson's reply to Staunton in *The Academy* for 11 April 1874.

25. Thus glossed by *O.E.D.* when citing Greene's words.

26. On the other hand, it may merely be intended to express Greene's contempt for an unlearned player thrusting himself in, like the crow in the fable, among his betters.

27. See Alexander, *op. cit.* p. 142; Greg, *The Editorial Problem in Shakespeare*, p. 52.

28. *Greenes Newes* (1593), and *Greenes Funeralls* (1594), ed. R. B. McKerrow (1911), p. 4.

29. Greene exploited this repentance up to the last. See e.g. the (to us) revolting sanctimony of *The Repentance of Robert Greene wherein by himselfe is laid open his loose life with the manner of his death* (1592).

30. *Greenes Newes*, etc., p. 81.

31. Cited Chambers, *Elizabethan Stage*, III, 325.

32. Smart, *op. cit.* p. 195; Alexander, *op. cit.* pp. 48–9.

33. *3 Henry VI*, I, iv, 162–6.

34. I am indebted for much in this paragraph to suggestions by my friend J. A. K. Thomson.

35. *Review of English Studies*, XVIII (October 1942), 385–94.

36. *Francescos Fortunes* (1590). See Greene's Works (ed. Grosart), VIII, 111, and Chambers, *Elizabethan Stage*, IV, 236.

37. The tale of the cobbler is found for instance in Erasmus's *Apophthegms* (Udall's trans. (1542), I, iv; cited McKerrow's *Nashe*, V, 105), and that of Cicero and Roscius in Cornelius Agrippa's *Of the Vanitie...of Artes and Sciences* (1569), ch. 20; cited Chambers, *Elizabethan Stage*, I, 377; IV, 195.

38. Sandys, *History of Classical Scholarship*, II, 192; a reference pointed out to me by my friend G. M. Young. Had the Phaedrus version been current in 1592, it might be held responsible for the epithet 'vpstart', as I suggested in my lecture at Oxford. But the moral of the Basle version, "Quod non oportet imitari praestantiores" shows that the idea was commonly associated with the Aesopian 'Cornicula'.

39. I give the traditional translation of *ampullatur* which, however, modern scholarship now interprets "lays on too thick" and associates with *coloribus* later.

40. *Epist.* I, iii, 9–20.

41. See McKerrow, *Nashe*, v, 134.

42. *Ulysses upon Ajax* (1596, ed. 1814), p. 8.

43. Cited from H. R. D. Anders, *Shakespeare's Books* (1904), p. 18 (my italics).

44. Since this article was set up in type I have come across another reference in Greene to "Aesop's crew" which directly associates it with plagiarism. In 1584 he published *The Mirror of Modesty*, a fanciful retelling of the story of Susanna, in the Apocrypha; and, apologizing for this fact in his Dedication to the Countess of Derby, he writes: "Your honor may thinke I play like *Ezops* Crowe, which deckt his selfe with others feathers, or like the proud Poet *Batyllus*, which subscribed his name to *Virgils* verses, and yet presented them to *Augustus*. In the behalfe therfore of this my offence, I excuse my selfe with the answere that Varro made, when he offered *Ennius* workes to the Emperour: I giue quoth he another mans picture but freshlie flourished with mine owne colours." The parallel with *A Groatsworth of Wit* is striking: though Aesop is named, 'mine owne colours' echoes the 'furtivis coloribus' of Horace, while the question in both cases is not of pilfering a few feathers but of rewriting a whole literary composition.

45. J. A. K. Thomson suggests to me that since the *Satires* were almost as well known to the Elizabethans as the *Epistles*, Chettle's tribute to Shakespeare: "facetious grace in writing" may well have been intended to reflect, in reply to Greene, the words "molle atque facetum" which Horace uses in praising Virgil (*Sat.* I, x, 44). "And if so," he asks, "what could be a higher compliment to Shakespeare?"

46. See *Review of English Studies*, XXIII, 70 ff.

47. *The Editorial Problem in Shakespeare*, pp. 50–1.

48. Boswell's *Malone*, XVIII, 571.

AN EARLY COPY OF SHAKESPEARE'S WILL

BY

LEVI FOX

In 1948 the Trustees and Guardians of Shakespeare's Birthplace acquired an early copy of Shakespeare's will which, so far as is known, ranks as the earliest transcript in existence.

Its immediate previous owner was Miss C. Hartwell Lucy, a descendant of a family prominent in Stratford-upon-Avon in the eighteenth and early nineteenth centuries. Miss Lucy's great-grandfather built the present mill on the Avon below the church at Stratford-upon-Avon and also the large residence, now a private hotel, called Avonside nearby. The copy of the will was discovered by Miss Lucy among a few papers in a deed box which belonged to her grandfather, the Reverend Edmund Lane, M.A., D.C.L.[1] This gentleman, born and educated in Stratford, was a brilliant but rather peculiar person, whose absorbing hobby was the collection of rare books, manuscripts and the like. He spent the last twenty years or so of his life as Episcopalian Rector of St John's, Selkirk, and died in 1898 or 1899. His library was subsequently dispersed to sundry dealers, and it was by extraordinary good fortune that the precious document, folded up in an insignificant foolscap-sized envelope, endorsed 'Shakespeare's will' in typical Victorian handwriting, survived among a few family papers. How it came into Lane's possession is not known.

The copy of the will consists of eleven numbered sheets of paper written on one side only, each measuring 12 by 15½ in. approximately, fastened together at the head by a parchment thong. When acquired by the Birthplace Trustees its condition was poor, the pages being much crumpled and weakened by folding over a long period; the last two pages in particular were much worn and torn, and several fragments had become detached and some were missing. The document has now been expertly repaired and restored to comparatively good condition, but the last two pages remain defective.

As indicated by the heading,[2] this copy of Shakespeare's will is an extract from the register of the Prerogative Court of Canterbury, and is therefore a transcript of a copy of the original in Somerset House. Unfortunately it is undated, but the handwriting places it beyond all reasonable doubt in the first half of the seventeenth century and does not exclude the probability of its having been written within a few years of Shakespeare's death.[3] Two other clues which might possibly assist in dating the document have been pursued but so far with inconclusive results. First, the watermark of the paper used is of a type common over a long period, and it has not been possible to identify this particular variant. Secondly, although the notary who was responsible for making the copy is known to have been a certain William (or ? Gilbert) Rothwell,[4] attempts to identify him with certainty have so far proved abortive.

Rothwell is not a very uncommon name, and several Williams were active in the first half of the seventeenth century.[5] Of these William Rothwell of Stapleford, a member of the Rothwell family of Ewerby and Stapleford[6] and father of Sir Richard Rothwell, was entered at Gray's Inn on 8 February 1614–15[7] and presumably qualified and practised as a lawyer. He died in 1630, but other persons of this name, whose occupations are uncertain, have been traced.[8] As a notary public Rothwell is likely to have been free of the Scriveners' Company, but his name does not appear in the old extant Common Paper of the Company, which ends at 1627; after that the records were apparently lost or destroyed and the present Common Paper starts in 1868.[9] Inquiries for information about Rothwell at other record repositories [10] have also yielded no results, though it is possible, indeed probable, that Rothwell's handwriting or signature may appear in documents preserved in any one of them. Any evidence about Rothwell's activities will be most welcome.

Apart from its provenance and date, the interest of the Birthplace copy of the will lies in the circumstances of its origin, the comparison of its text with that of the original, and its later history.

The question naturally arises as to the purpose for which the copy was made and for whom. No certain answer can at present be advanced. It may have been made for any one of the beneficiaries or for any other interested person. A cross appears in the margin of the third sheet against the name of Elizabeth Hall, but though it is tempting to conjecture that this may indicate that the copy was made for one of the Halls there is no proof. The language of the will is quoted as early as 1618 in the deed by which "according to the true intent and meaning of the last will and testament of the said William Shakespeare" the Blackfriars property was conveyed to trustees for Susanna Hall, but though the study of the two documents raises some interesting points of speculation there is no certain link between the Birthplace copy and this deed.[11]

Again, it may have originated as one of the papers in connexion with legal proceedings or depositions. Both the handwriting and format of the document are of a type commonly met with in records which have formed part of the pleadings in lawsuits. Such an occasion may well have been the suit in Chancery brought by Baldwin Brookes against Mrs Hall and her son-in-law Thomas Nash shortly after the death of Dr John Hall in November 1635, to which attention was first drawn by Frank Marcham.[12] In the "Joynte and severall answeres of Susan Hall widowe and Thomas Nashe gent' defendants to the Bill of Complaynte of Baldwyn Brooks complaynaunte", dated 5 May 1637, reference is made to the properties in Stratford and London, "given to her the said Susan by the last will and testament of Willm̄ Shackspeare gent' her late Father deceassed as in and by the said last will and testament proved in due forme of lawe wherevnto for more precise certayntye theis defendantes referre themselues relacion beinge therevnto hadd at large yt doth and maye appeare…". Baldwin Brookes was a mercer of Stratford-upon-Avon who served as a member of the Corporation and filled the office of Bailiff (i.e. Mayor) in 1640-1.[13] Apparently he obtained, in Easter Term 1635, a judgement in the Court of King's Bench against John Hall for payment of a debt of £77. 13s. 4d., but Hall died in November the same year. Brookes proceeded against Susanna Hall as executrix, but was non-suited presumably because no executor or executrix was named in the will. Hall's will [14] was nuncupative, being made and declared 25 November 1635 and witnessed by Thomas Nash and Simon Trapp, but administration was not granted until a year later, 29 November 1636. Shortly afterwards, in February 1636-7, Brookes filed his Chancery bill, alleging undue delay on the part of the Halls in closing the estate. Their answer (cited above) was taken by commission and is dated 5 May 1637. A week later Susanna Hall filed her own bill against Brookes, complaining that execution had already been levied by the Undersheriff, Edward Raynsford of Warwick, and that Brookes with various bailiffs from Warwick, who are named, and James Newell of Stratford, forcibly entered New Place and took "divers bookes boxes deskes monyes bondes bills and other goodes of greate value",[15] subsequently stated to be "to the value of £1000", a palpable exaggeration. This produced an injunction for stay of proceedings. What followed subsequently is not known.

Alternatively, the Birthplace copy may have been made either in 1639 or in 1647 when settlements were concluded of the estates which passed under Shakespeare's will. The first arrangement followed the death of Dr John Hall in 1635 and provided for his widow with remainder to her daughter Elizabeth and son-in-law Thomas Nash. The second, a resettlement on Mrs Hall and Elizabeth Nash, was necessitated by the death of the latter's husband early in 1647. Shakespeare's will is cited in both documents[16] and a copy would have been a *sine qua non*.

There is of course nothing precise to connect the Birthplace copy with any one of these three events. But there remains a strong presumption that it was made between the years 1635 and 1639, a period of much uncertainty in the life of the Halls when the controlling hand of Dr John Hall was removed by death in 1635. He left a nuncupative will, administration of which was only formally granted a year later. The lawsuit with Baldwin Brookes was depending all this time and continued into the following year 1637. Differences between Susanna and her son-in-law may perhaps be indicated by the statement that the latter entered a caveat in the Prerogative Court of Canterbury to prevent the administration being granted until some agreement was reached with him about Hall's personal estate, part of which was his by right of his wife. This chapter of difficulties seems to have closed with the settlement of 1639. An agreement was concluded on 27 May of that year[17] whereby the properties willed by Shakespeare were vested in trustees for the benefit of Mrs Hall for her life, and thereafter of Thomas and Elizabeth Nash.

The subject-matter of the copy being the same as the original will, the textual importance and interest of this document lies in the scribal variations or discrepancies it exhibits when compared with the original at Somerset House and the transcript in the Register of the Prerogative Court of Canterbury. The copy is in the handwriting of one writer but has been checked and corrected by another using a different coloured ink. A full transcript of the copy, indicating the additions of the corrector, is appended for easy comparison with the text of the original.[18] Here a few of the most interesting discrepancies may be noted. On sheet 5 the Christian name *Thomas* is inserted by the copyist in the blank before the second of the Hart brothers, whereas the name is omitted in the original will and in the probate register. On sheet 4 the passage which appears in the original as "maryed and couert Baron" is rendered by the copyist "married and Couert Baren", and Baren is altered by the corrector to Barne. On the same sheet, what has been read from the original as "marryed unto or attaine after" is rendered by the copyist "married vnto or at anie after", and the corrector has added a second *t* to make *att anie*. This version accordingly reinforces the view that what was written was "or att anie *time* after", *time* being omitted in the original and copies. Interesting spellings of the copyist are 'nuncke' for 'nunc', 'wardrope' for 'wardrobe', 'hamblettes' for 'hamlettes', 'guilt boule' for 'gilt bole', '*Villimo* Bird' for 'Willelmo Bird'. Other variations include the use of *was* instead of *ys* in the sentence "to the earth whereof it ys made"; the omission of eightpence after twenty shillings in the legacy to William Renolds; the rendering of eightpence in John Nash's legacy in Roman numerals, whereas all the other legacies are spelt out in full; the omission of *of* after *enabling* (sheet 6); and the spelling of many of the surnames.

What happened to this copy of the will after it had served the purpose for which it was made is another question at present unanswerable. The only certain facts are that it survived and that its existence in Stratford-upon-Avon in the middle of the eighteenth century can be proved. On 17 September 1747 the Reverend Joseph Greene, vicar of Stratford-upon-Avon and head-master of the Grammar School there, wrote to the Honourable James West at Alscot (near Stratford-upon-Avon) as follows: [19]

Sr

I have been extremely concern'd I shou'd disappoint you in your expectation of seeing Shakespear's will: As soon as you left me I made a diligent search, and at length had ye luck to meet with it, and hope for the time to come I shall have more prudence than to promise what I cannot readily perform: I have now transcrib'd it a second time, which Transcript, as some small attonement, I humbly beg your acceptance of.

I am pretty certain the thing it self will not come up to the Idea you may have entertain'd of it, as it bears the name of Shakespear's Will: The Legacies and Bequests therein, are undoubtedly as he intended; but the manner of introducing them, appears to me so dull and irregular, so absolutely void of ye least particle of that spirit which animated our great Poet; that it must lessen his Character as a Writer, to imagine ye least sentence of it his production.

The only satisfaction I receive in reading it, is to know who were his Relations, and what he left them, which perhaps may just make you also amends for ye trouble of perusing it.

I am Sir

With all Dutiful Respect

Your most Humble Servant

Joseph Greene

Stratford upon Avon
Septemb: 17. 1747.

To

The Honourable James West Esqr.

at Alscott.

Greene does not say where or in whose possession the document was, though it is reasonably certain that it was in Stratford or neighbourhood. Did he have to make 'a diligent search' for it among his own private papers or was it in the possession of a friend or acquaintance? Was it at that time among the parish records kept in the Church of which he was vicar, or among the Borough records which were stored in a room attached to the Grammar School over which he presided? Until some other reference to the existence of the document is found these questions must remain unanswered.

From the evidence of his own letter Greene apparently made two transcripts of the copy of the will, both of which are extant, as follows:

(*a*) The transcript which accompanied Greene's letter to James West, made in 1747. This is now Lansdowne MS. 721, fol. 4 *et seq*. in the British Museum.[20]

(*b*) Greene's other transcript, undated, which varies in a few details from (*a*). This was acquired by J. O. Halliwell-Phillipps and is now in the Folger Shakespeare Library.[21]

These two transcripts reveal some slight discrepancies of detail which reflect the varying interpretations of Greene as he wrote out two different copies, probably at two different times. On the whole, transcript (a) seems to be the more careful copy, though in transcript (b) Greene took the trouble to mark the sheet numbers and also attempted an elucidation of Gi^{um} Rothwell N.P. as Gi^{um} Rothwell (vel Gilbertum) Notariũ Publicum. In both transcripts Greene made a serious error by mistranscribing the surname Nash as *Marsh*, though in transcript (a) he queried this in the margin.

A careful collation of these transcripts with the Birthplace copy leaves no doubt that it was the latter, and not the original will, which Greene had access to and used. Apart from other points of agreement, including the indications of sheet divisions, the note relating to probate on Greene's transcripts is identical with the wording on the last page of the Birthplace copy and differs considerably from the notes of probate on the original will and in the probate register (the last two are almost identical). As in the Birthplace copy there is in Greene's transcripts a lacuna marked by asterisks, after the letter *m* of the word *Iuramento*; where the former breaks off, after the word *eodem*, Greene's transcripts continue:

T xxx/ Commissa fuit Adminis xxxxx./ Concordat cum Registro, facta collacõe per me / Gi^{um} Rothwell N[otarium] P[ublicum].

This conclusion that Greene's transcripts were not taken from the original will is contrary to the belief which has been generally accepted by scholars from Halliwell-Phillipps onwards, but the source of the error is not far to seek. Halliwell-Phillipps knew of the existence of Greene's letter and transcript sent to West in 1747, and even noted one or two of the verbal discrepancies the transcript exhibited when compared with the original which he printed;[22] but he completely ignored other important variations and particularly the difference in the note relating to probate which Greene's transcript shows when compared with the original.[23] In fact Halliwell-Phillipps, without making an attempt to reconcile this all-important discrepancy, described Greene's transcript as "a copy of the probate of Shakespeare's will" and quoted the 'curious observations' contained in Greene's letter to West.[24] Somewhat later Halliwell-Phillipps himself acquired the Folger version of Greene's transcript; but whilst appreciating its similarity to the Lansdowne version he claimed it (incorrectly as now shown) to be "the earliest copy out of Somerset House known to exist".[25]

Subsequent scholars have failed to realize that Greene copied from a copy and not from the original will. For the same reason Greene has come to be credited with having discovered the will.[26] The wording of his letter to James West has been read to indicate that he found the original will, whereas what he was referring to was the early copy of the will now under consideration. Hence this has resulted in statements such as the following, that "in 1747 Rev. Joseph Greene of Stratford-upon-Avon found the document among the wills in the Doctors' Commons in London".[27]

The emergence of this early copy of Shakespeare's will after being lost sight of for two centuries raises the query whether any similar copies, or indeed any other valuable Shakespearian records, still lie hidden in private ownership. There is no record of comparable copies of the will, and though at the moment the Birthplace acquisition provokes more questions than answers it must be regarded as one of the most interesting finds of the century.

NOTES

1. These family details have been supplied by Miss C. Hartwell Lucy.

2. "E Registro Curiae Prerogat' Cant' Extract'."

3. This view is shared by A. J. Collins, Keeper in the Department of Manuscripts at the British Museum, and his colleague A. Mayor, to whom I record my thanks and indebtedness for having examined, and furnished useful observations about, the Birthplace copy.

4. The foot of p. 11 on which this information was recorded is now missing. It was there, however, when Greene made his transcripts of the document (see below).

5. I have received much help in trying to identify Rothwell from J. H. Ellis, Records Assistant at the Birthplace Library.

6. *Lincolnshire Pedigrees*, ed. Maddison (Harleian Soc. 1902–4), III, 835.

7. *Gray's Inn Admission Register*, ed. Foster (1889), p. 136.

8. Another interesting William Rothwell was Mayor of Warwick in 1680, but there is nothing to connect him with the will.

9. Thanks are due to A. A. Pitcairn, Clerk of the Scriveners' Company, for permission to consult these records.

10. I am indebted to those who have dealt with my inquiries at Somerset House, the Faculty Office of the Archbishop of Canterbury, the British Museum, the Public Record Office, the Records Office of the Corporation of London, the Guildhall Library, the Bodleian Library, the Birthplace Library, and the Folger Library, Washington.

11. This document, the original of which is in the Folger Shakespeare Library, is reproduced in B. Roland Lewis, *The Shakespeare Documents*, II, no. 250. The section of it relating to uses (beginning *to the vse and behoofe of the aforesaid Susanna Hall...*down to...*to the vse and behoofe of the right heires of the said William Shakespeare*) is substantially a quotation from the will (Birthplace copy, sheets 8–10), particularizing, however, "my said Neece Hall" as "Elizabeth Hall daughter of the said Susanna Hall" and "my daughter Judith" as "Judyth Quiney now wife of Thomas Quiney of Stretford aforesaid Vintiner one other of the daughters of the said William Shakespeare". The one instance where the wording seems to have been altered with a view to making it legally more precise (viz. "the seuerall heires males of the seuerall bodies of the said fowerth fiveth sixt and seaventh sonnes" substituted for "the heires males of the bodies of the said fourth fifth Sixte and Seventh sonnes") so happens to be at one of the two places marked with a cross in the text of the Birthplace copy of the will (sheet 9). Is this merely a coincidence?

12. Frank Marcham, *William Shakespeare and his daughter Susannah* (1931).

13. Stratford Corporation Council Book, C. 189.

14. P.C.C., 115 Pile.

15. This statement is also of great interest as showing what happened to some of Shakespeare's books, etc., at New Place.

16. Both documents are in the Birthplace Trust's collection.

17. Also in the Birthplace Trust's collection.

18. For a modern transcript and facsimile of the will see E. K. Chambers, *William Shakespeare: A Study of Facts and Problems* (1930), II, 169–74.

19. Lansdowne MS. 721, fol. 2.

20. See *The Probate Copy of the Will of Shakespeare, now first printed from a Manuscript Copy of it made by the Rev. Joseph Greene, of Stratford-on-Avon, in the Year 1747*, printed for private circulation by J. O. Halliwell-Phillipps in 1872.

21. It appears as item 114 in Halliwell-Phillipps, *Calendar of Shakespearean Rarities*.

22. James Orchard Halliwell, *The Life of William Shakespeare* (1848), pp. 275–8.

23. For the probate note on the original see E. K. Chambers, *op. cit.* II, 174.

24. Halliwell, *op. cit.* p. 274 note.

25. Halliwell-Phillipps, *Rarities*, p. 42.

26. Sir E. K. Chambers states that "the will was found by Joseph Greene" and quotes a reference to Greene's letter to West (*op. cit.* II, 169).

27. B. Roland Lewis, *The Shakespeare Documents*, II, 471.

AN EARLY COPY OF SHAKESPEARE'S WILL

E REGISTRO CURIAE PREROGAT' CANT' EXTRACT'*

[Sheet 1] Vicesimo Quinto die Martij Anno Regni Domini nostri Jacobi nuncke Regis Anglie &c decimo quarto &c Scotie xlix°. Annoque Dominj 1616

IN THE NAME OF GOD AMEN I William Shackspeare of Stratford vppon Avon in the County of Warr' gent (in perfect health and memorie God be praysed) ~~doe~~ doe make and ordaine this my last will and Testament in manner and forme followinge, That is to saie First I Comend my Soule into the handes of God my Creator Hopinge and Assured*ly* beleevinge through thonelie merrittes of Jesus Christ my Saviour to be made partaker of life Everlastinge. And my body to the Earth Whereof it was made Item I giue and bequeath vnto my daughter Judith one Hundreth and fiftie poundes of Lawfull English money to be paied vnto her in manner and forme Followinge That is to saie one Hundred poundes in discharge of her Marriage porcion within one yeare after my decease with Consideracion after the rate of Two shillinges in the pounde for soe longe tyme as the same shall be unpaied vnto her [Sheet 2] after my decease and the fiftie poundes Residue theireof vpon her surrendringe of or giuinge of such Sufficient securitie as the ouerseers of this my will shall lyke of to Surrendor or graunt all her Estate and Right that shall descend or come vnto her after my decease or that shee nowe hath of in or to one Copihold Tenement' with thappurtenaunces Lyinge and beinge in Stratford vpon Avon aforesaid in the said County of Warr' beinge parcell or houlden of the mannor of Rowington vnto my daughter Susanna Hall and her heires for ever, Item I give and bequeath vnto my said daughter Judith one hundred and Fiftie poundes more if shee or anie Issue of her Bodye be Livinge att the end of three yeares nexte Ensuinge the day of the date of this my will duringe which tyme my Executors [Sheet 3] to paie her Consideracion from my decease according to the Rate aforesaid, And if shee dye within the said Terme without Issue of her body then my will is and I doe giue and bequeath one hundred poundes thereof to my Neece Elizabeth Hall, and the fiftie poundes to be sett forth by my Executors during the life of my Sister Johane Hart and the vse and proffitt theire of cominge shall be paied to my said Sister Joane and after her decease the said l. li' shall Remeane amongst the Children of my said Sister Equallie to be devided amongst them But if my said daughter Judith be livinge att thend of the said Three yeares or anie Issue of her bodie, then my will is and soe I devise and bequeath the said Hundred and fiftie poundes to be sett out by my Executors and overseers for the best benefitt of her and her Issue and the [Sheet 4] the stock not to be paied vnto her soe long as shee shall be married and Covert ~~Baren~~ *Barne*, but my will is that shee shall haue the Consideracion yearelie paied vnto her duringe her life and after her decease the said stocke and Consideracion to be paied to her Children if she have anie, and if not to her Executors or assignes shee Livinge the said Terme after my decease, Provided that if such Husband as shee shall att thend of the said three yeares be married vnto or at*t* anie after doe Sufficiently assure vnto her and Thissue of her bodie landes answerable to the porcion by this my will given vnto her and to be adiudged soe by my Executors and ouerseers, then my will is that the said Cl. li' shall be paied to such Husband as shall make such Assurance to his owne vse, Item I giue and bequeath vnto my said Sister Joane [Sheet 5] Twentie pounde and all my wearinge apparell to be paied and deliuered within one yeare after my decease And I doe will and devise *vnto her* the house with thappurtenaunces in Stratford wherein shee ~~nowe~~ dwelleth for her naturall lyfe vnder the yearelie Rent of twelue pence Item I giue and bequeath vnto her three sonnes William Hart Thomas Hart and Michaell Hart fiue poundes apeece to

---

* The letters and words printed in italics are written in a different ink by the corrector.

F*

be paied within one yeare after my decease Item I giue and bequeath vnto the said Elizabeth Hall All my plate (*Except my broad silver and guilt boule that I nowe haue att the date of this my will Item I giue and bequeath vnto the poore of Stratford aforesaid Tenne poundes, to Mr Thomas Combe my sword, To Thomas Russell Esquire five poundes and to Frauncis Collins of the Borough of Warr' in the County of Warr' gent' thirteene poundes [Sheet 6] sixe shillinges and Eightpence to be paied within one yeare after my decease, Item I giue and bequeath ~~Item I g~~ to hamlett Sadler ~~sixe and~~ Twentie *sixe* shillinges eightpence to buy him a Ringe, To William Renoldes gent' ~~sixe and~~ Twentie *sixe* shillinges to buy him a Ringe, to my Godsonne William Walker Twenty shillinges in Gould, To Anthony Nash gent' *sixe* and Twentie *sixe* shillinges viij^d. And to Mr. John Nash ~~sixe and~~ Twentie *sixe* shillinges and eight pence, And to my Fellowes John Heaminges Richard Burbage And Henrie Cundell ~~sixe and~~ Twenty *sixe* shillinges ~~Apeece~~ Eightpence apeece to buy them Ringes Item I giue will bequeath and devise vnto my daughter Susanna Hall for better Enablinge her to performe this my will and towardes the ~~per~~ [Sheet 7] performance theireof All that Capitall Messuage or tenemente with thappurtenaunces in Stratford aforesaid called the newe place where in I nowe dwell and two Messuages or tenementes with thappurtenaunces scituate lyinge and beinge in Henley Streete within the Borough of Stratford aforesaid, And all my barnes stables Orchardes Gardens land Tenementes and hereditamentes whatsoeuer Lyinge and beinge or to be hadd Receaved perseaved or taken within the townes hamblettes villages Feildes and growndes of Stratford vpon Avon Oldstratford Bushopton and Welcombe or in anie of them in the said County of Warrwicke and allsoe all that messuage or tenement with Thappurtenaunces wherein one John Robinson dwelleth seituate lyinge and beinge in the Blackfriers in [Sheet 8] London neere the Wardrope and all other my landes Tenementes and hereditamentes whatsoeuer, To haue and to hould all and Singuler the said premisses with theire appurtenaunces vnto the said Susanna Hall for and duringe the Terme of her naturall lyfe   And after her decease to the first sonne of her bodye lawfully Issuinge and to the heires males of the Body of the said First sonne Lawfully Issuinge and for default of such Issue to the second sonne of her bodye lawfully Issuinge And for default of such heires to the third sonne of the bodie of the said ~~susanna~~ Susanna lawfully Issuinge and of the heires males of the bodie of the said [Sheet 9] Third sonne lawfully Issuinge And for default of such Issue the same soe to be and Remeane to the fowerth fift sixet and seventh sonnes of her bodie lawfullie Issuinge one after another and to the heires males of the bodies of the said fourth fifth Sixte and Seventh sonnes Lawfully Issuinge in such manner as it is before Lymitted to be and Remaine to the first second and Third sonnes of her body and to the heires males, And for default of such Issue the said premises to be and Remaine to my said Neece Hall and the heires males of her bodie lawfullie Issuinge and for default' of such Issue to my daughter Judith and the Heires males of Her bodie lawfully Issuinge And for default of such Issue to the Right heires [Sheet 10] Heires of mee the said William Shackspeare for ~~euer~~ Ever, Item I giue vnto my wiffe my second Best bedd with the furniture Item I giue and bequeath vnto my said dawghter Judith my broad silver guilt boule All the Rest of my Goodes Chattells Leases plate Juells and howshould stuffe whatsoeuer after my debtes and legacies paied and my Funerall Expences discharged I giue devise and bequeath to my sonne in lawe John Hall gent' and my daughter Susanna his wiffe whome l ordaine and make Executors of this my last will and Testament And I doe Intreate and apoynt the said Thomas Russell Esquire †...auncis Collins gent' to be ouerseers.....I doe Revoke all former.....my.....[Sheet 11] In wittnesse whereof

* Second bracket wanting.
† This sheet and the next are defective at the bottom, the missing portions being indicated by dots.

AN EARLY COPY OF SHAKESPEARE'S WILL

I haue herevnto putt my hand the daye and yeare First aboue written by me William Shackspeare. Witnesse to the publishinge hereof Frauncis Collyns Julyus Shawe John Robinsonne Hamnett Sadler Robert Whatcott.

Probatum fuit Testamentum suprascriptum apud London coram.....venarabili viro Magistro Villimo Bird Legum doctore Curie Prerogatiue Cantuariensis Magistro Custodis.....siue Comisario legitime Const..... vicesimo secundo die mensis Junij Anno Domini mill.....sexcentesimo decimo sexto Iuram.....(unius Ex[ecut] orum in eodem.........

THE SHAKESPEARE COLLECTION IN THE BODLEIAN LIBRARY, OXFORD

BY

L. W. HANSON

The Bodleian Library was formally opened by the Vice-Chancellor of the University on 8 November 1602.[1] Yet we cannot suppose that in the last thirteen years of his life Shakespeare ever saw the transformation effected by Sir Thomas Bodley in that "great desolate roome" which he had found over the Divinity School. The use of the Library was restricted to graduates of the University. At best we may conjecture that Shakespeare on his visits to Oxford saw the outside of the original library building and may have seen the new quadrangle in course of construction. It was begun in 1610 but not finally completed until 1623.

HISTORY

The University Library which Sir Thomas Bodley refounded was naturally enough a library built up by scholars for scholars, and more particularly a library built up by Protestant theological scholars for Protestant theologians. Bodley himself had lectured in Greek to the University before he entered the diplomatic service of Queen Elizabeth. But it is more important that he began his education in Geneva, whither his parents had fled to escape the Marian persecution, and had there studied under Calvin. His diplomatic career had for the most part been spent amongst the congenial and Calvinistic Dutch. Thomas James, Bodley's choice as the first librarian of his foundation, left behind him, according to Anthony Wood, "this character that 'he was the most industrious and indefatigable writer against the Papists, that had been educated in Oxon since the reformation of religion'". The Library was therefore primarily intended by the Founder and the Librarian as a Protestant armoury in the paper war against the Counter-Reformation. This intention was enthusiastically supported by the University, then Puritanically inclined, in which theology was, as it still is, the senior faculty. It is not surprising therefore to find that of the 5611 books recorded in the Catalogue of 1605, nearly half, 2456, are classified as theological; that most of the books were in Latin, the language of scholarship; and that of the 1868 Arts books only thirty-six were in English, of which only three can be considered of any interest to the student of English literature: Chaucer's *Works*, 1561, Lydgate's *Fall of Princes*, 1554, and Puttenham's *Arte of English Poesie*, 1589.

The theological and scholarly intent, so plain in the Library's foundation, seemed likely to be modified by an arrangement with the Stationers' Company which Bodley concluded in 1610. In return for a piece of plate which has not survived, the Company agreed to send to the Library a copy of every book entered in their Register on condition that the books thus given might be borrowed if needed for reprinting, and that the books given to the Library by others might be examined, collated and copied by the Company. This generosity of the Stationers was a great compliment to Bodley and an indication of the national character which the Library had achieved within eight years of its opening. It was to keep this national character until the

PLATE I

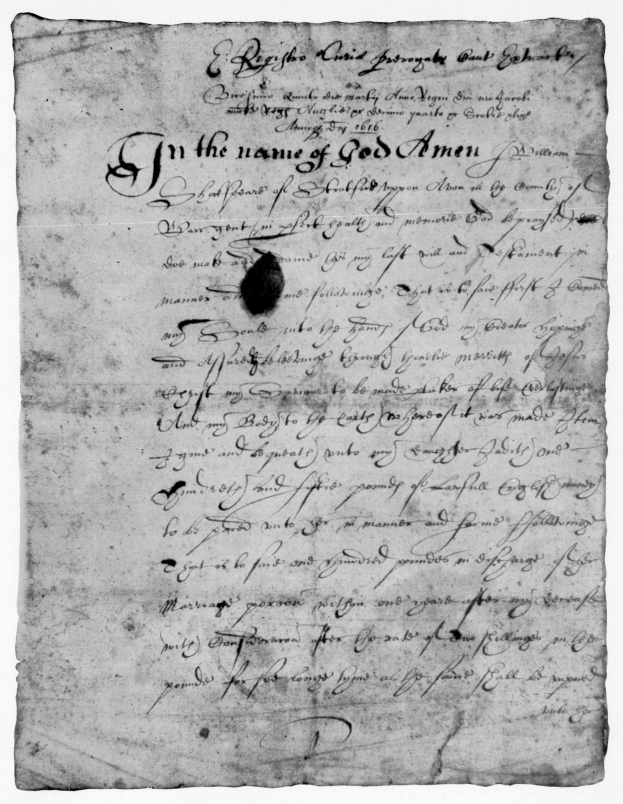

AN EARLY COPY OF SHAKESPEARE'S WILL. First sheet

PLATE II

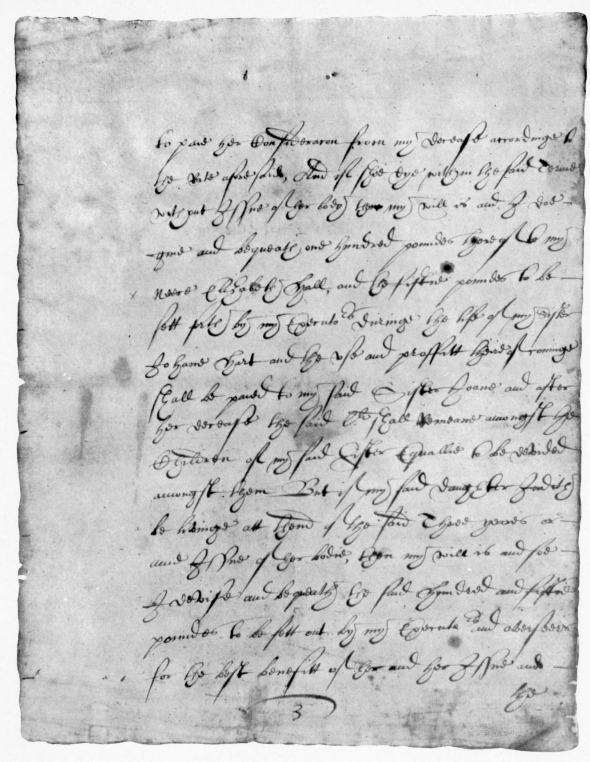

AN EARLY COPY OF SHAKESPEARE'S WILL. Sheet three

PLATE III

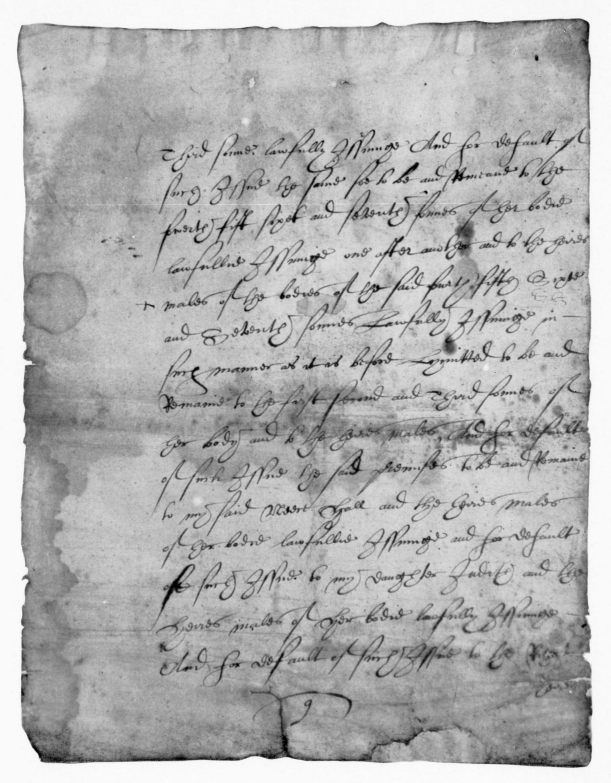

PLATE IV

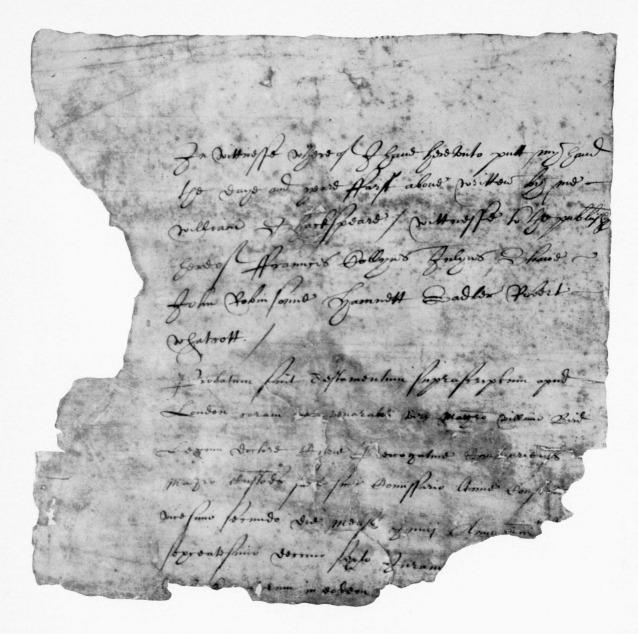

AN EARLY COPY OF SHAKESPEARE'S WILL. Final sheet

PLATE V

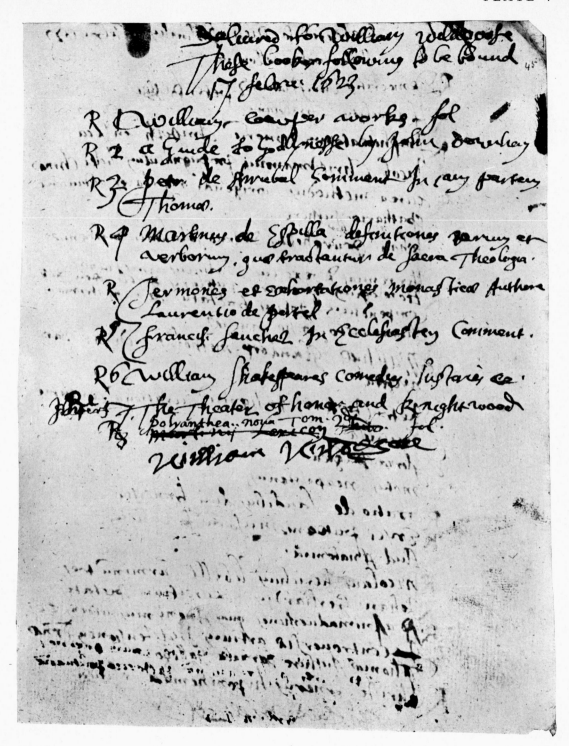

THE BODLEIAN BINDER'S BOOK. The First Folio was delivered to WILLIAM WILD-GOOSE to be bound on 17 February 1623–4. The R indicates that it was duly returned by him to the Library

PLATE VI

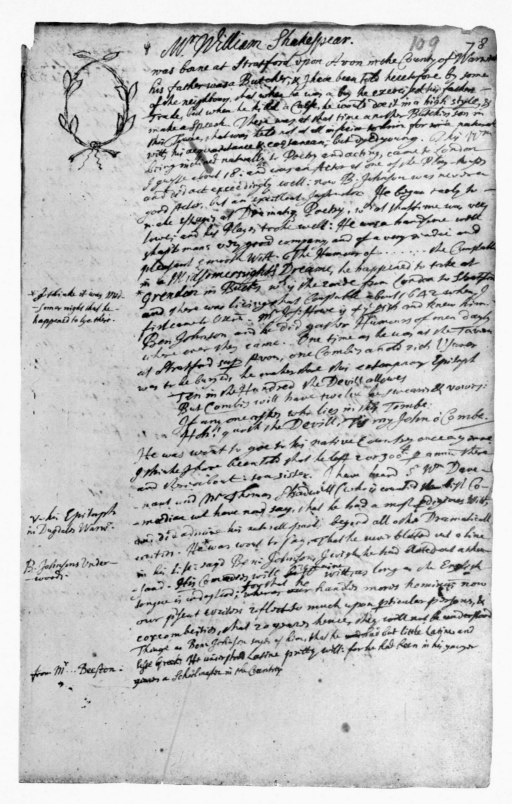

JOHN AUBREY'S *'Life of Shakespeare'*

PLATE VII

A Chriftian and heavenly treatife called phyficke for the foule, written by Mafter *Iohn Abernethy* Bifhop of Cathnes, printed for *Iohn Budge* in 4.

The hiftorie of the Iewes deliuerance out of Babylon, and the myfterie of our redemption, plainly demonftrated in ten fermons vpon the 126. Pfalme. By *Iohn Hume*. Printed by *William Stansby* in 4.

The firft and fecond booke of queftions and anfwers upon the booke of Genefis, containing thofe queftions that are moft eminent and pertinent, vpon the foureteene firft chapters of the fame booke: by *Alexander Roffe*, printed for *Francis Conftable*, 1622.

Playes, written by M. *William Shakeſpeare*, all in one volume, printed by *Iſaack Iaggard*, in fol.

The Theater of Honor and Knighthood, printed by *William Iaggard*, in fol.

Phyficke for body and foule: fhewing that the maladies of the one, proceed from the finnes of the other: with a remedie againft both, prefcribed by our heavenly Phyfitian Iefus Chrift: A fermon preached at Buckden in Huntington, before the Right Reuerend Father in God the Lord Bifhop of Lincolne: by *Edward Heron*, printed for *Francis Conftable*, 1622.

A. The 1622 advertisement of the First Folio (see p. 89)

Pilgah Euangelica, or a Commentary on the Reuelation of Saint *Iohn*, by Doctor *Symonds*, printed for *Edmund Weauer*, in 4.

Abrahams faith, that is, the old Religion, wherein is proued that the Religion now publikely taught and defended by order in the Church of England is the onely true, Catholike, ancient and vnchangeable faith of Gods Elect: and the pretenfed Religion of the Sea of Rome is a falfe, baftard, new, vpftart, hereticall and variable fuperftitious deuice of man. By *Iofias Nichols*: printed for *Edmund Weauer* in 4.

Mafter *William Shakeſperes* workes, printed for *Edward Blount*, in fol.

Shifts and euafions vfed by Mafter *Arnox* the Iefuit, a Treatife wherein the caufes why he refufeth to anfwer to 17. queftions made by the Minifters of the Church of *Paris*, are examined, &c. by *Peter D. Moulin*, printed for *Nathaniel Newbery*.

A Catechifme made by Mafter *Daniel Votier*, Minifter of Gods Word, printed for *Nathaniel Newbery*.

B. The 1624 advertisement of the First Folio (see p. 89)

establishment of the British Museum in 1753. The agreement was the foundation of the copy-right privilege, for the obligation of the members of the Company to deliver books to the Library was enforced by the Star Chamber decree of 1637 which regulated printing. This strengthening of the Library's privilege was doubtless inspired by Laud, Chancellor of the University, and a great benefactor of the Library. There can be no doubt that James prompted the conclusion of the 1610 agreement, and that he would have taken full advantage of it. But Bodley soon showed that he meant to exercise his rights with discrimination, and was determined to keep to that high and serious intention which had prompted him to set up his "Staffe at the Librarie dore in Oxon". On 1 January 1612 he wrote to James,

Sir, I would yow had foreborne, to catalogue our London bookes, till I had bin priuie to your purpose. There are many idle bookes, & riffe raffes among them, which shall neuer com into the Librarie, & I feare me that litle, which yow haue done alreadie, will raise a scandal vpon it, when it shall be giuen out, by suche as would disgrace it, that I haue made vp a number, with Almanackes, plaies, & pro-clamacions: of which I will haue none, but such as are singular.

A fortnight later he was even more outspoken:

I can see no good reason to alter my opinion, for excluding suche bookes, as almanackes, plaies, & an infinit number, that are daily printed, of very vnworthy maters & handling, suche as, me thinkes, both the keeper & vnderkeeper should disdaine to seeke out, to deliuer vnto any man. Happely some plaies may be worthy the keeping: but hardly one in fortie. For it is not alike in English plaies, & others of other nations: because they are most esteemed, for learning the languages & many of them compiled, by men of great fame, for wisedome & learning, which is seeldom or neuer seene among vs. Were it so againe, that some litle profit might be reaped (which God knowes is very litle) out of some of our playbookes, the benefit thereof will nothing neere counteruaile, the harme that the scandal will bring vnto the Librarie, when it shal be giuen out, that we stuffe it full of baggage bookes. And though they should be but a fewe, as they would be very many, if your course should take place, yet the hauing of those fewe (such is the nature of malicious reporters) would be mightily multiplied by suche as purpose to speake in disgrace of the Librarie. This is my opinion, wherin if I erre, I think I shall erre with infinit others: & the more I thinke vpon it, the more it doth distast me, that such kinde of bookes, should be vouchesafed a rowme, in so noble a Librarie.[2]

It is not surprising, therefore, that there was no Shakespeare in the Library whilst Bodley lived and none in the Catalogue of 1620. The First Folio was received on publication, presumably, though not certainly, under the arrangement with the Stationers' Company. It was kept, we may suppose, as much for its form as for its content. Folios were ideal accessions in a chained library; octavos a constant embarrassment. In 1640 two Shakespeares from Robert Burton's library joined the First Folio. Fortunately by this time the Library was showing a more catholic taste, and John Rous, the Librarian, accepted all Burton's books not already in the Bodleian. These included, in the words of the Benefactors Book, "Comoediarum, Tragediarum, et Schediasmatûm Ludicrorum (praesertim idiomate vernaculo) aliquot centurias". Amongst Burton's bequest was the 1602 [1607/8] *Venus and Adonis* and the 1600 *Lucrece*. The *Venus and Adonis* has long been recognized as a Burton book. It bears his name and his peculiar symbol.

The *Lucrece* has not hitherto been identified as his, but I have no doubt that this is so,[3] and that this is the copy from which Burton (not quite correctly) took the quotation:

> For Princes are the glasse, the schoole, the booke,
> Where subiects eyes doe learne, doe read, doe looke.

This couplet first appears in the preface to the 1624 edition of the *Anatomy* of which the Library also possesses Burton's copy.

In 1659 the Bodleian acquired its first Shakespeare quarto play, and that a very late one. This was a copy of the 1637 *Hamlet*, one of the 8000 volumes from John Selden's library, presented to the Bodleian by his executors. For the next 150 years the Library acquired, apart from the Third Folio, no Shakespearian item of any early interest or importance. Two editions of Davenant's and Dryden's adaptation of *The Tempest* and Davenant's adaptation of *Macbeth*, 1674, were received from Stationers' Hall. These represent the sum total of additions of note to the end of the seventeenth century. In the eighteenth century no seventeenth-century edition of any Shakespeare play came into the Library.

In 1812 Edmond Malone died, bequeathing his library to his brother Lord Sunderlin, to keep as an heirloom if he thought fit, or else to hand on to some public library. In 1815 Lord Sunderlin announced that he proposed to give the cream of the collection to the Bodleian as soon as the younger Boswell had finished the new edition of Malone's *Shakespeare*. In 1821 the Variorum Shakespeare was published and the transfer was completed. The Bodleian became possessed of the collection to which it owes its fame as a Shakespeare library. With Malone the friend of Johnson, Reynolds, Burke and Boswell we are not here concerned. Our matter is with Malone the Shakespearian scholar. For his library was above all a working library, gathered to further his scholarship and for no other purpose. He read his books and he annotated them when he thought necessary. He did not collect books as beautiful things in themselves. He did not pay for wide margins. Indeed, he had margins made for his Shakespeare quartos; they are all inlaid. He was not interested in bindings, and it is known that he discarded the royal binding in which Charles I had housed his Beaumont and Fletcher quartos. It is deplorable that in this instance he should have preferred Kalthoeber and convenience, but too much can be made of his philistinism. Where the text was concerned he was utterly scrupulous. He gave his continual patronage to Kalthoeber because he was trained to treat his books "with proper respect, recognizing that these venerable relics of antiquity require more than common care".

Malone's published contribution to Shakespearian studies began in 1778, when he contributed to Johnson and Steevens's Shakespeare an 'Attempt to ascertain the Order in which the Plays attributed to Shakespeare were written'. In 1780 he published his supplement to that edition, in which he edited the Poems, *Pericles* and six Shakespeare Apocrypha. In 1790 his own edition of Shakespeare was published. In 1796 he exposed the Ireland forgeries. The second edition of his Shakespeare was, as we have seen, published posthumously in 1821. As a scholar Malone is remarkable not for brilliance but for integrity and hard work. He himself said, "I claim no other merit than industry". But his application, "his inflexible adherence to truth", were such that our greatest living bibliographer, who is not given to undue praise, has called him "the greatest of Shakespeare's editors". Malone did not confine himself to editing the plays. He threw much new light on Shakespeare's life, and his edition included "An Historical Account of the Rise and Progress of the English Stage". It was these virtues of thoroughness and application, when devoted to book collecting, which enabled him to build up the best Shakespeare library of his time. Indeed, he built up two great libraries, for he was largely responsible for the formation of the Charlemont Library, most of which was destroyed in the fire at Sotheby's in 1865.

Unfortunately the records of the Bodleian, which are generally so rich and so rewarding, preserve no details of the transfer of the Malone collection. We do not know who picked the books nor on what principle they were selected. Some 800 volumes containing about 3000 items were reserved for the Bodleian. The rest of the library was sold in 1818 at Sotheby's in a sale of 2544 lots.

The early Shakespeares of the collection are best described in Malone's own words, written on 1 January 1801:

This Collection of Shakespeare's Plays and Poems in seven Quarto volumes...forms perhaps the most complete Assemblage of the early editions of his productions that has ever been made. It wants only the *Hamlet* of 1604, *King Richard* II. 1597, *King Henry* IV. Part I. 1598, and *Venus and Adonis*, 4to 1593, to make it complete; and of those three plays it contains very early copies, carefully collated with those original editions; and of the fourth piece [the Venus and Adonis of 1593] no copy was ever seen by any of the Collectors of these precious rarities, or is now known to exist, though I have no doubt that at some future time it will be discovered.

Malone goes on to justify his claim. He describes in detail the collections of Pope, Capell, Steevens, Garrick, Kemble and Charles Jennens. He shows that although each of them possessed plays not in his own library, none could match the general excellence of his own collection. And in 1805 he went one more step ahead of his rivals. His confidence that the 1593 *Venus* would be found was justified. It turned up in Manchester and he bought it.

In 1821 the Bodleian found itself the best Shakespeare library in the country, and for some years the influence of the Malone collection is evident in the gifts the Library received and in its purchases. In 1833 Thomas Caldecott presented to the Library his collection of the poems of Shakespeare. At the Heber sale in 1834, and subsequently, some of the gaps in the Malone collection were filled. This was largely due to the enterprise of Bulkeley Bandinel, Bodley's Librarian from 1812 to 1860 and himself a considerable collector. There was no pressure within the University to improve the collection of English literature, which was not a subject of study in the Schools. The Professorship of Poetry had indeed been founded in 1708, but it had never been expressly connected with English poetry, and in 1842 the chair became a bone of contention between the supporters and opponents of the Oxford Movement. When the question of attaching a Professorship of English Literature to the History School was debated in 1877 Professor Stubbs said firmly, "I think that to have the History School hampered with dilletante teaching, such as the teaching of English literature, must necessarily do harm to the school". The Merton Professorship was established in 1885, but the English faculty can hardly be said to have existed before this century. The foundation meeting of the Malone Society was held, we must confess, at University College, London, not at Oxford. Unfortunately Bandinel was not able to buy any of those first quartos which Malone's library had lacked. When these later came into the market the resources of the Library were totally inadequate to secure them.

In 1905, however, the Library was for once able to compete successfully with Folger. The story begins in the latter half of the seventeenth century. We have seen that the Library acquired a copy of the First Folio on publication. This copy was sent to be bound by William Wildgoose on 17 February 1624 and was returned by him to the Library. It was entered in the shelf lists provided for the Curators of the Library and duly appears in the appendix to the 1620 Catalogue which was published in 1635. It does not appear in the Catalogue of 1674, where the Third Folio only is recorded. The presumption is that the First Folio was considered out of date and

Malone's note in his copy of *Venus and Adonis*, 1593. (Bodleian Library.)

was sold as a superseded edition upon the receipt of the Third Folio. We know from the Library accounts that in 1663–4 Richard Davis, the Oxford bookseller, paid £24 for "superfluous Library Books sold by order of the Curators". The First Folio may well have been amongst these. It is barely possible that the book may have been stolen. It has certainly been unchained somewhat roughly. But theft is improbable because there is no contemporary notice of it among the Library papers and none in Thomas Hearne's diary, who must have heard of the theft by report, and who would certainly not have let it pass unrecorded.

By whatever means it went, the First Folio was lost to the Library for 240 years. But on 23 January 1905 G. M. R. Turbutt, an undergraduate, brought to Falconer Madan, then sub-librarian, his father's copy of the First Folio, which had been in the possession of the family for over 150 years. The book was shown to Strickland Gibson. He recognized that it was in a contemporary Oxford binding, and had obviously come from a chained library. The most exciting possibilities began to present themselves. The binder's book was sent for (see Plate V). "A comparison of the volume with the books sent to Wildgoose for binding on the same day shows the tooling of the leather to be identical. The boards of four of the books are lined with leaves of the *De Officiis* and the *Cato Major*, printed at Deventer in the fifteenth century." The Turbutt Shakespeare was the original Bodleian First Folio. Madan was not slow to broadcast this discovery. He wrote a note for the *Athenaeum* in which he described the volume as "a standard copy in a sense which no other copy could be", since it had been deliberately picked out by the Stationers' Company for permanent preservation! On 20 February the book was shown at a meeting of the Bibliographical Society in London at which Gibson read a paper on 'The Localization of Books by their Binding'. No paper read before the Society can ever have had, or hope to have, a more splendid example to illustrate its points. And certainly no praise can be too high for Gibson's recognition of the book by its binding alone. Bodleian books remained unstamped until the nineteenth century, and their only mark of recognition is the shelfmark. In the Turbutt Shakespeare this probably appeared at the foot of the title-page which had been torn away. There is no internal evidence to connect the book with the Library in any way.

Nicholson, the Librarian, had offered to buy the volume at an independent valuation the moment he had been told of its existence. The possibility that Turbutt might be induced to part with the volume seems not to have occurred to Madan. He was soon enlightened. The day his article appeared in the *Athenaeum* one London bookseller wrote: "We write to ask whether there would be an opportunity of purchasing this book privately. We have a client who requires a good working copy of the first folio, & we should imagine from its condition, that it would be just such a copy to suit him." Madan was horrified. "I really could not have believed", he wrote to Turbutt, "that any one was so depraved as to think that that notice [in the *Athenaeum*] was intended as an advertisement of a private copy of the First Folio for sale." On 17 March 1905 Henry Sotheran & Co., who were Folger's agents, wrote to Madan: "An important foreign customer of ours is anxious to obtain, for purely bibliographical reasons, further particulars respecting the Shakespeare described in the Athenaeum for February 25th." We cannot be sure of the identity of the customer, but presumably it was Folger. In June the monograph on the copy was published. In it Madan wrote: "Mr Turbutt may be congratulated on possessing perhaps the most interesting copy of the most important printed book in English Literature, and the only copy which can claim to be the standard exemplar of that great work." And to bibliographical desirability was added romantic appeal. The wear and tear of the volume was said to prove that the young graduates of the University read *Romeo and Juliet* more often than any other play. By this time Folger's interest in the volume had ceased to be purely bibliographical. He ordered Sotheran's to offer Turbutt £3000 for the book. This was about twice the current market value of an ordinary copy of the First Folio, and was a brilliant business stroke, for it made Turbutt think for the first time of selling the volume. To Nicholson's previous offer to buy the book he had made no definite reply. Now he wrote to Madan: "The amount of the offer somewhat alters the opinion I had previously formed i.e. of making it a family heirloom." He went on to ask the Bodleian to make an offer within the next month. Subsequently he agreed to sell the book to the Library for the price offered by Folger. Nicholson reported that state of affairs to the Curators. "The Curators were of opinion that no public appeal should be made but that the

Librarian or individual Curators might communicate privately with persons likely to be willing to assist in providing the sum of £3000 required for the purpose." What prompted this decision is not apparent, but Nicholson set to work energetically to try to raise the money. He wrote to all the college bursars for lists of their wealthy members. The response was disappointing. From the bursars' replies one would gather that the University had been educating a generation of paupers. Nicholson, nothing discouraged, turned to the bursary clerks. They were paid to address envelopes to all the members on the books of the colleges. Money came in very slowly. Turbutt had given the Librarian until 31 March 1906 to find the money. By the beginning of the month not much more than a third of the sum had been raised and Nicholson asked leave of the Curators to make a public appeal. This was granted on condition that the Curators themselves were not associated with it. On 12 March Nicholson's letter appeared in *The Times*. Sir William Osler lent his great influence. Lord Strathcona's aid was enlisted. Turbutt himself abated £200 of the purchase price. The money was raised, but only just in time. Nicholson without the backing of his Curators had performed a notable service for the Bodleian. The magnitude of the task in the scale of Bodleian finance may be measured by the fact that up to that time the largest sum ever paid by the Library for a single volume was the £221. 10s. 0d. spent on a collection of Anglo-Saxon charters in 1891. The moral was well pointed by A. W. Pollard: "It's a bad way of going to work to advertise a book for its owner first and then try to buy it of him." But the advice should have been addressed to Madan, not to Nicholson.[4]

The Text

The late Joseph Quincy Adams, in an interesting analysis of the second edition of Bartlett and Pollard's *Census of Shakespeare's Plays in Quarto*, shows that the work records 77 quartos printed before 1710 in the Bodleian, compared with 205 in the Folger Shakespeare Library, 125 in the Henry E. Huntington Library and 101 in the British Museum.[5] This puts the Bodleian a very bad fourth, although the recent purchase of three late quartos brings the total up to 80, and to 87 if we include the seven quartos lent by the Earl of Verulam to the Library for exhibition. If we confine our attention to the quartos published before 1623, which alone are of any textual significance, and if we consider different editions and issues only, ignoring duplicates, the picture takes on rather a different shape. Omitting the Folger fragment of the first edition of *Henry IV, Part 1*, Bartlett and Pollard record 47 quartos before 1623. Of these the Henry E. Huntington Library is credited with 42, the British Museum with 39, the Folger Shakespeare Library with 38 and the Bodleian with 35—37 if we count the Verulam copies. If we include *Pericles*, *The true Tragedie of Richard Duke of Yorke*, *The First part of the Contention betwixt the two famous Houses of Yorke and Lancaster* and *The Whole Contention* in the Shakespeare canon, the total of quartos is increased to 53 of which the Huntington has 47, the British Museum and the Folger 44 and the Bodleian 43. Of these the Bodleian copy of the *True Tragedie* is unique, as is its copy of the second issue of the 1608 *Richard II*.

It is in its collection of early editions of the poems of Shakespeare that the Bodleian can best challenge its rivals. We have seen that Malone found in Manchester a copy of the first edition of *Venus and Adonis*. No other copy of Shakespeare's first published work is known. Ten editions of the poem were published in Shakespeare's lifetime. The last of these is known only from the title-page in the British Museum. Of the other nine the Bodleian has copies of five, the British Museum three, the Folger and the Huntington Libraries two each. Of the five Bodleian editions three are represented in unique copies. We have unique copies too of the editions of 1617 and 1630 and of the undated edition of *c.* 1630. Of the six editions of *Lucrece* up to 1616 the Bodleian has copies of three. It has two copies of the first quarto and its copy of the fourth quarto is unique. The Folger and the Huntington have also three, whilst the British Museum has two, of which one is imperfect. Of *The Passionate Pilgrim* Malone had a copy of the third quarto of 1612 with both title-pages. Unfortunately the Bodleian has Robert Chester's *Loues Martyr* neither in the original edition of 1601 nor in the reissue of 1611 entitled *The Annals of Great Brittaine*. The *Sonnets* of 1609 are present in the Bodleian in both imprints. It may fairly be claimed therefore that the Bodleian has as many early editions of the poems as any other library, although of course it is by no means so rich in duplicates as is the Folger Shakespeare Library.

Bodley has only two copies of the First Folio. I should not myself like to maintain all the claims put forward by Madan on behalf of the Turbutt copy. But it is one of the few copies surviving in a contemporary binding, and it is perhaps the only copy of which we know the name of the binder. The Malone copy is one of the three recorded with the Droeshout portrait in its earliest state. Of the Second Folio there are three copies in the Library. Two of them have the Allot IV imprint; the other has the Hawkins imprint. This is Bishop Percy's copy, presented to the Library by the Delegates of the University Press in 1946. A note inside it reads: "This Second Edition in 1632, was very accurately collated with the First and Third Impressions, and the Variations noted in the Margin, by the Revd. Thomas Hawkins, M. A. of Magd. College, Oxon who was appointed by the Delegates of the Oxford Press to superintend the 2d. Edition of Sir Thos. Hanmer's Shakespeare in 1771." It is pleasant to recall that he was paid £250 for his pains. The Third Folio is represented in the Bodleian in one copy only. This is the second issue with the additional plays. Our copy also contains the title-page of the first issue without the portrait. It is the Malone copy. The copyright copy which ousted the First Folio seems itself to have been discarded as a duplicate. There are two copies of the Fourth Folio with variant title-pages.

The great English libraries are notoriously deficient in eighteenth-century books. The Bodleian is no exception. It has, of course, most of the principal editions of Shakespeare's works, but its collection of single plays is a poor one, and with present resources is not likely much to increase except by gift. Of the eighteenth-century collections piety demands some mention of Sir Thomas Hanmer's edition, the first Oxford Shakespeare, printed at the expense of the University in 1744 and in bland defiance of the copyright claimed by Tonson. The Bodleian has Hanmer's copy of Pope's Shakespeare, annotated by him in preparation for his own edition. A manuscript note at the beginning of this copy shows the growth of his confidence in the course of the work, and explains the defects which distinguish his editorial work:

To doe justice to this incomparable Author, and to make this Edition of his works as perfect as I can; I have with my pen corrected all the errors which have occurr'd to my observation, admitting also such of the emendations contained in Mr. Theobald's Edition as I judge to be well grounded and material.

Note. There are still several passages wherein, from the corruptions of the text through all the Editions, the sense remains defective and obscure: If in those the true words and meaning are ever to be restored it must be owing to some lucky conjecture hereafter.

But since I wrote the foregoing note I have carefully review'd the whole work again: and I hope I have retrieved the true reading and sense throughout, and have made every passage intelligible, either by an amendment of the words noted in the margin, or by an explanatory note at the bottom of the page, or by an explanation of the obsolete and difficult terms in a Glossary which I have made for that purpose.

Whatever its critical defects the edition sold. The accounts which survive in the University Archives show that the book cost over £1300 to produce. The paper cost £800 and the press-work of the text £305. Hayman was paid three guineas for designing each of the thirty-six plates. Gravelot the engraver was paid fourteen guineas. In the first year of publication 575 sets of the book were sold, and the sale of "three sets of Shakespeare, being the last", is recorded in the accounts for 1746/7. When the editions of Pope and Warburton were remaindered in 1767, Hanmer's edition was fetching nine or ten guineas.

The Library possesses Malone's own copy of his Shakespeare of 1790, heavily annotated in preparation for the the second edition which he did not live to publish. This was purchased, and ever since it received his collection the Library has tried to buy as much of Malone's correspondence and papers as it could. In 1851 Thomas Percy's letters to him were acquired, and in 1858 his notes on his researches at Oxford. From these it appears that he discovered Aubrey and meant to edit him. In 1864 a volume of letters to him was purchased, which included some from Johnson and Mrs Siddons. In 1878 came some 300 letters to him. Some of Malone's printed books have also been acquired. As early as 1835 B. H. Bright presented to the Library Malone's copy of Wood's *Athenae*. In 1838 Rodd sold to the Library seventy-six volumes of eighteenth-century pamphlets which had been Malone's.

The Bodleian has no autograph of Shakespeare. Malone had at least one forgery, which he recognized as such. But in 1865 the Library somewhat hopefully paid £9 for a copy of the Aldine 1502 edition of Ovid's *Metamorphoses*. This has a note on the paste-down: "This little Booke of Ovid was given to me by W Hall who sayd it was once Will Shaksperes T N 1682." On the title-page are the initials W^m Sh^e. Madan cherished the hope that this might be genuine as late as 1916 when he reproduced it in the Shakespeare Exhibition Catalogue. In the following year, however, it was exposed as a forgery with ruthless vigour by Sir E. Maunde Thompson.

SOURCE AND ALLUSION BOOKS

The Bodleian collection of source books is a good one without being particularly outstanding. One of Shakespeare's schoolbooks was William Lily's *A Shorte Introduction of Grammar*. Bodley has the only known copy of the first edition of 1549. To pass from grammar to another part of the trivium, rhetoric, Thomas Wilson's *The Arte of Rhetorique* (the first edition of 1553 and five later editions before 1586), and Abraham Fraunce's *The Arcadian Rhetorike*, 1588, are both in the Library. Early poetry is most famously represented by the only known copy of the first edition of the *Songes and Sonettes* (1557), known to us (but not to Slender) as 'Tottel's Miscellany', a miscellany which provides the first appearance in print of the gravedigger's song in *Hamlet*. This from the collection of Thomas Tanner, bishop of St Asaph, whose library was largely formed in preparation of his *Bibliotheca Britannico-Hibernica*. It is especially rich in sixteenth-century theology. Unfortunately the barge containing the collection sank in the Thames on the last stage of its journey from Norwich to Oxford, and the condition of the books is not all that a fastidious collector would wish.

Of the books which provided Shakespeare with the immediate sources of his plays Arthur Brooke's *The Tragical Historye of Romeus and Iuliet* is among the rarest and most important. The Bodleian has a copy of the first edition of 1562. This was a late acquisition of Malone's, for when he printed it in the Supplement to Johnson and Steevens's *Shakespeare* he took his text from Capell's copy. One of the two known copies of *The Famous Victories of Henry the fifth*, 1598, is also in the Library. Barnabe Riche's *Farewell to Militarie Profession*, considered by many to be a source of *Twelfth Night*, is in the Bodleian both in the edition of 1581 and in that of 1606. Of the sources of *Pericles*, all the sixteenth-century editions of Gower's *Confessio Amantis* are in the Library, as is the only known copy of the 1607 edition of Laurence Twyne's *Patterne of painefull Aduentures*. Corpus has a copy of the earliest surviving edition (that of 1594) bequeathed to the College by Brian Twyne, Laurence's nephew. This is a variant of the Huth copy in the British Museum, the only other copy known. Arthur Golding's translation of the *Metamorphoses* is well represented in the Library in the editions of 1565, 1567, 1575 and 1578. The first edition of Holinshed has long been in Bodley, but the first edition of North's Plutarch is a very recent acquisition. It was a gift in 1948 from the Friends of the Bodleian, who have filled so many of the Library's gaps in the twenty-five years of their existence. But there are still many gaps, some of them surprising. We have early, but not first, editions of Thomas Lodge's *Rosalynde*, Sir Philip Sidney's *Arcadia*, *The Troublesome Raigne of Iohn King of England*, *The Taming of a Shrew*, Robert Greene's *Pandosto* and *The Paradyse of daynty deuises*. Most of these are rare books in any edition. Capell especially coveted Malone's *Shrew* of 1607. In 1779 he wrote to ask, "Could Mr Malone be prevail'd upon to accept two or even three 4° Shakespeares of elder date then his Shrew, in exchange for that one? I have duplicates by me, and he shall take his choice, if he will honour me with a call." Malone was not tempted by the exchange, but he agreed to lend the play to Capell in return for the sight of *Romeus and Iuliet*.

Among the printed allusion books mention may be made of two rare collections of epigrams, the unique copy of John Cooke's *Epigrammes*, of *c.* 1604, and one of the two known copies of John Weever's *Epigrammes* of 1599. This last speaks of "Honie-tong'd Shakespeare". A similar metaphor was used by Richard Barnfield who speaks of Shakespeare's "hony-flowing Vaine". His *Encomion of Lady Pecunia* is also in the Library.

Most of the allusion books come from Malone, but a few are found in the Douce collection. Francis Douce, sometime Keeper of Manuscripts in the British Museum, died in 1834. He bequeathed to the Bodleian nearly 400 manuscripts and 17,000 printed books. In 1807 he had published his *Illustrations of Shakespeare*, and he compiled for his own use a bibliography of Shakespeariana. He interleaved his copy of the *Catalogue of Mr Capell's Shakesperiana* published by Steevens in 1779, added considerably to it, and marked all the books in his own possession with an asterisk. The reception of the *Illustrations* was most disappointing, and seems to have deterred Douce from collecting Shakespeare seriously. He turned to illuminated manuscripts and early printed books. But he had Scoloker's *Diaphantus*, 1604, in the preface to which the author hopes that his work may "come home to the vulgars Element, like Friendly Shake-speares Tragedies, where the Commedian rides, when the Tragedian stands on Tip-toe: Faith

G

it should please all, like Prince Hamlet". The Douce copy was long thought unique, but is now known to have a fellow in America. Of the two most famous allusion books of all, Greene's *Groats-worth of Witte* is not in the Bodleian in its first edition of 1592, and *Willobie his Auisa* in any of the four early editions.

Among the rarest allusion books may be rated the two catalogues of the Frankfurt Book Fair in which the publication of the First Folio was advertised. These catalogues were, of course, the regular tools of the early seventeenth-century librarian and book collector. In 1614 the Curators of the Bodleian decided that they would examine the catalogues within a week of their receipt in the Library. Robert Burton's copies are marked, presumably with a view to purchase. The First Folio was advertised not in the original German edition, but in the London edition, which included a supplement of books in English. The announcement by F. P. Wilson that the First Folio had been advertised in 1622 induced E. E. Willoughby "to examine the Folio for signs of an interruption in the printing", an examination which had such happy results in *The Printing of the First Folio of Shakespeare.*

Of the manuscripts of Shakespearian interest in the Bodleian the most important are Aubrey's *Life* and Simon Forman's *Bocke of Plaies*. The former is the first real biography of Shakespeare, for the account in Fuller's *Worthies* is a formal recital without personal anecdote. No one could ever say that Aubrey was formal; it is his great charm that he is not. But one could wish that the final draft of his Shakespeare had been written. We should then know for certain if the famous note beginning "the more to be admired q. he was not a company keeper" referred to Shakespeare. What we have is his first draft, with a memorandum that he should ask the actor Beeston for more information (see Plate VI); and this tantalizing note. Aubrey's notes are supplemented by those of Richard Davies among the Fulman papers at Corpus Christi. Davies is the first to tell us of Shakespeare's "unluckinesse in stealing venison & Rabbits", and that he died a Papist.

Simon Forman's *Bocke of Plaies* records the impressions of a London doctor after seeing performances of an otherwise unknown *Richard II*, *The Winter's Tale*, *Cymbeline* and *Macbeth* at the Globe in 1611. The authenticity of these impressions has lately been questioned by Samuel Tannenbaum. This attack has given Dover Wilson and R. W. Hunt the opportunity of examining the manuscript afresh. They have shown conclusively that the manuscript is completely genuine, and that Collier, far from having forged the book, had in fact been sent a transcript of it by W. H. Black, then engaged in compiling his catalogue of the Ashmole manuscripts.[6]

There are other references to the performances of Shakespeare's plays among the Rawlinson manuscripts. The draft accounts of Lord Stanhope, Treasurer of the Chamber, preserve the names of some of the plays acted at Court which are not to be found in the final state of the accounts in the Public Record Office. They tell us, for instance, that the fourteen plays presented before the Princess Elizabeth and the Prince Palatine in 1613 included *Much Ado about Nothing*, *The Tempest*, "The Winter's Tale, Sr John Falstafe, The Moore of Venice, The Nobleman, Caesars Tragedye And one other called Love lyes a bleedinge". Closely allied to these Chamber Accounts are the Revels Accounts. Malone preserved among his manuscripts a transcript from these accounts sent to him by Sir William Musgrave of the Audit Office. When the authenticity of the Revels Accounts was first questioned this 'Malone scrap' was cited as an important piece

A Chriſtian and heavenly treatiſe called phyſicke for the ſoule, written by Maſter *Iohn Abernethy* Biſhop of Cathnes, printed for *Iohn Budge* in 4.

The hiſtorie of the Iewes deliuerance out of Babylon, and the myſterie of our redemption, plainly demonſtrated in ten ſermons vpon the 126. Pſalme. By *Iohn Hume.* Printed by *William Stansby* in 4.

The firſt and ſecond booke of queſtions and anſwers upon the booke of Geneſis, containing thoſe queſtions that are moſt eminent and pertinent, vpon the foureteene firſt chapters of the ſame booke: by *Alexander Roſſe*, printed for *Francis Conſtable*, 1622.

Playes, written by M. *William Shakeſpeare*, all in one volume, printed by *Iſaack Iaggard*, in fol.

The Theater of Honor and Knighthood, printed by *William Iaggard*, in fol.

Phyſicke for body and ſoule: ſhewing that the maladies of the one, proceed from the ſinnes of the other: with a remedie againſt both, preſcribed by our heavenly Phyſitian Ieſus Chriſt: A ſermon preached at Buckden in Huntington, before the Right Reuerend Father in God the Lord Biſhop of Lincolne: by *Edward Heron*, printed for *Francis Conſtable*, 1622.

A. The 1622 advertisement of the First Folio. (See Plate VII.)

Pilgah Euangelica, or a Commentary on the Reuelation of Saint *Iohn*, by Doctor *Symonds*, printed for *Edmund Weauer*, in 4.

Abrahams faith, that is, the old Religion, wherein is proued that the Religion now publikely taught and defended by order in the Church of England is the onely true, Catholike, ancient and vnchangeable faith of Gods Elect: and the pretenſed Religion of the Sea of Rome is a falſe, baſtard, new, vpſtart, hereticall and variable ſuperſtitious deuice of man. By *Ioſias Nichols:* printed for *Edmund Weauer* in 4.

Maſter *William Shakeſperes* workes, printed for *Edward Blount*, in fol.

Shifts and euaſions vſed by Maſter *Arnox* the Ieſuit, a Treatiſe wherein the cauſes why he refuſeth to anſwer to 17. queſtions made by the Miniſters of the Church of *Paris*, are examined, &c. by *Peter D. Moulin*, printed for *Nathaniel Newbery*.

A Catechiſme made by Maſter *Daniel Votier*, Miniſter of Gods Word, printed for *Nathaniel Newbery*.

B. The 1624 advertisement of the First Folio. (See Plate VII.)

of evidence for the defence. The genuineness of the Accounts had now been vindicated without recourse to "this rather elusive witness", to quote W. W. Greg. But if the scrap has lost a great deal of its importance, it remains a museum piece of some interest.

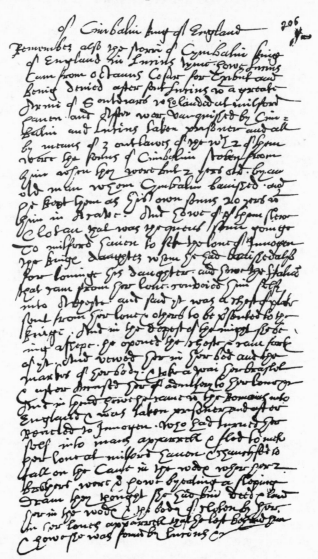

Simon Forman's account of *Cymbeline*.

Early references to and extracts from Shakespeare are to be found in several Bodleian manuscripts. The commonplace book of Edward Pudsey, written 1610–15, contains two extracts from Shakespeare. A later anonymous commonplace book written chiefly from 1620 to 1630 contains a statement that Nicholas Richardson of Magdalen quoted *Romeo and Juliet* in the pulpit of St Mary's in University sermons preached in 1620 and 1621. The manuscript contains two other references to Shakespeare. The comments on the Fourth Folio in the commonplace book of a late seventeenth-century reader have recently been analysed by G. Blakemore Evans.[7] And to carry the record into the eighteenth century we have the earlier of the two surviving assignments of the copyright in Shakespeare to Jacob Tonson. The Bodleian document assigning to Tonson the property of Henry Herringman was executed on 20 May 1707.

PLAYS TO 1640

Of the dramatic manuscripts of the Elizabethan and Jacobean age in the Bodleian the most important is Ralph Crane's private transcript of *The Witch*. Middleton's songs from the play were interpolated into *Macbeth*, and this manuscript is the earliest authority for the text of them. Another play of Thomas Middleton's, *A Game at Chess*, is also in the Bodleian in a transcript by Crane. The dedication is in Middleton's autograph. Two non-dramatic manuscripts transcribed by Crane are in the Library.

The Rawlinson collection, among its 1300 volumes, has a number of manuscript plays. *The Pilgrimage to Parnassus* and *The Returne from Parnassus* are perhaps the most important. W. D. Macray discovered that these were the first two parts of a trilogy of which only the third, *The Returne from Parnassus*, 1606, has survived in print. There are references to Shakespeare in all three parts. The trilogy was written for performance at St John's College, Cambridge, between 1598/9 and 1602/3.[8] The Bodleian is strong in academic plays, for Douce as well as Rawlinson collected them. Of the manuscript plays recorded in Alfred Harbage's 'Census of Anglo-Latin Plays' about one-fifth are in the Bodleian. They include Walter Hawkesworth's *Labyrinthus*, Thomas Legge's *Richardus Tertius* and George Ruggle's *Ignoramus*. The Library also has the epilogue to Richard Eedes's *Caesar Interfectus* as it was spoken at the performance at Christ Church in 1582. The play itself has not survived. Of the work of the Christ Church dramatist, William Gager, friend of George Peele, the Library possesses copies of his extremely rare *Meleager* and *Ulysses Redux*, both printed in 1592, but no manuscript: a manuscript of his *Dido*, however, is at Christ Church.

Of records relating to the performance of plays in the seventeenth century the lost Office Book of Sir Henry Herbert was of prime importance. Most of it had been fortunately printed either by Malone in his edition of Shakespeare, or by George Chalmers in his *Supplemental Apology for the Believers in the Shakespeare-Papers*. Malone did not print all he transcribed, and some of the entries have survived as annotations in the Malone copies of the plays to which they relate. I have already mentioned the draft accounts of Lord Stanhope. Eight papers of payments made by Sir Robert Cary as Chamberlain to Prince Charles throw some light on the obscure history of the Prince's Company. They would seem to suggest that Middleton and Rowley's *A Fair Quarrel* was acted in November 1617 and that the Company was occupying the Curtain in 1620.

The collection of printed plays up to 1640 is a strong one, thanks again to Malone's wide interests. In the first volume of his *Bibliography* W. W. Greg lists 326 plays separately published up to 1616 in some 600 editions. The Bodleian has 264 of these plays in just over 400 editions. A count of plays first published between 1616 and 1640 shows the Library to hold over four-fifths of the recorded editions up to 1700. Among the unique copies are *The Beauty and Good Properties of Women*, c. 1530; John Bale's *The Temptation of Christ*, 1547/8; Ulpian Fulwell's

Like Will to Like, 1568; *The Marriage of Wit and Science*, 1569; George Peele's *The Pageant before Woolstone Dixie*, 1585; *Fair Em, c.* 1593; the first edition of Marlowe's *The Tragicall History of D. Faustus*, 1604; and Ben Jonson's *Lovers made Men*, 1617. Of the plays wrongly attributed to Shakespeare the Library has first editions of *Arden of Feversham, Locrine, Sir John Oldcastle, Thomas Lord Cromwell, The London Prodigal, The Puritan,* and *A Yorkshire Tragedy.* Its earliest edition of *Mucedorus* is the fourth. Malone had an especially good collection of Massinger. A. K. McIlwraith has recently paid this tribute to it:

Malone had two copies of most of Massinger's plays. It happens too often to be a probable result of blind chance that, among the ten or twenty copies of each quarto which can now be traced, one of Malone's copies has the earliest recorded state of the text in most formes and the other has the latest state. In at least two instances, the title-page of *The Virgin Martir* (1622) and one forme in *The Emperour of the East* (1632), one of Malone's copies is unique among those now known in preserving the least corrected state of a forme.[9]

BACKGROUND LITERATURE

The poet Samuel Daniel printed a special dedication for the copy of his *Works* which he presented to the Library. It begins:

> Heere in this goodly Magazine of witte,
> This Storehouse of the choicest furniture
> The world doth yeelde, heere in this exquisite,
> And most rare monument, that dooth immure
> The glorious reliques of the best of men;
> Thou, part imperfect worke, voutsafed art
> A little roome, by him whose care hath beene
> To gather all whatever might impart
> Delight or Profite to Posteritie.

Bodley was indeed more interested in profiting than in delighting posterity. But so great was his zeal and energy that within five years of the foundation of the Library he could report that "the general conceat as well of other nations, as of our owne at home, of the Librarie stoare, is so great, that they imagine in a maner, there is nothing wanting in it". Most of the books recorded in the Catalogue of 1605 are still in the Library. A great many of them are still in their original bindings, a tribute alike to the excellence of the work of the Oxford binders, the clemency of the Oxford climate, and, perhaps, to the paucity of Oxford readers. The reading room still known as Duke Humfrey is substantially the same as when the Library was opened. The atmosphere of the early seventeenth century is thus preserved to a remarkable degree.

Contemporaries of Sir Thomas Bodley thought his Library the almost perfect university library. He was the prince of beggars, and fortunately the success of the Library in attracting gifts did not cease with his death. The present resources of the Bodleian in English and foreign books of the fifteenth, sixteenth and seventeenth centuries have come from many benefactors in the past 350 years. The libraries of Robert Burton and John Selden have already been mentioned. The latter had books from the collections of John Donne, Ben Jonson, Thomas Crashaw and Edward Gwynne. Thomas Barlow, Bodley's Librarian, 1652–60, and afterwards Bishop of Lincoln, bequeathed his library in 1691. It is strong in early theology, and included a copy of the first book printed in Oxford, the *Exposicio sancti Hieronymi*. The bequest of Richard Gough's library in 1809 added considerably to our resources in English topography and early Service Books. In 1860 the printed books and manuscripts from the Ashmolean Museum were transferred to the Library. They included not only the library of Ashmole himself but also that of Anthony Wood. The books in both these collections are remarkable not only for their rarity, but for their condition. The result of these donations, with those already mentioned, aided by the buying policy of the Library, is that the Bodleian possesses copies of just over half the books recorded in the *Short-Title Catalogue*. The recent generosity of the Rockefeller Foundation to English universities has enabled the Library to tap American sources for material which would not otherwise have been procurable. Photostats have been obtained of all English books before 1640 in the Henry E. Huntington Library not available in this country. Two essential American catalogues have also been acquired, the catalogue of English books to 1640 in the Folger Shakespeare Library, and the Harvard rearrangement of the *Short-Title Catalogue* in chronological order.

The Bodleian has a good representative collection of fifteenth- and sixteenth-century foreign books. Here the Douce collection brought a notable accession of strength. The Library had been buying incunables steadily for forty years before it received Douce's 300 in 1834. It now has well over 6000. Two comparatively recent donations have made notable the Library's already good collection of early printed Italian and humanist literature. Between 1912 and 1932 Paget Toynbee presented his collections of Dante, Boccaccio and Petrarch, and in 1914 Ingram Bywater bequeathed to the Library some 4000 volumes of early humanist scholarship, especially rich in editions and commentaries on Aristotle.

The printed collection of early humanist literature is, however, more than matched by the Library's manuscript resources in this field. For its exhibition of Italian illuminated manuscripts from 1400 to 1550 held in 1948 the Library drew principally on the Canonici collection which it had bought in 1817. But a dozen other collections, including those of Douce, Laud, Digby and Humfrey, Duke of Gloucester, were also represented in this memorable display. The general collection of medieval manuscripts is, of course, second only to that of the British Museum in the English-speaking world.

ENGLISH PLAYS, 1641–1700

Malone was not only a great editor of Shakespeare. His edition of Dryden has not yet been superseded and the life of Dryden prefixed to his edition was so well done that Hugh Macdonald has said, "I do not know that we know or can know enough about Dryden to justify another serious biography". As in his Shakespeare so in his Dryden, Malone's thoroughness led him to the study and collection of the works of his author's contemporaries. Malone's good collection has in recent years been further improved. The Friends of the Bodleian have contributed notably with money and expert advice to the play collection. The Library now holds copies of four-fifths of the separate plays recorded in Woodward and McManaway's *Check List*.

The Rawlinson collection is especially strong in manuscript copies of plays of this period. It has Aphra Behn's *The Younger Brother*, Orrery's *Henry the Fifth* (two manuscripts), *Mustapha* and *Tryphon*, Sir William Killigrew's *Siege of Urbin*, said to be unacted, but here provided with a cast, Thomas Neale's *The Ward* and Elkanah Settle's *Pastor Fido*. Later accessions include Carleton's *The Concealed Royalty* and *The Martial Queen*.

THE COLLEGE LIBRARIES

Sir Thomas Bodley was no innovator. He set no new fashion in book-collecting. New Bodleian in 1602 was only old college library writ large. And the college librarians were no more eager than Bodley himself to fill their shelves with plays. We cannot imagine that John Rainolds, the author of *Th'overthrow of Stage-Playes*, allowed a printed play within the walls of either Queen's or Corpus whilst he had any influence in those colleges. Though the statement that the colleges never spent money on buying books in the sixteenth century has been disproved, it is certainly true that they never spent money buying English books. Corpus Christi has preserved its catalogue of 1589, and the library of that date has been described as "a representative library of the renaissance". Among the 371 chained books there was 'Chaucerus Anglice', apparently the only work in the vernacular.[10] Such Shakespeare as the colleges possess they owe to later benefactors, and it is not surprising to find that there are only nine Shakespeare quartos in college libraries. Balliol has the two earliest, a *Hamlet* of 1611 and a *Merry Wives of Windsor* of 1619. Worcester has five quartos: *Henry IV*, 1632, *The Merchant of Venice*, 1637, *Richard II*, 1634, *Richard III*, 1629 and *Romeo and Juliet*, 1637. Three other quartos, *The Merry Wives of Windsor*, 1630, *Richard III*, 1634, and *The Taming of the Shrew*, 1631, were at one time in the library, but were stolen in the nineteen-thirties and have not since been recovered. Lincoln has two late quartos, the *Hamlet* of 1676 and the *Othello* of 1681.

Three colleges have copies of the First Folio, Oriel, Queen's and Wadham, and there are nine copies of the Second Folio in college libraries. Queen's and Wadham alone have all four Folios. Wadham owes its set to the botanist Richard Warner who died in 1775 and left his library to his college. Queen's has had its Third Folio from the seventeenth century. It was the gift of Sir Joseph Williamson. Its other three folios it owes to the Reverend Robert Mason, who was also a great benefactor of the Bodleian. In 1841 he bequeathed £30,000 to the college on condition that the money was spent in three years. The college started well by buying Garrick's copy of the First Folio, which came up at the Jolley sale, and also acquired the Second and the Fourth.

The general resources of the colleges in early printed books have been disclosed in the preparation of the Inter-Collegiate Catalogue of books up to 1640. It is estimated that about 11,000 English and about 39,000 foreign books will be recorded in over 100,000 copies. The manuscripts of the colleges have already been catalogued by H. O. Coxe. Many of them are deposited in the Bodleian. From amongst this vast wealth of material I can only single out the general collection of plays at Worcester and a few special items of interest. Worcester owes its plays for the most part to two eighteenth-century benefactors, George Clarke, Member of Parliament for the University, who died in 1736, and William Gower, Provost of the College, who died forty-one years later.[11] Among the early plays, which mostly come from Gower, are *New Custome*, 1573, George Gascoigne's *The Glasse of Gouernement*, 1575, *George a Greene*, 1599, and three editions not in the Bodleian, Lyly's *Sapho and Phao*, 1584, *Worke for Cutlers*, 1615, and *The Famous Victories of Henry the Fifth*, 1617. In all, the college has nearly 1000 plays printed before 1700. Among other rare plays in college libraries are one of the two recorded copies of *The Play of the Wether*, 1533, at St John's and Robert Greene's *The Honorable Historie of frier Bacon, and frier Bongay*, 1594, at Corpus Christi.

Oxford archives have already yielded a great deal of information about theatrical performances in the city in the sixteenth and seventeenth centuries. In 1584 professional performances had been forbidden in the University, but the ban seems to have been ineffective. The accounts of successive Vice-Chancellors preserved in the University Archives show that payments were made regularly to travelling companies of players from 1588 onwards to leave the University peaceably. The accounts of the City Chamberlains record payments to travelling companies from 1584/5, when 6s. 8d. was paid to "the Erle of Oxfordes musytians". These two sets of accounts supplement each other, and together they furnish in many instances both the name of the company and the date at which it visited Oxford.[12] They do not tell us in what year *Hamlet* was played in the University, but we know from a letter[13] in the Fulman papers at Corpus Christi that *Othello* and *The Alchemist* were seen at Oxford in 1610. The performances which the King's Men gave attracted even the theologians "qui (pudet dicere) avidissime confluebant". This is a surprising change of attitude from that of twenty-five years earlier, but already in 1607 Ben Jonson had dedicated *Volpone* to the Universities. Oxford returned the compliment by giving him an honorary degree in 1619.

The prohibiton of 1584 had allowed the continuance of academic plays, and the archives of the colleges preserve details of their performance. Those of Christ Church have been studied most intensely.[14] Christmas entertainments were a regular feature of the life of the House. When distinguished visitors came to the University special pains were taken. In 1583 George Peele was paid £20 for producing plays by William Gager for the entertainment of Prince Albertus Alasco. In 1592 Queen Elizabeth saw Leonard Hutten's *Bellum Grammaticale* and Gager's *Rivales* in Christ Church Hall. When her successor came to Oxford in 1605 the plays presented for his pleasure included Samuel Daniel's *The Queenes Arcadia*. The lists of the properties hired for these performances have survived in the University Archives. There is still unpublished material to be brought to light in college archives. The present researches of R. E. Alton will furnish a future volume for the Malone Society.

It is impossible to exaggerate the debt which the Bodleian Shakespeare collection owes to Malone. The few accessions to that collection in the last fifty years might suggest that the Library was not conscious of its great heritage. Nothing could be further from the truth, especially at present when the English Faculty is providing the Library with a record number of readers for higher degrees. Unfortunately the resources of the Bodleian for the purchase of old books have never been great. The will has always been there; for it has long been the policy of the Library to concentrate on making its good collections better. Judged even by the highest modern standards the Malone collection is a good one.

NOTES

1. I am greatly indebted to F. P. Wilson for very generous help and also to my colleagues R. W. Hunt and I. G. Philip. The standard history of the Library is W. D. Macray's *Annals of the Bodleian Library*. The second edition was published in 1890 by the Clarendon Press and is still in print. The more one uses it the more one is impressed by the width of the author's knowledge. I am also much indebted to *Specimens of Shakespeariana in the Bodleian Library at Oxford*, published by the Library in 1927. This is now out of print. It supersedes the earlier *Catalogue of the Shakespeare Exhibition held in the Bodleian Library*, 1916.

2. *Letters of Sir Thomas Bodley to Thomas James*, edited by G. W. Wheeler, 1926, nos. 220, 221.

3. In 'A note of Mr Robert Burtons books given to the Library by his last Will and testament' John Rous lists 'The rape of Lucrece by Wm Shakespear, Impfect'. The copy now in the Library lacks the title-page and the last leaf. It is bound in a mid-seventeenth-century binding and has a shelfmark entirely consistent with it being a Burton book. It does not appear under Shakespeare in the 1674 Catalogue. The cataloguer obviously had not troubled to read the dedication. He entered it under the heading *Lucrece*. The 1738 Catalogue did not correct this error. Now that we know that the book was in the Library in 1674 its provenance is reasonably certain.

4. Robert M. Smith has drawn on material in the Folger Shakespeare Library in 'Why a First Folio Shakespeare remained in England' (*Review of English Studies*, XV (1939), 257–64). I have based my account mainly on the Bodleian records. The monograph published by Madan was *The Original Bodleian Copy of the First Folio of Shakespeare*.

5. *Journal of English and Germanic Philology*, XXXIX (1940), 405–7.

6. 'The Authenticity of Simon Forman's *Bocke of Plaies*' (*Review of English Studies*, XXIII (1947), 193–200).

7. In *Review of English Studies*, XXI (1945), 271–9.

8. *The Three Parnassus Plays* (1598–1601), edited by J. B. Leishman, 1949.

9. *The Library*, Fourth Series, XXIV (1944), 186*n*.

10. J. R. Liddell, 'The Library of Corpus Christi College, Oxford, in the Sixteenth Century' (*The Library*, Fourth Series, XVIII (1938), 385–416).

11. C. H. Wilkinson, 'Worcester College Library' (*Oxford Bibliographical Society Proceedings and Papers*, I (1927), 263–320).

12. F. S. Boas, *Shakespeare and the Universities* (1923), pp. 14–83.

13. Printed by Geoffrey Tillotson in *The Times Literary Supplement*, 20 July 1933, p. 494.

14. The best and most recent account is that of W. G. Hiscock in his *Christ Church Miscellany* (1946), 165–96.

WAS THERE A 'TARRAS' IN SHAKESPEARE'S GLOBE?

BY

GEORGE F. REYNOLDS

Whether there was or was not a 'tarras' in Shakespeare's Globe and its successor is in itself perhaps of minor importance. But the question has a wider significance, because the arguments advanced for the tarras are typical of a distinctive point of view toward the whole of Elizabethan stagecraft, not to say of drama in general. Discussion of the tarras is possible in a limited space, but leads to conclusions of broad significance.

John C. Adams has presented the latest and longest argument in support of the existence of a tarras.[1] He describes it as part of the balcony in the second story of the theatre, twenty-four feet long stretching across the back of the stage from one obliquely placed window to the other, and as three or four feet deep, this depth being secured by letting it project over the lower stage from the tiring-house wall. A light railing protected its front edge, and a curtain at the rear separated it from what Adams calls the 'chamber'. This arrangement of the balcony is consistently thought out and sounds convincing, even obvious, and it is scarcely to be wondered at that C. Walter Hodges in his attractive little book, *Shakespeare and the Players* (1948), accepts it, as have also some other scholars in various modern reconstructions of the old stage.

But when one looks for the evidence for this tarras one cannot feel so sure. The contemporary Elizabethan stage pictures offer little confirmation, and they, in spite of their admitted limitations are, we have always to remember, our most tangible evidence. The Swan drawing shows for the gallery above the stage only a series of window-like openings. The *Roxana* engraving has two similar openings, also without curtains. The so-called Red Bull engraving does show curtains over the centre of the balcony, but they clearly fall outside the railing. Only the *Messalina* picture has a detail which could be interpreted as such a shelf,[2] but it is so precariously narrow as to be useless for acting, and can more sensibly be interpreted as a protective coping above the lower stage curtain. Adams does not bring it into his argument at all. Nor do the pictures of continental stages show such a tarras arrangement.[3]

And when we turn to Adams for specific evidence offered by the plays, it turns out to be meagre indeed. Of Adams's numerous citations in his sixteen pages only four plays mention the tarras (or terrace) as such at all and only one of these names it in a stage direction, D'Avenant's *The Rivals*, written 1663, not acted till 1668, and not therefore a pre-Restoration play, and certainly hardly pertinent to the Globe. To Adams's list, however, may be added two more mentions in stage directions, *2 Henry VI*, "Enter King, Queene, and Somerset on the Tarras" (Folio; Kittredge's scene number, IV, ix) and in *The White Devil* (at the Red Bull, 1609–12), "A Cardinal on the Tarras" (IV, iii, 40), described a little later as "on the Church battlements". Adams's other evidence, besides the specific references to tarras, are all to scenes below a penthouse (interpreted as this projecting tarras) or on the walls, in a gallery, above, aloft, and in *Love's Cure*, V, iii, to some women, "How in the Devil Got these Cats into the gutter". In every case where 'tarras' ('terrace') is used in the text or directions it is dramatically suitable to the scene and is therefore of dubious weight in proving an actual theatrical detail. Why suppose some special part of the stage which was a tarras and not also suppose another that was, for instance, a gutter? Even Adams does not go that far. All these references to scenes 'above' can be more simply explained as dramatically appropriate names for the same balcony. Scenes under a penthouse, if one insists on literalness, could equally well have been played under the projecting bay-windows which some assume above the stage doors. In short, none of the evidence submitted to prove the existence of some special acting-place, a tarras, does really do so or even make it probable.

What would have some force would be the citation of some scenes surely in the balcony in which an actor in front of the upper curtain opens it to discover something or somebody in the curtained space, especially if not in a bed when the bed-curtain might serve. None of Adams's instances suggests such business, but he could of course find several such scenes in which he would think this does occur, because, as we shall see, he places so many scenes 'above' which other scholars would not place there. One much discussed such scene may serve for many, *Romeo and Juliet*, IV, v, where the Nurse discovers the 'dead' Juliet. W. J. Lawrence and Granville-Barker, in a considerable correspondence with Adams,[4] decisively dismissed as unfounded and theatrically ineffective Adams's arguments for staging this scene above. To this matter of theatrical effectiveness, to which Adams seems unresponsive, I shall return presently. It is strange if an acting place did exist in front of the balcony curtain that no certain use of it has been so far cited.

No doubt Adams would still argue for the tarras because it so nicely fits into his conjectured reconstruction by filling in the space between the projecting bay-windows at either end. I shall not press the point that this plan may be less likely if I. A. Shapiro's opinion is accepted that the Globe was not octagonal but round,[5] but the possibility must be faced that the *Messalina* picture's projecting structure is a more practical arrangement in a public theatre for the curtained spaces than an alcove. Nobody has yet made clear how spectators in the side galleries could very well see action in the alcove curtained spaces above or below, unless these did project in some such fashion, and could open on three sides. The *Messalina* upper stage obviously does not permit this, but this idea of a projecting instead of an alcove rear stage has scarcely been sufficiently considered. With such a projecting structure Adams's tarras would be an awkward detail. Here a projecting stage need not further be considered, but it does serve as a reminder that Adams's reconstruction is not the only possible one and that it is not as completely satisfactory as it at first appears.

More significant, however, is the underlying principle which causes Adams to look for a tarras at all, and which motivates his whole book; the idea that the more realistically and literally every hint of stage directions and textual allusions as to stage settings and equipment is carried out the better. Applying similar interpretations to the Elizabethans that one would to Ibsen or Pinero or any other realistic modern dramatist, Adams arrives at a detailed inventory of stage equipment and construction and tries for a naturalistic consistency easy for a modern reader to accept, but quite foreign not only to the Elizabethan stage but to that of the eighteenth century and the early nineteenth as well. Lawrence and Granville-Barker, in the correspondence already referred to, emphasized the inapplicability of this theory to the Elizabethans, and I have submitted evidence that shows how far their actual practice was from carrying it out.[6] Not only does Adams's theory show a fundamental misunderstanding of Elizabethan stage-craft; it seems to indicate a misconception of dramatic illusion in general. This is a late date to have to insist that dramatic illusion has little to do with an illusion of reality. Yet that is the basis on which Adams seems to be arguing all through his book. One point may serve as illustration: scenes in which a character is told to 'come up', as in 2 *Henry IV*, II, iv (between Falstaff, Doll, a Drawer and Pistol, who is about to enter), are placed 'above' apparently only for that reason. There are, of course, numerous such scenes. Moreover, having named the balcony curtained space the 'chamber', Adams is naturally inclined to place all chamber scenes there, though he is himself aware that this is not always true (p. 276). In his article, 'The Original Staging of King Lear',[7] he goes further still in pressing the upper stage into service. On p. 318 he states as "a basic principle of Elizabethan drama that a given stage may not be used in two successive scenes to represent two essentially different or widely separated places". The statement is open to a variety of interpretations, but it would seem that a sufficient answer is the journeying scenes of Eliza-bethan drama and the convention of showing a change of scene by exit at one door and immediate entrance at another.[8] Adams uses his principle to place all the scenes in Gloucester's castle in the 'chamber' on the balcony level and finds it 'theatrically convincing' (p. 319) for Edgar to come down from the third story level when thus summoned by Edmund, who by this theory is in the balcony. Literalism could scarcely go further. Adams's shifting the direction for Edgar's entrance to a few lines later does not allow Edmund to continue his speech to him without a break, and Adams does not specify whether Gloucester and the servants enter above or below— if below, how does Edmund get down to him; if above, what about Cornwall and his party? Adams says that by his plan five of the twenty-six scenes of the play are in the balcony, "a normal ratio", but this 'ratio' corresponds naturally enough only to his own ideas.[9] These call, as here, for many scenes in the balcony with nobody on the stage below. Actually, I know of no such scenes in Elizabethan drama definitely placed 'above' by the directions. In short, Adams, in pursuing a literal realism, binds the Elizabethan stage as strictly as our most realistic drama— more strictly indeed, for even it does not place on an upper stage all scenes conceived of as in second story rooms.

Moreover, his plans deprive the Elizabethan stage of one of its most distinctive and effective characteristics. Even if the upper stage was, in spite of its elevation and its protecting railing, as easily visible as Adams insists it was (pp. 296–7)—this seems highly doubtful, but can only be proved or disproved by experimental productions—it would still be more remote from the audience than the lower stage (twelve feet is quite a height), and scenes placed there would lose their psychological immediacy, if we may speak of it so. Of course for some scenes this remote-ness would be desirable, but generally speaking the Elizabethan stage tended to bring its action forward into as immediate contact with the audience as possible.

Its actual practice and its advantages were very well illustrated at the Edinburgh Festival in Tyrone Guthrie's *Satire of the Three Estates*, and in some points at Stratford-upon-Avon by his production of *King Henry VIII* and by John Gielgud's *Much Ado About Nothing*. These pro-ductions corrected some misconceptions that studies of the Elizabethan staging based mostly on reading the plays have fallen into. Insisting that there must be no delay in the progress of the play for the placing of properties, some students have made the use of two or three stools a sufficient reason for placing a scene in the curtained space, and any scene requiring a table with several seats about it was likely to be imagined in the rear stage as a matter of course. But in *King Henry VIII* two large tables with numerous chairs and stools were twice placed before the audience and as swiftly removed, with no decrease in interest or illusion, indeed rather an increase. Clearly the supposed rule is not valid at all. In *Much Ado* a whole house façade was right before our eyes and in defiance of realism pushed about to display the interior of a church. The *Satire*, staged on a platform extending into the audience and open on three sides, was even more instructive. There was a throne for the king, Sensualitie took her place with her maidens at some distance from him, progress from one point to another was visually indicated by going two or three times about the stage, stocks, at first standing out of the way at the back of the stage, were moved up to the front where all could see and hear the actors confined in them, two gibbets were later brought in and swiftly erected. To have placed these back in the curtained space or to have insisted on such a position for the tables of *King Henry VIII* would have completely destroyed their dramatic effect. And one of the most favourable circumstances for the *Satire* was that the actors in it, all the time, were in immediate touch with their audience, not separated from it by proscenium arch or orchestra pit or a wide expanse of stage, circumstances which the actors at Stratford found inescapable hindrances.

It is this freedom and this immediacy that Adams and those who insist on literal realism of staging would surrender. Adams's book is admirable in its clarity of imagination, its precision and its consistency, but its imagination is too much conditioned by modern ideas. Acceptance of them by students of Shakespeare and by theatrical producers would be regrettable. Instead of a well-developed theatrical medium with peculiar advantages the Elizabethan stage would be made into a poor approximation to our own when most naturalism-ridden.

NOTES

1. *The Globe Playhouse* (1942), pp. 241–56, besides scattered references listed in the index.
2. As by Arthur Skemp, *Shakespeare Jahrbuch* (1909), p. 103; Victor Albright, *The Shakespearean Stage* (1909), p. 66.
3. See, for example, George Kernodle, *From Art to Theatre* (1944), pp. 65, 120, 126; also his restoration of an Elizabethan stage on p. 152. The Rubens triumphal arch at Antwerp (1635), p. 105, does show two speakers in a gallery before a curtain, but the space is obviously so circumscribed that it can scarcely be thought of as a suggestion of a place for acting.
4. In *The Times Literary Supplement*, 19 September 1935; 15, 22 February, 23, 30 May 1936.
5. *Shakespeare Survey* 1 (1948), 25–37.
6. *The Staging of Elizabethan Plays at the Red Bull* (1940), pp. 39–48.
7. *Adams Memorial Volume*, pp. 315–35.
8. For examples see my *Staging of Elizabethan Plays at the Red Bull*, index, under 'Journeying scenes' and 'Exit-Reenter' convention.
9. I add for what it may be worth a comparison of the twenty-two plays given by the King's company in the last five years before the closing of the theatres, a group I have recently been examining, with twenty-two similar new plays given by them after taking over the Blackfriars in 1608. This older group has 419 scenes, of which only eleven are suggested by precise stage directions to have been in the balcony. The group written for the company after 1636 has 413 scenes of which twelve used the balcony. In both groups I include scenes said to have been given at a window above. The comparison with Adams's ratio is striking, even if my system of scene division differs from his; I have tried to notice every clearing of the stage. Adams suggests that the upper stage was less and less used (p. 297) and I expected a similar result, but my examination does not bear this out. I on purpose chose the earlier period at a time when history plays were no longer common or the comparison would have shown a sharper contrast, but one not so fair.

TRADITION, STYLE AND THE THEATRE TO-DAY

BY

JOHN GIELGUD

Tradition, according to the dictionary, is "the handing down of customs, opinion or doctrines from ancestors to posterity, from the past to the present, by oral communication: an opinion, custom or doctrine thus handed down: principles or accumulated experiences of earlier generations handed on to others".

It is often said that the English stage has none of the great tradition of acting which has given dignity and substance to the theatres of France, Germany and Russia in their finest days. The National Theatre, we are told, will create a similar tradition in England, a permanent company for acting classic plays with style. Style (I read again in my dictionary) is "the general formal characteristics of any fine art". A broad generalization, surely, and not a particularly illuminating definition. What exactly is style in acting and stage production? Does it mean the correct wearing of costume, appropriate deportment and the nice conduct of a clouded cane? Does it mean correct interpretation of the text without extravagance or eccentricity, an elegant sense of period, and beautiful (but unself-conscious) speaking, by a balanced and versatile company of actors, used to working together, flexible instruments under the hand of an inspired director? Such were the theatres of Stanislavsky in Russia, of Copeau and, afterwards, the Compagnie des Quinze in France, and, during certain years of Reinhardt's supremacy, in Germany.

An individual actor can have style. A production can achieve a general style. A company can be said to play with style. And this word 'style' can apply equally to a modern play or to a costume piece, to comedy and tragedy alike.

It is a doubtful question whether tradition and style can be studied and learnt in a dramatic school, or acquired by watching fine actors; still less by reading accounts of the performances of the great players of the past. Every year students flock to the Old Vic and Stratford from many parts of the world (and especially from America) to learn the way to act Shakespeare and to interpret his texts. It would be interesting to know what conclusions they carry away with them. For the glamour, the past traditions of the theatre, merge so imperceptibly into the theatre of to-day that it is hard to know which influence is the stronger. Both actors and audiences know the familiar plays of Shakespeare far too well, and the unfamiliar ones far too little.

Some actors and directors try to escape altogether from the web of tradition, especially in the best known Shakespearian plays and parts. Too often in the last twenty years they have achieved sensational modern innovations and freakish quirks of originality at the expense of the plays themselves. The actors who play Shakespeare dressed in clothes of some other period—Macbeth in Byronic costume, Rosalind as a Watteau lady—have a double task, for they have to play in the manner of one period as regards deportment and behaviour while interpreting characters conceived in the Renaissance. Shakespeare has already confused the issue with his anachronisms, and too much ingenuity in decorating his plays will only add to the confusion. Granville-Barker has of course suggested that some of the plays should be staged with Renaissance-classical costumes, in the manner of Paolo Veronese and Tintoretto, and this legitimate experiment has been tried with varying success, most happily no doubt in the obvious case of *Antony and Cleopatra*, to which it is particularly suited.

But style in acting does not consist solely of the external elegances. Diaghilev introduced painters into the theatre, and a designer of fine taste can, of course, help the pictorial side of a production by insisting upon correct detail, not only in scenery, costume, properties, but also with wigs, make-up and every kind of accessory (though he cannot teach the actor how to wear them). But this is only the beginning. Each actor has his own qualities and method of approach, and it is the subtle task of the producer to study his players before trying to weld them into a particular unity of manner, pace, grouping and variety of attack. He is probably influenced considerably by his designer, and by the limitations as well as the outstanding qualities of his leading players. (He should, of course, influence the designer too, in planning the production, and together they will have considered the physical limitations of the theatre in which the play is to be given, as well as those of each player in the cast.)

Now, in the process of invention and interpretation many strange complications may ensue. A designer of genius, as Lovat Fraser was, may invent an original version of the period he is to represent. In his famous designs for the *Beggar's Opera* Fraser stripped the costumes of all trimmings and superfluous detail (preserving the line and using plain colours), and simplified his backgrounds to the barest suggestion. Playfair invented a presentational style for the actors and singers that also simplified and stylized the eighteenth-century atmosphere, and, in complete harmony with his designer, a new and delightful effect was achieved. This was a rare example in the theatre of a marriage of true minds, but subsequent developments of the same kind and treatment (even by Playfair himself) seemed comparatively inferior, imitative, and sometimes quite indifferent.

True originality comes from within—an instinctive feeling on the part of some person connected with a production which is strong enough to influence everybody concerned. But if this originality, however brilliant, runs counter to the intrinsic quality of the author and his text, the result will not be a happy one.

It is seldom customary nowadays for the author to read his new play to the company at the first rehearsal, though this was often done in the past by men like Pinero, himself a masterly director, and by Bernard Shaw, who always read with a rare vivacity and sense of character. Irving, too, always read a play to his company, whether by Shakespeare or anyone else. But readings are apt to be unsatisfactory occasions, since the interest of each actor in his own part is apt to make him inattentive to everybody else's. Also, if the author or director attempts to give too many theoretical hints of what he hopes to achieve at such an early stage, he may only succeed in confusing his actors before they get down to work. He will have some main essentials worked out for himself through his preliminary talks with the author and designer, and he will often find it best to wait to elaborate his views until he has seen from the first few rehearsals how the cast he has to work with fits into the imaginary pattern he has in mind. As regards a classical play, however, several readings will be found needful, though not necessarily at the first rehearsal, for elucidating meanings, discussion of rhythm and phrasing, and a broad suggestion of character drawing, interplay and the manner in which the director wishes to proceed.

Most actors like to set their movements and business at an early stage, and they find it very exasperating when the director changes his mind continually on these matters up to the very last minute. Some extremely skilled directors (Granville-Barker, St Denis, Komisarjevsky) who have their plan worked out in great detail in advance, can bring an almost perfect scheme, prepared in every detail, to the early rehearsals, and the movement of the play can then be rehearsed and set in the first weeks, leaving two weeks or more for the development of detail, pace, character, and the finishing touches. This is certainly the ideal method of production—but few directors are sufficiently clear-headed, or certain enough of the abilities of their company to achieve it. There is also a danger that, if the director provides too much set detail, the actors will become lazy, and cease to contribute their share in the creative work they have to do. They begin to move to order like puppets. It is important that they should feel they are bringing something of their own to add to the effect which the director is trying to contrive. Naturally, he remains the guiding influence, since he sees them from the front, and must be the final judge of their efforts, but they may easily, amongst themselves, create a somewhat different result from what he had imagined, and he must remain alive to the possibility of exciting developments throughout the play which he never envisaged from his own conception in reading it. The author, too, must be prepared to be similarly influenced in the matter of cuts and rewriting.

The actors, then, should be receptive but not dumbly submissive, obedient but not slavishly imitative, and the director, if he is also an actor, must not try to force his own personality upon the members of his cast who seem to him lacking in personality of their own. It is better for him to indicate subtleties of mood and character than to go up on the stage and illustrate what he requires by showing off his own superior technical skill or caricaturing faults— a cruel discouragement to self-conscious or inexperienced actors. Only if he finds an actor negligent and deliberately unco-operative is he justified in making an example of him before his fellows.

What are the most important qualities in an actor? Imagination, sensibility and power. Relaxation, repose and the art of listening. To speak well and move gracefully, these are elementary feats which can be mastered with hard work and practice—some great actors, Irving in particular, seem to have succeeded without them. At first the young actor is bound to be greatly influenced by the acting he admires, and a love of tradition combined with a natural respect for experience may lead him to admire the less subtle excellences of the actors he watches at work. His own taste may not be good. But as he grows older, he will be increasingly influenced by the pictures he sees, the books he reads, the music he hears, rather than by the acting of other players. He will come to trust more to his own instinct, and to his increasing knowledge of character and emotion, as well as his experience of acting in several different kinds of plays. A fine actor of modern parts who plays for the first time in a costume play may bring a far truer sense of style to his performance than an actor who is steeped in tradition and can boast of a long career in Shakespeare.

As he grows in experience and power, the actor discovers more and more how the make-believe side of acting has to be strangely combined with a naked admission of self-revelation. At first he enjoys pretending, living in another character. But he has at the same time to imagine himself, say, into the character of Macbeth, a warrior capable of committing a murder for the sake of ambition, and also to discover his own personal reactions to the speeches and situations

H

with absolute truth and sympathy. However well he may simulate the externals of the part—the age, deportment and physical aspects of his impersonation—he can only execute the promptings of his imagination within the limits of his own technical instrument and range of personality. And it is here that Shakespeare provides so wonderfully for the actor. In his great characters there is such a wide sweep of creation, such subtle variety of temperament, that a dozen actors may choose a dozen ways of playing them and, if only they succeed within their own personal expression to the full, the result will be a fine performance.

Similarly the director has his most subtle task in conducting the rehearsals so that the actors may feel confident that he is stretching them to the extreme limit of their potentialities, yet not demanding the impossible. Only with this object in view is he justified in any liberties he may take in adjusting the balance of a scene—for the total effect of the play will of course be greatly influenced by the qualities of the leading performers, and they need all the assistance possible to enable them to dominate the action wherever it is required by the text.

Some directors, as I have said, believe in preliminary discussions and many days of readings. Others work without trying to explain their views to the actors. Others, again, look to the leading players to set the pace and style. They try to teach, parrot-fashion, the actors of the smaller parts, or seek to cover their deficiencies with a mass of movement, comic invention, and pretty groupings. But how seldom is the intrinsic atmosphere of a period achieved (especially when the play is written in prose or verse of complicated pattern and full of archaic references and jokes) and how often is a false one superimposed as a result!

I have said that relaxation is all-important in acting. For myself, I have always found it the most difficult quality to attain. Relaxation is best learnt, perhaps, in acting the plays of Chekhov. I believe any actor who has appeared in one of his plays will agree with me. There is a lack of urgency, an inner truth of domestic substance in his characters that comforts the actor. Though the Chekhov men and women are frustrated, unhappy, nervous, yearning, they are very natural. It is curious that it seems easier for our actors to interpret the humours and tragedies of these Russians than to give true performances of the simple English rustics of Shakespeare, Sheridan and Goldsmith. It may be that the mixture of comedy and tragedy in the Chekhov plays makes the burden easier to sustain. The mood is continually flexible and changing, and the director may exercise his talents to the full in controlling these varieties of mood and atmosphere, leaving the actors to concentrate on details of characterization. Besides, the parts are very evenly divided, no single character dominates the action, and the period style is comparatively unimportant.

Of course it is very difficult to sustain the tragic plane in a tragedy like *Macbeth* or *Othello*, where the principal characters are of such heroic size and there is little comic relief. But it is equally difficult to sustain the changing moods of Shakespeare's comedies, with their alternating scenes of verse and prose, romance and knockabout, or the brilliant heartlessness of Congreve and Wilde without wearying the audience, especially to-day, when the restlessness of modern life and the familiar hectic rattle—and whisper—of the microphone and the cinema makes it hard for an audience to listen attentively to a long performance in the theatre. Pace, in classical playing, is of course essential, but it is much more important for the actors to play closely with one another, picking up cues, welding scenes together in contrasts of varying speeds and intensity, than for the producer to achieve a general effect of violent hurry and restless vivacity.

Unless the leisure of an earlier generation is achieved upon the stage, the brilliant talk seems wearisome and over-elaborate, the characters jerky puppets, grimacing and posing in a wealth of improbable affectation.

Tradition can only be handed down, a delightful but ephemeral mixture of legend, history and hearsay, but style evolves afresh in the finest players and directors of each succeeding generation, and influences, in its own particular era, the quality of acting and production. The theatre needs both, thrives on both, for both are the result of discipline, of endless experiment, trial and error, of individual brilliance and devotion. And genius may always be relied on to appear suddenly from nowhere, breaking all rules and confounding all theory by sheer magnetism and originality.

Poel and Granville-Barker worked continually to clear away the melodramatic gestures, slow delivery, and old-fashioned declamatory manner of the Victorian and Edwardian theatre. Thanks to their influence, Shakespeare's plays began to be acted for the first time in the right order of scenes and with a minimum of cuts. Business was allowed only if it seemed to arise naturally from the text, not spun out or elaborated into effective tableaux, or as a means for working up applause. All this was greatly to the good. But the director, however forceful in personality, has to withdraw once the curtain goes up. The actors have the final word. After six weeks of consecutive performances, the pace has dragged, new business has been introduced. Even the most conscientious players tend to flag when the audience is unresponsive and they begin to find their parts monotonous and devoid of spontaneity. Rehearsal is the only remedy, and English actors do not relish rehearsing a play in which they are already acting eight times a week. So it is obviously an advantage from the actors' point of view to be playing several plays in a changing repertoire. But such a programme confuses the public, costs a fortune in scenery changes and lighting rehearsals, and risks the dangers of miscasting, since the same actors must somehow be fitted to several parts at once.

Can we ever achieve a permanent classical company in this country? Granville-Barker attempted it, achieved one or two brilliant beginnings, and foundered with the first World War. Nigel Playfair and J. B. Fagan benefited by his example, and (to a limited extent) created theatres of integrity and style, using a nucleus of actors and actresses whose early training under the actor-manager stars, Tree, Benson, Alexander, had developed their talents to a point when they were admirably fitted to become members of a company where the policy was bent towards interpreting good plays without sacrificing their balance. Our character actors are surely as fine as any in the world, and, as the body of every repertory company, they are of course, essential. They are versatile and loyal. But, curiously enough, they seem to do their best work under an autocrat—whether he be actor, director, or a combination of both. For it is the leaders of companies who create their own tradition of style and ensemble playing. But soon the more brilliant among the younger members of such a company begin to find themselves cramped. They break away from the nursery and, as they become increasingly successful, they begin a new tradition of their own. So it happened with Mrs Kendal, Ellen Terry, Irving, Forbes-Robertson, Tree, Alexander, Granville-Barker, and in our own day with Sybil Thorndike, Edith Evans, Richardson, Olivier, Guinness and my humble self.

The struggle is always the same. Between the actor's personal magnetism, the public's demand for outstanding personalities and the author's dependence on them to interpret the leading roles they write, and that ideal theatre in which author, designer, actors and director are all bent to an unselfish, perfectly balanced creation in which no part shall be greater than the whole.

It is evident that the star must always exist. Is he to sacrifice his choice of parts and the development of his personal career to the establishment of a theatre of which he is the head? If so, he must stand down in certain productions, and either play a small part, or direct, or not appear at all. In that case he must have in his company one or two actors at least of equal talent and drawing-power with himself—a very difficult achievement, since star actors are always greatly in demand. In addition, he must guarantee his company long-term engagements—but not so long that they will become exhausted and dissatisfied. Also his actors must agree not to accept film and radio work since they will be required to rehearse continually, and sufficiently attractive parts must be provided for each player—at least one good part in a season, say, of four plays. Experimental plays must be alternated with some of the well-known classics (which are most certain to attract the public), and modern authors must accept a ready-made cast (which may imperil the chances of their work, since in a repertory company a certain amount of less-than-perfect casting is inevitable) as well as a limited run. Yet it is essential that a classical company should sometimes work on an original script, even though a Shakespearian team is seldom well suited to act a modern play, in which the women's parts are so often predominant and there are seldom enough parts to accommodate the whole company. If actors are laid off for a certain play (which may be an admirable respite for them), they must be paid or they will go elsewhere. Economically, as well as artistically, the prospect is a bleak one; and it seems to me remarkable that, with the interruption of the two wars, the advent of films, radio and television, and the enormous rise in expenses in every department of the theatre—all these crises following one another in rapid succession—the experiments in classic repertory and semi-permanent companies made in this country during the last thirty years have succeeded as well as they have.

Patrons such as Lord Howard de Walden, Lord Lathom, Sir Barry Jackson and Anmer Hall have cheerfully risked and lost fortunes in the theatre, but distinguished work has been achieved through their enthusiasm and altruism. The Old Vic has triumphed over a succession of financial crises and has now a world-wide reputation. The much criticized Arts Council has helped repertory schemes and encouraged experimental and classical theatrical ventures throughout the country. We have had, during the last decade, productions of *Peer Gynt*, *Three Sisters*, *Murder in the Cathedral*, *Back to Methuselah*, and at least half a dozen Shakespearian plays, which could challenge comparison with any in the world.

But the struggle is unending. It seems sad, of course, that when at long last a really fine production is achieved, it cannot be kept in the repertoire of a theatre, to be revived at intervals over several years, and shown in America and the great capitals of Europe too. But that is the glory of the theatre as well as its fallibility. Talented players develop quickly and cannot be kept in a subordinate position for long. The best ensemble will deteriorate after a hundred performances of the same play. Actors cannot work together happily for too many years at a time. Directors become stale. Style changes. Stars become too old to wish to continue playing the great parts in which they made their reputation a few years ago (this was not always so, and surely it is a sign of grace).

The repertory theatre and the classical theatre must always be nurseries. They will attract talented young people who wish to learn their business. A few of the best stars and character actors will always be glad to work in them—but only for a limited period, for the work is intensely concentrated and demanding, and the rewards financially inferior. In addition there are the purely material considerations to deter an actor who is no longer young—continuous rehearsals and learning of new parts, sharing of dressing-rooms, unfeatured billing, and the binding terms of a long contract.

Practical men of vision are rare in the theatre. It is seldom that one man can combine the talents of impresario, financial manager, director and actor. He may have a smattering of all these qualifications, but if so he is best fitted to work in a theatre building which belongs to him and to devise his own policy for running it. He will certainly not work so well under a committee or board of governors. But if he makes wrong decisions, or becomes tired or ill after a concentrated period of hard work, he will collapse as Irving did. Under present-day conditions there is little possibility that he can back his own ventures, so that he is bound to be financially responsible to a patron or a syndicate, or else he must work under someone else's management, in whatever theatre that management is able to provide for him and, to some degree, under their supervision. The conditions cannot be ideal, however one looks at them. The demand is always far greater than the supply as far as talent is concerned—and the temperament of theatre people notoriously incalculable. Actors are inclined to be loyal in adversity and difficult when things are going well.

But there is a great new public for the theatre since the last war. The little clique of middle-class theatre-lovers of the Victorian and Edwardian days is gone. They were regular and critical playgoers, but conventionally minded, following the favourite authors and actors of their day, fearful of experiment and suspicious of innovation. They loved Shakespeare chiefly as a stamping-ground for stars and spectacle, and revelled in the melodramas which the cinema has now usurped for ever. To-day books are more widely read, films and radio have increased the public demand for entertainment, and an appetite for literature, acting, spectacle and the spoken word has spread to millions of potential playgoers who would never have dreamed of entering a theatre twenty years ago. Plays are read, listened to and discussed as well as seen. There is a much wider interest in the production of intelligent work. Criticism is more general, if often less well informed and expert. And though one may venture to resent pipes and open shirts in the stalls of a theatre, they represent a far more widely representative audience than the snobbish socially divided house of former days.

Audiences are still traditionally minded. They still applaud (as a rule) and hiss (a good deal less frequently than of old). They still stand in queues, arrive late, drop tea-trays, and demand speeches and autographs from their favourites.

Behind the curtain too tradition remains, as much an inevitable part of the theatre magic as the plush curtain, the jumbled property room, the narrow bleak passages and staircases where the actors pass, now in costume, now in their street clothes, and the dressing rooms with their pinned-up yellowing telegrams, strangely assorted mascots, and the reminders scribbled in grease-paint across the mirrors. An age-old tradition, even in a young company playing in a theatre that has been newly built (though how much happier actors feel when playing in an old one— the Haymarket, or the Theatre Royal in Bath or Bristol). But Tradition is not a God to be worshipped in the theatre. It encourages sentimentality and looking backward. We may use it as a warning as well as an example, a danger as well as an ideal.

To play with style—the style which expresses the actor's individual personality, serves his author intelligently, and is flexible enough to give and take for the benefit of his fellow actors, either in classical or modern plays, this is a more worthy and constructive aspiration for a talented young actor to pursue. He may achieve it, perhaps, when he comes to his maturity, in a different, yet equally brilliant, way from his predecessors. But the theatre muddles on. I believe it will muddle forward and muddle through.

SHAKESPEARE IN SLOVAKIA

BY

JÁN ŠIMKO

So far as can be determined, the history of Shakespeare in Slovakia starts with the year 1806.[1] It was then that a voluminous collection of poems entitled *Poezye* was published by the poet Bohuslav Tablic, who later made a great contribution to Anglo-Czechoslovak cultural relations by publishing in 1831 an anthology of translations from English poets called 'The English Muses in Czechoslovak Garb'. His *Poezye* contained a translation of the famous 'To be or not to be', wherein the spirit of the original was not unsuccessfully rendered, even though the Slovak poet permitted himself much freedom and changed Shakespeare's iambic measure into trochaics.

The first attempt at a systematic translation of Shakespeare's plays was made by Bohuslav Križák (d. 1847). He produced versions of *Hamlet*,[2] *Macbeth* and *The Two Gentlemen of Verona*, but none of these has come down to us complete.[3] At the same time, the impress of Shakespeare was laid heavily on the work of many of the young romantic poets and dramatists active about the middle of the nineteenth century.[4] Other translations were made later,[5] but it is only when we come to the great Slovak poet Hviezdoslav (1849–1921), that we find anything of real value. Hviezdoslav produced his translation of *Hamlet* (1903) and of *A Midsummer Night's Dream* (1905) after much fruitful activity in the fields of poetry and drama, and his seriousness of purpose is shown by his own declaration that he was "imbued with true piety towards the author's masterpiece", and "inspired by a special reverence for each word that had come from his pen".[6] Hviezdoslav's knowledge of English was, however, deficient, and he followed a common practice by drawing upon versions in other languages (Czech, Hungarian, Polish, German). He also sought for help from friends with a better knowledge of English. Although Schlegel's German translation, in those times and even later considered as an authority, did not leave any marked traces in his work, striking correspondences in the use of certain special words in Hviezdoslav's *Hamlet* and in the modern Czech version produced in 1941 by E. Saudek[7] appear to indicate that both Hviezdoslav and Saudek probably drew upon an earlier Czech translation. The Slovak literary critics of those days hailed the translation of *Hamlet* as a great achievement.[8] Before 1918, the Slovak nation had suffered terribly from political and cultural oppression, and the publication of this and other similar works had a considerable cultural and moral significance. To quote Paul Selver:[9] "By these translations Hviezdoslav carried out a task of great educative value to the Slovak people and extended the resources of the Slovak language. In this respect he deserves to be compared with Vrchlický (1853–1912) whose services to Czech literature were of a similar order, though wider in scope." For a long time, these translations ranked as classics, although the fact that the poet's language is interspersed with elements of his native dialect and consequently is not the accepted literary language in its pure form has had the curious result that, just as Shakespeare's plays are nowadays sacred rather than wholly comprehensible pieces of literature to an average Englishman, Hviezdoslav's translations now require close study if they are to be understood.[10]

No doubt Hviezdoslav's achievements will become ever more and more historical literary documents, giving way as translation to later attempts by men better equipped in knowledge of the original English texts and writing in standard Slovak diction—such men, for example, as Vladimír Roy (1885–1936), a symbolist poet, who after spending some time in Great Britain, has bequeathed to us versions of *Macbeth* and *The Comedy of Errors*.

SHAKESPEARE ON THE SLOVAK STAGE

As the Slovak professional theatre has existed only since 1921, it has obviously not been able to create any tradition of its own in Shakespearian production. From this point of view, the earlier amateur productions (such as those of *The Comedy of Errors* in 1864 and *The Taming of the Shrew* in 1866) may be neglected. The unusual development of the Slovak theatre[11] after the recent war, however, and the fact that in the 1946–7 season each of the five Slovak theatre companies had one Shakespearian play in its repertory, indicate that the foundations of such a tradition are about to be laid. The programme directors of our theatres realize that without Shakespeare serious work is impossible in the theatre.[12] It is true that only comedies were acted in the season mentioned (*As You Like It*, *The Taming of the Shrew*, *Much Ado About Nothing*, *The Comedy of Errors*), but this should not be considered a poor achievement. Comedies were chosen because the producers felt that they were more likely to arouse general public interest in Shakespeare than a series of tragedies.

TWO MODERN PRODUCTIONS

(1) *As You Like It*

Let us examine *As You Like It* first, considering the problems in translation, ideas, and staging which it presents.

The translated text used by the theatre was produced by two people. It was my task to provide the literal translation of the text into Slovak. Its further refinement was the work of Miss Zora Jesenská, a poet and a first-rate master of the Slovak language. Let me quote her own words about the problems she had to face in the course of her work:[13]

The first problem, the verse, whether rhymed or unrhymed. And along with this the first principle: no poetic licence, on any account. Say what you like, for a poet such licence is merely a crutch, and he has recourse to its help only when there is no other way out for him. We do not accept it in non-dramatic poems—and still less on the stage. Then, obviously, clarity of expression is demanded, not too complicated, with no violence done to it; and yet it must be verse—with a certain elevation, a slight pathetic tinge hardly noticeable, and the whole to be at the same time natural, elastic, fresh; a simple sentence structure, choice of words….Yes, choice of words. Obviously, when we are dealing with other than 'conversational' plays, we need not restrict ourselves solely to words in current use. But is not *As You Like It*, in parts at least, something like a conversational play from the times of the Renaissance? It was in this sense that I conceived it when translating—as a non-realistic, conversational fairy-play; to this conception a translator is forced by its constant sallies of wit, of verbal attack and defence, a flash here and a flash there, and occasionally whole passages, all based on word play and brisk dialogue. Its very spirit depends on dialogue that is lively, fresh and pointed. Here enters the second problem. When Rosalind and Celia lighten their idle moments by talking; when Rosalind is exchanging her repartees with the love-sick Orlando; when Touchstone is exercising his wit—this is the conversation of 350 years ago, and courtly conversation at that. I must confess that this was a tougher problem than the question of verse. Here are puns, idioms and jokes of quite a different period, milieu and culture. Make a literal translation—and the point is lost, it sounds strained and unnatural, leaving the actor with no alternative but to rush hurriedly over such a passage lest it should offend the ears of the audience. And yet our audience is supposed to laugh at it as did the English audience three and a half centuries ago! A choice example of Touchstone's wit: "When a man's verses cannot be understood, nor a man's wit seconded with the forward child understanding, it strikes a man more dead than a great reckoning in a little room...". What can we do in a case like this but make a cross against it and transform the literal translation into something *sui generis*, which would remain nearly the same, yet reveal Touchstone's sophistry and wit, which would be both ingenious and clear, and which would be in the spirit of the Slovak language (not just Slovak words—this is not enough), and sound well on the stage.

Yes, decidedly, to give it the spirit of the Slovak language and not just Slovak words was the third problem. The contrast is severe—the English court of Shakespeare's time, and the Slovak language which has never undergone the discipline of a duke's court. Yet, the task of relating these two was not impossible, for Slovak, as a relatively young language, is fortunately quite elastic. The only thing to be borne in mind was this: neither a slavish word-for-word translation nor a misplaced 'topicality' must be allowed. Nothing that would be too evidently of 1946, and yet a living language which would help to make the personages seem real beings of flesh and blood endowed with a natural human sensitiveness, not merely reciting puppets....

Well, the main principle? A translation which is neither bookish nor too much concerned about scholastic accuracy, but a translation designed for the stage, for the actors, for the audience. A translation which will not be read, but listened to; lively, clear, and well sounding, so that it can be spoken well.

The method of staging was determined by the internal values and significance of the play. Let me quote the words of J. Felix on this point:[14]

Shakespeare's *As You Like It* is one of a series of radiant comedies, almost fantasies, where reality shakes hands with unreality, where most of the play is projected into a dream (as in *A Midsummer Night's Dream*), and where Shakespeare revels in words, optimism, and the glorification of life. Clowns and fools appear on the stage in order to talk foolish sense in splendid improvisations. A certain critic has, indeed, characterised these plays as ingenious improvisations where using a few formulae, cosmic, tragic and clownish at the same time, Shakespeare, releasing his imagination, has summed up the whole of human life. Yet it does not seem to us that these plays are entirely the expression of this wonderful Shakespearian vitality, that they sprang solely from this strange positive attachment to life as such. We know what followed after this period. We know how quickly—in spite of the fact that "the heavens were still full blue" and England was daily growing into a world-power—Shakespeare plunged into the extreme tragic mood: *Hamlet, Othello, Macbeth, Timon of Athens, The Tempest* are landmarks in this tragic progress; and if, earlier, these various 'Forests of Arden' of his represented the romantic ideal of nature where there is complete harmony between things and man, to Hamlet the whole beauty of the earth seems to be but "a sterile promontory", and "this most excellent canopy, the air, ..appears no other thing to" him "than a foul and pestilent congregation of vapours". Timon of Athens even disavowed man completely and put the "tigers, dragons, wolves and bears" morally above mankind.

And here we put a question to ourselves: is the so-called optimism of *As You Like It* really the optimism of an idyll in which there are no problems, a state of pure happiness? Is this the expression of the complete harmony of world and man? Or is it perhaps only a pious desire, a proclamation, a manifesto of the *poet* in the world of strife, of disharmony? It seems to us that the latter is the truth. It is not quite certain that this play was woven of nothing but an idyll, even if it tends towards the idyllic, or simply of optimism, even if it tends towards optimism. This world existing and shining in the comedy of *As You Like It* was created by Shakespeare in a dream about a better, more beautiful society represented here symbolically by 'The Forest of Arden', this fairy land where wonders of love and mutual brotherhood appear, where people love each other, and where the abysses gaping between them are overcome. Yet this is 'the land of dreams' contrasted with the land of reality, the country for which Shakespeare longs optimistically in spite of everything. As if he were exclaiming in his time and consequently in our time: "You, people, it is only you yourselves who are spoiling your lives, you are forgetting that a Forest of Arden, a life 'as you like it', actually exists or is within the reach of possibility."

We are conscious of the conditions with which Shakespeare was contrasting this picture of an ideal 'land of tenderness'; we know what were the social and spiritual realities that stimulated his protest against reason ("the more reason the more folly") and his 'yes' to Touchstone the fool ("The fool doth think he is wise, but the wise man knows himself to be a fool"). Obviously, *As You Like It* is directed against the puritanism and the religious dogmatism which in those days were beginning to thrust themselves vehemently into the foreground of English spiritual life and which by their narrow-minded, low, and non-pathetic conception of life tried to make the world poorer by bereaving it of beauty and love, the goodly relation of man to man. Shakespeare's protest is directed against all that puritanism—or any kind of dogmatism—takes away from life. Shakespeare laid stress on the heart and on all that stands as a symbol for the heart, not hesitating to create this imaginary country of the Forest of Arden, a romantic, devout idealisation of society where all conflicts are resolved in peaceful agreement and love.

Is all this topical? There is, I think, a straight-forward answer to this question. By its emphasis on humanity, by its bitter accent on the stupid pains which we inflict upon ourselves by that 'little foolery that wise men have', and, finally, by the resolution of the last act, this comedy is obviously more than ever capable of speaking to the present-day world of conflicting ideologies. This is one of the most humanistic of Shakespearian comedies.

We have conceived its stage realisation as a proclamation in the terms of a fairy-tale, and in optimistic tones, of the rights of the human heart. It is not an operetta-like optimism, but one wrought, by the strength of genius, out of the bitter antagonistic forces of life. And this is the only optimism which does not seem like a vain paper-proclamation—this is the only sincere optimism, since it arises from the abysmal pain and eternal tragedy of human life.

These are the ideological foundations on which Joseph Budský, the producer, based his stage work. Let me in conclusion quote his words:[15]

Joy, optimism, sunshine, sadness. This is where two worlds stand in sharp contrast to each other. The world of Duke Frederick's court, at first sight a magnificent one, in reality, however, nothing but a rotten prison full of intrigues dictated by the egoistic needs of individuals, a court where humiliation protests and demands its rights—and the world of people living in the Forest of Arden, a world of people bound in a Rousseau-like manner to nature which chastises them, and brings them nearer to one another, and forces them to respect one common interest—that of the whole.

The plot of the comedy lacks any probability and reality. This lack does not interfere, however, in any respect with our willingness to be carried away by the free intermingling of scenes, now full of charm and playful spirit and now of melancholy, which gather here into a splendid picture of freedom. Starting from the poet and from his conscious negation of any logic, he and we are led to flee from all that makes life heavy, dreary, and monotonous. Society has blocked itself in with ponderous shutters: its complicated system does not allow it to break through towards the ideal.... The forest which we are presenting on the stage supports, in contrast with the courtly society of Act I, the central idea of our production, and its optimism is expressed in the words of the banished Duke:

> the winter's wind,
> Which, when it bites and blows upon my body
> Even till I shrink with cold, I smile and say
> This is no flattery: these are counsellors
> That feelingly persuade me what I am.

The polarity of sadness and joy, of reason and heart, was therefore the leading principle of the staging of this drama. All its elements were subordinated to this principle. The depressed, packed atmosphere of Duke Frederick's prison-like court was expressively symbolized by the lattice-like setting for Act I, and intensified by the dimmed lighting. Celia's words at the end of Act I, "now go we in content to *liberty*...", emphasized by strong, clear light coming from a distance, announced the break-away from the stifling prison into the longed-for land of freedom. The attractiveness and beauty of the forest life of the subsequent acts were stressed in the rich decorations and in the tuneful music.

(2) *The Taming of the Shrew*

It is most significant that it was *The Taming of the Shrew* which was chosen for the opening performance of the New Stage of the National Theatre, Bratislava, in December 1946. The text was a co-operative effort by Emil Saudek, the outstanding Czech Shakespearian of to-day, and the Slovak poet M. M. Dedinský.

The Slovak theatre could not accept the play in its entirety. For example, there is a general avoidance on our boards of strong oaths and other base expressions. This accounts for the fact that in our production the Sly prologue was omitted—in sharp contrast to the 1947 Old Vic performance, wherein the concept of a play within a play was kept strongly to the fore, as it was at Stratford-upon-Avon in 1948. It seemed to me that the English producer's aim was to exaggerate the rudeness of the play, while our producer, Drahoš Želenský, seemed to go in the opposite direction. His starting point was the principle that

in our eyes, the poet must not sink to a mere supplier of the plot. Shakespeare must be approached with the intention of shaping his play and not with an *a priori* aim of re-shaping it. The order of the scenes is unchangeable in *The Taming of the Shrew*, and the secondary plots (concerning the fair Bianca, the disguised servants, the disavowed father) are not less important and interesting than the main theme with which they may be balanced proportionally. The metaphors, the shades and niceties of expression are of a nature to give this comedy the air of a poetical work *par excellence*. The language takes a foremost part, and in this case the poet Shakespeare seems to have surpassed the dramatist Shakespeare. The words have become a superior element transcending the plot and casting a strong light on the characters. In dramatic poetry, it is the task of the word to create spiritual space and to assume material existence by its own means. The metrical grouping of words into verse makes of them one *synthetic* word. According to Šalda, verse is magic. In setting out to conquer the indifferent world and fill it with sound and light, the verse becomes the instrument of the poet's will. The transformation of indifference into sympathy, this is the poet's aim. And just as the poet must not sink to be a mere supplier of the libretto, the actor must not sink to be a mere clown. The actor must loyally subserve the words of the poet. There is always plenty of opportunity for activity of movement. The intonation of sentences, the rhythmical speaking of words, and the balancing of the dynamic phrases create subtleties of voice which may be accompanied by actions, the actor's subtleties. If we go this way we can avoid those unrelated details of both production and acting which are so often capable of spoiling any conception of style whatsoever.[16]

In this way, the production of *The Taming of the Shrew* acquired more of a poetic character, the edge of rudeness was made smoother. Stress was laid on good speaking, and the contrast of prose (the empirical word) and poetry (the synthetic word) was underlined. As a whole, the play gave the impression of a true jest, of a series of amusing episodes rather than the clowneries of a 'crazy gang'. Interesting was the producer's innovation in increasing the number of Petruchio's staff by persons storming the stage from the orchestra. The settings were in keeping with the conception of the play. They were rather simple, but expressive of the moods of various scenes. Contrasts of light and colour added much to the youthful acting. As to the success of this play—it was acted for two seasons and has been one of the most frequently performed plays of this company.

Problems of Translation

Let me say finally something about the Slovak language as used on the stage. It will already be seen that the exploitation of its possibilities in the theatre is rather limited. Standard or literary Slovak in its present form has undergone not much more than a hundred years of systematic development. Though we have distinct *regional* dialects with differing systems of pronunciation, phonology, morphology, and syntax of their own, apart from the literary language we have not developed many separate *social* dialects as distinct systems with a different linguistic structure. The social differences are to be found mostly in specialized vocabularies, although many peculiarities of a social character have also a regional flavour. The Slovak stage is dedicated, as a rule, almost exclusively to the cultivated standard speech, the reason for which is educational—to foster and spread the knowledge of fine Slovak speech among the widest public.[17] Dialect is rarely used throughout a whole play as a means of characterization. To give a certain social or regional flavour to the language, the most that is done is to impose a few typical features (syntactical or lexical), and the selected words or phrases are presented to the audience usually with the 'correct' accent. This lends a certain uniformity to stage Slovak speech. It sometimes prevents the achievement of a necessary dramatic effect and sometimes gives a false impression of refinement, as, for example, when it is put into the mouth of a shepherd or peasant. The result is that shades of characterization which on the English stage would be expressed linguistically, on the Slovak stage can often be conveyed only by the help of outward signs, such as movements, gestures, and costumes. Yet Slovak is relatively rich in its vocabulary, especially in its possibilities of word-formation and derivation. In terms for abstract ideas it is sometimes superior to English. Its richness in inflexions and in the so-called verbal aspects and their synthetic formal quality lend a certain compactness to our language. Though its rhythmic possibilities are poorer (the stress accent always falling on the first syllable) than those of English, yet it is well qualified for poetic use.

The richness of Shakespeare's language (archaisms, foreign words, new coinings of his own, dialectal and vulgar expressions, syntactical and semantic peculiarites) can hardly be reproduced in its full vigour by Slovak, and I wonder whether indeed any other language is capable of this. Moreover, I do not think that it should be the aim of translations to reproduce it. It is the unchallengeable quality of the original. The translator's task is to catch the spirit and meaning of the original. And what should always be prominent in the translator's mind is the existence of the actor, which should affect his approach to his task. It should be made easy for the actor to learn parts of the classic plays which abound in thoughts of high complexity. These should be so rendered that the actor has no special difficulty in making their meaning clear to the audience. Our actors have not been able as yet to devote themselves to a systematic study of and training in Shakespeare's language. Neither could a special speech style have been developed such as is sometimes used by English actors in Shakespearian plays. Yet the greater the number of good Slovak translations, the more easily and intensely will the various groups of people concerned (producers, actors, audiences) be able to get to the heart of Shakespeare.

NOTES

1. The first Shakespeare translation in Czech was that of *Macbeth* by K. I. Thám, published in Prague in 1786.

2. Act IV, sc.v was published in the periodical *Hronka*, III, in 1838; Act I, sc.iii was edited from the translator's MSS. posthumously by P. Dobšinský in the *Slovak Review* (*Slovenské Pohľady*), v, 1885. (See Ľ. Rizner, *A Bibliography of Slovak Writings up to 1900* (T. Sv. Martin, 1933), vol. I.)

3. A. Mráz in the introduction to his school edition of Hviezodoslav's *Hamlet* (T. Sv. Martin, 1931).

4. "Among the dramatists, J. Záborský (1812–76) considered Shakespeare as his ideal, and his attachment to the great master led him to write historical dramas." "J. Palárik (1822–70) imitated Shakespeare in so far as he formed his own plays into a succession of comic, sentimental and pathetic scenes." (See Jan Jakubec, *A History of Czech Literature*, Prague (1934), II, 863, 907.)

5. A *Julius Caesar* translation by Bohuslav Nosák (1818–77) remained in manuscript. (See J. Vlček, *A History of Slovak Literature* (T. Sv. Martin, 1923), p. 326.) Ľ. Rizner (in *A Bibliography...*, III, 218; v, 60) mentions Štefan Mišík (1843–1919) as a prolific translator who published translations from *The Tempest, A Midsummer Night's Dream, The Winter's Tale, Much Ado About Nothing, As You Like It* (in *The National Gazette*=*Národnie Noviny*, XIV, 1883), *King Lear* (ibid. XVIII, 1887).

6. In a letter to A. Kolísek, written on 10 January 1916 (as quoted by Mráz).

7. Emil Saudek, author of several outstanding translations from Shakespeare into Czech.

8. Sv. H. Vajanský in *The National Gazette* (CXLVIII, 1903); Professor P. Bujnák in his article 'Shakespeare with us' (*Slovak Review* (1916), p. 118, as quoted by Mráz).

9. *Czechoslovak Literature*, London (1942), p. 48. See also Fr. Chudoba, *A Short Survey of Czech Literature*, London (1924), p. 143.

10. This contention is supported by the existence of a glossary added to the school edition of Hviezdoslav's *Hamlet* (1931), explaining difficult words in the translation.

11. Against *two* professional theatre companies before the late war, we have had *five* resident companies since 1946 in Slovakia, *nine* in 1950.

12. See M. M. Dedinský's article 'The Slovak Theatre and its Revival by Shakespeare' (in *The Bulletin of the New Stage*, Bratislava, 1946).

13. *The Bulletin of the National Theatre of Bratislava*, published on the occasion of the first performance of *As You Like It*, 12 October 1946.

14. *Ibid.*

15. *Ibid.*

16. D. Želenský in *The Bulletin of the New Stage*, Bratislava.

17. Cf. Orlovský-Arany, *A Grammar of the Slovak Language*, Bratislava (1946), p. 33.

SHAKESPEARE IN POST-WAR YUGOSLAVIA

BY

VLADETA POPOVIĆ

The translation, interpretation and performance of Shakespeare in the South Slav lands have passed through two phases and are now in the third. The first began in the forties of last century and lasted until the first World War, a period when only a minority of the South Slavs had an independent State, the majority being under Austria-Hungary or Turkey. The second phase covers the period between the two World Wars, after the South Slav peoples had attained political independence, and were united in the sovereign state of Yugoslavia. The third phase begins after the second World War, in the new, socialist Yugoslavia (a federation of the republics of Serbia, Croatia, Slovenia, Bosnia and Herzegovina, Macedonia, Montenegro). The quality of translation, acting and staging has improved in the course of time; in the second phase they reached a fairly high level, and have touched a still higher one in the third.

Before 1914 twenty-one of Shakespeare's plays had been performed in Croatia, in translation from the German, except in the case of two which were possibly from the English and of one from the French. Of the printed translations of nine of Shakespeare's plays, only one was from the English original.[1] In the Serbian lands, six of Shakespeare's plays were acted in translations from the English and five from the German, while altogether thirteen translations were printed, ten of which were from the original English.[2] The principal translators of Shakespeare during this period were: in Croatia, the novelist A. Šenoa and the poets A. Harambašić, H. Badalić and V. Nazor; in the Serbian lands, the poets L. Kostić and S. Stefanović; in Slovenia, the short-story writer I. Cankar and the poets A. Funtek and O. Župančič.

Between 1919 and 1941, almost all the translations of Shakespeare printed in Yugoslavia were from the English originals, as were the acting versions. In Serbia, S. Stefanović published his translations of fourteen plays; in Croatia, M. Bogdanović published ten, and in Slovenia, Oton Župančič nine. The best of these were Župančič's.

In the first, and even in the second phase, the translation of Shakespeare was a haphazard undertaking, without a fixed plan; a personal venture, the issue of which depended on many circumstances. Thus some plays were translated, whether from German, English, or some other language, more than once, by different people, and some not at all. Publishers would publish one or more translations, and then discontinue.

In the third phase, in the new Yugoslavia, the systematic publication of the whole of Shakespeare in Serbo-Croat has been ensured. The cultural institution of 'Matica hrvatska' in Zagreb (Croatia) has begun publication of translations of the complete works, under one general editor, and also a study of Shakespeare's life and times.[3] The great State publishing house of 'Prosveta' in Belgrade (Serbia) has started a similar undertaking. Translation and publication have at last become work of communal importance and of great responsibility, and there is every hope that the plans will be carried out.

The celebrated Slovene poet, Oton Župančič, whose death occurred in 1949, had up to 1945 translated into Slovenian ten of Shakespeare's plays, of which five were reprinted after that date (*A Midsummer Night's Dream*, *The Comedy of Errors*, *Twelfth Night*, *Julius Caesar*, *The Merchant of Venice*). He published two new translations after the war (*Coriolanus* and *Romeo and Juliet*). All the post-war translations have short notes and *Coriolanus* has a lively and well-informed introduction by F. Koblar.

In Zagreb there have already appeared, under the editorship of Josip Torbarina, Professor of English Language and Literature in the University of Zagreb, *A Midsummer Night's Dream* and *The Merchant of Venice* in the translation of the late Milan Bogdanović, revised by the editor; and *The Merry Wives of Windsor* in Torbarina's own translation. The editor states that he has collated Bogdanović's translations with the latest critical editions of the plays. All these translations have short, interesting, well-written introductions and notes by the editor of the series. The introductions include, among other factual information, a discussion of the date of the play and the elements and sources of the plot, and a survey of important performances in Zagreb. The introduction to *A Midsummer Night's Dream* emphasizes the realism of the artisan-actor scenes and the need for simple staging of the comedy. In the introduction to *The Merchant of Venice*, the general excellence of the play and its great stage qualities are recognized, but its weaknesses are also indicated. In the introduction to *The Merry Wives of Windsor*, the editor treats Falstaff as a 'decadent knight', a representative of the dying feudal system, and at the same time as a typical man of the Renaissance, who rebels against both the ascetic ideals of the Middle Ages and the hypocrisy of contemporary Puritans. All the characters in the play, he says, are of flesh and blood and give a realistic picture of the life of a provincial town in sixteenth-century England. With the understandable exaggeration of a translator, Torbarina affirms that in *The Merry Wives* Shakespeare has "more clearly than in any other work expressed the progressive ideas of his time and represented those forces in the English middle class which a few years later were to drive it into the struggle against the king and the privileged nobility".

At present translating Shakespeare in Belgrade are B. Nedić and V. Zivojinović. The former is well known as the translator from English of numerous prose works, and the latter as a poet and the translator of Goethe and Schiller. In practice, Nedić translates Shakespeare into prose, line for line, and Zivojinović versifies this faithful prose translation.

The Nedić–Zivojinović translation of *Julius Caesar* has appeared since the war; their translation of *As You Like It* was printed before the war, and has lately been reissued in a revised edition. Both translations have notes and introductions by Nedić, concisely written, clear and well-informed, like those of the Zagreb edition, except that they only give details of the date of the play and its sources. The same translators announce that they have ready for the press their translations of *The Winter's Tale* and *Romeo and Juliet*, and that they are at present engaged on *Antony and Cleopatra* and *The Merchant of Venice*.

The first translators of Shakespeare into Macedonian are V. Iljovski and I. Milčin. Their translation of *As You Like It* was published in 1949 in Skoplje. Twelve of Shakespeare's sonnets were translated into Croatian by the poet D. Andjelinović and published in the Zagreb periodical *Republika* in 1949.

It will be asked how the post-war Yugoslav translators have approached the problem of translating Shakespeare, with all his subtleties of style and rhythm, his mastery in the use of poetic language, his powers of suggestion and of evocative associations. Of problems there are many. The English language, containing many monosyllables and many words of two syllables with the accent on the second, falls easily into iambic; Serbo-Croatian, however, has comparatively few monosyllabic words which can take an accented position at the end of a line, and hardly any words of two syllables stressed on the second; consequently, it does not readily adapt itself to the iambic metre, and has, indeed, prevailingly used the trochaic. In addition, the fact that the plurals of many monosyllabic words are expanded to make three or four syllables makes a sharp difference between this language and the English. How, then, have the Yugoslav translators approached the translation of Shakespeare's iambics? Has fidelity to the sense of the original been achieved at the expense of terseness?

The Yugoslav post-war translators always render verse into verse, prose into prose. Župančič and Torbarina endeavour to make the number of lines in the translation correspond to the number in the original, but in the Bogdanović and Nedić-Zivojinović versions the text is usually expanded.

For example, Hippolyta's lines in the opening scene of *A Midsummer Night's Dream*:

> Four days will quickly steep themselves in night;
> Four nights will quickly dream away the time;
> And then the moon, like to a silver bow
> New-bent in heaven, shall behold the night
> Of our solemnities...

are translated by Bogdanović as follows:

> Al četir dana brzo će u noći
> Uroniti, i brzo će nam sanci
> Progutat vrijeme četirju noći—
> I tad će mladjak kao srebrn luk,
> Na nebu zapet, svadbenu nam noć
> Promatrat.

Although Bogdanović keeps to ten or eleven syllables in the line, and obtains an iambic effect, his version corresponds literally to the following:

> But four days quickly will in night
> Sink down, and quickly will our dreams
> Devour the time of those four nights—
> And then the young moon like a silver bow,
> In heaven bent, will our nuptial night
> Behold.

Almost every image in the original is retained, but it has not the lovely movement of Shakespeare's lines (Four days will...night; Four nights will...), where the significant words are effectively repeated and contrasted in rhythmic symmetry.

In the Nedić-Zivojinović translation of *Julius Caesar*, Shakespeare's line is sometimes made to appear forced, because Zivojinović, to obtain the iambic effect, has placed the adjective after the noun, whereas its natural position in Serbo-Croat is before the noun, as in English. But the Nedić-Zivojinović translation of *As You Like It*, perhaps thanks to its longer polishing, reads much more smoothly. The same is true of the verse portions of Torbarina's translation of *The Merry Wives* and of all Župančič's translations.

I

After this necessarily short survey of translations of Shakespeare in post-war Yugoslavia, we may pass on to a consideration of the performance of Shakespeare on the stage.

The Yugoslav national theatres are of the repertory type: in addition to Yugoslav drama and opera they produce foreign works in translation. The Belgrade National Theatre, for instance, has since the second World War given works by Molière, Capek, Galsworthy, Gogol, Priestley, Tolstoi, Ostrovski, Chekhov, Gorki, Sheridan, Shaw and others. A considerable amount of time is devoted to the preparation and rehearsal of famous works of world literature, although the theatres give regular performances every day from September to June. Intensive work on *Hamlet* occupied four months before its production at the Belgrade National Theatre. Such preparatory work is done in all the Yugoslav theatres, at least in the larger towns.

Public interest in Shakespeare since the war has been great, greater than ever before, and greater than in the case of any other foreign dramatist. All seats for a performance are often booked up in advance by syndicates and other bodies.

In Zagreb, *A Midsummer Night's Dream* was given in 1945–6, *Othello* very successfully in 1947. In Belgrade *Othello* was also given with great success (both by Belgrade and Zagreb companies) in 1947, *Hamlet* with still greater success in 1949, while *As You Like It* and *The Merchant of Venice* are in preparation. In Ljubljana, *Macbeth* was produced in 1948–9, *Hamlet* and, most successfully, *King Lear*, in 1949; *Romeo and Juliet* is in rehearsal. In Skoplje, to great public satisfaction, the first Macedonian translation of a play by Shakespeare, *As You Like It*, was given in 1948–9. The following plays were produced in 1948–9 or are to be given in 1950: *The Merchant of Venice* in Sarajevo; *Romeo and Juliet* in Jasenice; *As You Like It* and *The Comedy of Errors* in Maribor; *The Taming of the Shrew* in Split; *Much Ado About Nothing* in Varaždin; *The Merchant of Venice* and *A Midsummer Night's Dream* in Šabac.

The great popularity of Shakespeare is seen from the fact that in the National Theatre in Belgrade, which is, as we have said, a repertory theatre like all the Yugoslav theatres, *Othello* has been given thirty-two times since May 1947, and *Hamlet* twenty-two times since March 1949.

The efforts of producers and actors to give fresh interpretations of Shakespeare's plays are best seen in the case of *Hamlet*, produced in Belgrade by Hugo Klain and the leading actor Raša Plaović. Before the opening, Klain published an article of thirty pages in the principal Belgrade literary journal, *Književnost*, expressing his conception of the play. Having considered the views of some outstanding critics, Klain declares that the question is not which of them is right, but what a Yugoslav can get out of *Hamlet* for himself here and now. According to Klain, Claudius is a 'canker of our nature', a sore on the body of society, which can only be made whole by the excision of the sore. Actually Hamlet, a man of Shakespeare's time, is trying to escape from "the outworn, ghostly, dead past" and to step into the new times. Those times are not ours, but Shakespeare's, and therefore it would be wrong to expect Hamlet to look with our eyes on the problems and people of those times.

According to Klain again, "the essence of Hamlet…is the hard and bitter mortal struggle with the conscience, the active man's withholding from action until he is sure that his act will not be a crime—a restraint which is hard and painful, for to such a man only action can bring peace, liberation, salvation".[4]

Klain's view is shared by Plaović, who not only co-operated with Klain in the production, but also played Hamlet, both before and after the war. In his pre-war performance, Plaović interpreted Hamlet as a man overwhelmed by disgust with life, disgust born of the closed perspectives of the social situation. Since the war, according to his own statement, he has come to consider Hamlet as a man predominantly conscious of the ugliness and evil in the social life around him. Hamlet's mind demands complete proofs, but when these are clear, they lead him to conscious action. In the pre-war interpretation, Hamlet's killing of Claudius was the outcome of extreme excitement, almost of rage. To-day, in Plaović's new interpretation, Hamlet's final act is quite deliberate, and is emphasized as such on the stage. Hamlet kills Claudius in full awareness, as a judge, not as an avenger.

Criticism of the performance of *Hamlet* was on the whole very favourable. The well-known Belgrade literary critic, Milan Bogdanović, in a long article in the daily paper, *Borba*, on 2 April 1949, wrote enthusiastically about Shakespeare and his times, the essence of Hamlet, and the excellent acting of Plaović. Shakespeare is for Bogdanović 'the greatest Titan of Titans' in Renaissance literature, and "of Shakespeare's characters Hamlet is the most complete expression of the humanism of the Renaissance,...the most human and the most realistic". In the production Bogdanović criticizes the presentation of the Ghost as a three-dimensional figure, and not as a vision, and he considers that the scenery in some places "overcrowds the stage, smothering it, with at times too pompous an effect". "From the excellence of Hamlet, from good solid creations which please us in the King, to some extent in Ophelia, sometimes in the Queen... Horatio...the Grave-digger, the production descends to ineffective theatrical posturing."

Hamlet attracted more attention from the Belgrade public than did *Othello*, which was given two years before. Some months before the first performance of *Othello* in Belgrade, Klain published an article entitled '*Othello* To-day'. For Klain, *Othello* is not a drama of jealousy or of slandered innocence, or of disappointed confidence, but "the tragedy of genuine humanity, surrounded by the inhumanity of 'higher' races and civilizations and the brutality of ambitious renegades and traitors. Iago is a renegade and a traitor...Othello does not kill Desdemona with hatred and the sadistic lust of the injured, jealous husband, but with the sorrow of a judge pronouncing the death sentence." *Othello*, for Klain, is a profoundly optimistic tragedy. The great love of Othello and Desdemona is the reflexion of a great love of mankind, of faith in the future, of the effort to realize the ideal of humanity. *Othello* "awakens and strengthens faith in the rights and duty of the true 'masters of life' to take over the control of life from the hands of the criminal 'puppet-masters'".[5]

The poet and critic M. Dedinac, in a criticism of this performance, finds that the actors did not show enough emotion and delicacy. He did not like their way of speaking Shakespeare's lines, and expressed the opinion that "Shakespeare must be translated all over again for us". He considers that "the adventurous, daring spirit of Renaissance man" was little felt in this production, and finds fault with the omission of the scene preceding Desdemona's arrival at Cyprus—a scene which, he says, "indicates the war-like background of the action". Dedinac praises the acting of Lj. Jovanović as Othello, and still more that of M. Živanović, who played the part alternately with him. He was not satisfied with Iago, for according to him, Raša Plaović played it "like a malicious, cold calculator", and M. Milošević, who played the part alternately with Plaović, "conceived it as a pathological phenomenon". It is characteristic that Dedinac considers that the players, after perfecting their acting, should tour the provinces "with the enviable task" of popularizing "this great work of Shakespeare's".[6]

Dramatic criticism in the new Yugoslavia demands of both producers and actors great efforts and high quality, so that the deep significance of Shakespeare's dramatic works may be revealed to the masses of the people. An attempt is being made to give fresh interpretations of *Othello*, *Hamlet*, and other plays, which shall correspond both to Shakespeare's conception and to the needs of the present time. Translators are endeavouring to rise to the height of their great task, and feel their responsibility to the public, which has long heard that Shakespeare is the world's greatest dramatic poet, and now wishes to feel this in the translations. The managements of all the national theatres are showing ever greater activity in bringing Shakespeare before the people. Editions of translations of Shakespeare's works are sold out in a few months. The actor Raša Plaović was awarded a State prize of 100,000 dinars for his performance of Hamlet. *Hamlet* has stirred intellectuals young and old, who discuss the play and its problems in study-circles and write about it in the press.[7] Such facts indubitably indicate that the long-felt wish that Shakespeare should be worthily installed in Yugoslav literature and on the Yugoslav stage is at last about to be realized.

NOTES

1. J. Hergešić, *Shakespeare u Hrvatskoj* (Hrvatsko kolo, Zagreb, 1949), pp. 505–28. R. Filipović, *Shakespeare Hrvati u 19. stoljecu* (Zagreb, 1948), p. 16.

2. Vl. Popović, *Shakespeare in Serbia* (1928), p. 128.

3. Yugoslav studies on Shakespeare published before 1941 include: S. Miletić, *Die ästhetische Form des abschliessenden Ausgleiches in den Shakespeareschen Dramen* (Agram, 1892); V. Krišković, *Shakespeare, Predgovori dramama* (2 vols. Zagreb, 1934–5); Vl. Popović, *Zivot i dela Viljema Šekspira* (Belgrade, 1938).

4. H. Klain, *Savremeni problemi u 'Hamletu'* (*Književnost*, Belgrade (March 1949), pp. 210–37).

5. H. Klain, '*Othello danas*' (*Naša književnost*, Belgrade (February 1947), pp. 138–50).

6. M. Dedinac, 'Povodom Šekspirovog "Otela" na Beogradskoj pozornici' (*Naša književnost* (June 1947), pp. 478–86).

7. The following works have exerted considerable influence: M. M. Morozov, *Viljem Šekspir* (Belgrade, 1947) and Marx-Engels, *O književnosti i umetnosti* (Belgrade, 1946).

ADDENDUM

In 1950, reprints of the following pre-war translations by M. Bogdanović have appeared in Zagreb: *Romeo and Juliet, Hamlet, Othello, King Lear*; and also a new translation by Danko Andjelinović of *Venus and Adonis*. A long article on Shakespeare in Slovenia by Dušan Moravec appeared in *Slavistična Revija*, Ljubljana, 1949, pp. 51–54, 250–291.

INTERNATIONAL NOTES

A selection has here been made from the reports received from our correspondents, those which present material of a particularly interesting kind being printed wholly or largely in their entirety. It should be emphasized that the choice of countries to be thus represented has depended on the nature of the information presented in the reports, not upon either the importance of the countries concerned or upon the character of the reports themselves.

U.S.A.: *Shakespeare Leads the Way*

If the Bard of Avon, touring the world in his astral body, had chosen the year 1949 to visit this benighted land, he would have found, on Broadway, his memory revered, but his plays neglected, while at the same time his *Hamlet* was leading the way in new fields of adventure and enterprise.

Only two productions have been seen in New York during the past twelve months: *Richard III* appeared briefly on the boards (in February) in a compact production designed, directed and performed by Richard Whorf; and a pleasant, fresh *Twelfth Night*, directed by one of our mid-western college producers, Valentine Windt, and employing an agreeable young cast, was seen in New York for a month or so in the autumn. Looming on the horizon is a Theatre Guild production of *As You Like It* starring Katharine Hepburn—recaptured from the films for the occasion—and directed by England's Michael Benthall (Plate VIII). This highly publicized production is a cause for rejoicing, for New York theatre-goers are starved for Shakespeare.

But I believe that none of these productions would surprise or delight the Bard as much as the ebullient musical comedy, *Kiss Me, Kate* (Plate IX), which riots around his own riotous farce, *The Taming of the Shrew*. Nothing could be gayer, more vigorous, more engaging than the musical that Sam and Bella Spewack have improvized on Shakespeare's play and for which Cole Porter has supplied appropriately rollicking and giddy music and lyrics. The authors have imagined a leading actor and his former wife, who is an equally successful star, coming together for a tour in Shakespeare's play. Off stage they exhibit in modern terms much the same characteristics as Shakespeare's mettlesome couple. Their violent personal quarrels and ultimate reconciliation wind in and out of their performance of *The Shrew*, which thereby becomes a play within a play in a new fashion. The supporting cast, the stage hands and the other characteristic hangers-on of a touring company supply the chorus and dancers a musical comedy must have as well as an absurd secondary plot hardly more far-fetched than those so often supplied by the Bard himself. Alfred Drake as the actor Petruchio and Patricia Morison as a spirited, singing Katharine give particular zest to the irreverent but highly successful raid on the Shakespearian canon.

If New York lacks 'straight' Shakespeare, there is more of him west of the Hudson than in previous seasons. In addition to the usual college and community theatre productions—the Valentine Windt *Twelfth Night*, already mentioned, was first produced at the Summer Theatre session of the University of Michigan—there have been several interesting professional developments. Margaret Webster, the Bard's ambassadress-at-large to the American playgoer, organized a touring company to take Shakespeare to the towns and cities that have long lacked any living theatre. Indefatigable and devoted, Miss Webster refused to be discouraged by the failure of the American Repertory Company, which was unable to weather more than its first season. In 1948-9 she organized a company on wheels, secured a bus, a truck-trailer and a station-wagon and sent *Hamlet* and *Macbeth* up and down and across the country on a twenty-two-week tour. New 'territory' was opened up by these courageous pioneers, for Miss Webster under the management of Sol Hurok and the National Concert and Artists Corporation sent her company to many places, chiefly colleges and high-schools, where Hurok's musical artists have performed but where no acting company had penetrated. During the first season the company played in some 200 spots, in thirty-four states and three Canadian provinces. The season was successful from the point of view of its major intention, but it inevitably lost money. A fully professional company of twenty-one, a technical and business crew of seven and the costs of travel, even when motorized, made the weekly expenses greater than the then possible guarantees. A second season, with *Julius Caesar* in modern uniforms and a spirited *Taming of the Shrew*, bids fair to

I*

succeed not only artistically but economically. So far the company has played 113 engagements in twenty-two states and is going ahead full steam.

This year's productions, which opened at Woodstock, New York, with the endorsement of the American National Theatre and Academy, show Miss Webster at her directorial best. Each play is interpreted with honesty and deep respect for the text, yet with so vivid a sense of its living values, its commentaries on the present, its illumination of the past, that it has the freshness of something new and unexpected. While the young players in the cast are receiving an invaluable training in classic playing (as well as in physical endurance—for the tours are extremely taxing) they are already sufficiently experienced to give first-rate performances and to provide their varied audiences with true theatrical enjoyment. It is greatly to be hoped that Miss Webster will be able to continue and expand her programme and that her courageous adventure in barnstorming will have the reward it deserves.

Another touring group of even longer standing, but only recently of professional calibre, is the State Theatre of Virginia—known as the Barter Theatre. The name is a relic of the depression days when its founder, Robert Porterfield, accepted potatoes, eggs and vegetables in lieu of dollars at the box-office of his theatre. From this summer theatre start, Porterfield has developed his project into a State Theatre, the first in the country, and has winter tours through Virginia and adjacent (as well as more distant) states. He had frequently offered Shakespeare in his repertory of classic and modern plays and finally as his two-hundredth production he invited Robert Breen to produce and play in *Hamlet*. Breen took leave of absence from his voluntary post as Executive Secretary of the American National Theatre and Academy and mounted a spirited version of the tragedy which when he was in the army he had played for soldier audiences. The Virginia production caught the attention of Danish authorities who invited Breen to bring this American *Hamlet* to Elsinore. Since the United States Government has nothing comparable to the British Council to underwrite such undertakings, Blevins Davis, whose interest in the theatre is as profound as his generosity toward it, stepped into the breach and supplied the needed funds. He sent the designer Nat Karson to Elsinore to see the courtyard where the play is given before creating his design, and he underwrote the expenses of gathering and rehearsing and costuming the company, which was headed by Robert Breen as Hamlet, Walter Abel as the King, Aline MacMahon as the Queen, Clarence Derwent as Polonius, and Ruth Ford as Ophelia.

The first American *Hamlet* to be shown in Hamlet's own historic Elsinore (Plate X A) caused a great deal of comment for its unconventionality, for the striking effects of its staging and lighting and for its generally unusual presentation. The Danish criticisms ranged from warm enthusiasm to horrified commentaries for such impieties as beginning the play with the council room instead of the parapet scene, for allowing pistols, historically possible but definitely not standard practice, to be carried by Rosencrantz and Guildenstern, for a Ghost whose recorded voice emanated from a loud speaker. But every one of the critics found the production and performances challenging and gave them serious and detailed consideration. The public was enthusiastic and the attendance records topped those of all previous productions.

Breen's arrangement of the *Hamlet* text included not only a realinement of some of the scenes and of the omission of others—notably the graveyard scene and those of Fortinbras—but the introduction of material from the first and second quarto as well as the first folio. His production was not modern in costume, but contemporary in spirit and original in concept. The setting designed by Nat Karson for the open reaches of the Kronenberg courtyard was also striking and imaginative. It consisted of flights of steps and platforms, the main acting space being surrounded by six huge statues, supposed monuments to Hamlet's royal forebears. These figures, made of simulated stone, seemed part of the palace itself, but they also served the purpose of masking the supports of the batteries of lights which played effectively on the scene. The following extracts from some of the more favourable commentaries of the Danish press reflect the impression made by the production as a whole:

"[Lighting effects and costumes] were perhaps the reason why most of the audience went away after the performance with a mind full of astonishment. The staging was imaginative and disclosed a fine sense of detail. The direction of the actors was carried through with the sharpest discipline with effective results. Episodes and scenes succeeded each other across the stage with steady precision. Not the smallest detail has been overlooked. The direction reached particularly effective heights in the fencing scene when full passion was let loose."

(Henrik Nejiendam, *Ekstrabladet*, Copenhagen, 18 June 1949.)

"The whole play is acted with naked, unafraid realism. Hamlet probably in no other version of the drama has so little of the legendary prince about him as in Breen's adroit, tense and modern characterization which plainly shows a doubting, tortured soul. Robert Breen plays without compromise. He gets everything out of the role. He is a vital person, swaying between night-black grief and brilliantly executed burlesque and pantomime. His movements and facial expressions are extraordinary."

(*Sydsvenska Dagbladet Snallposten.*)

From Denmark the company was flown by the U.S. Air Force to the American sector of Germany and proceeded to give five performances for the Air Force—a different but equally challenging audience. The company played in the gilded opera house at Wiesbaden with a full orchestra, and under less ample conditions in Erding, Nauheim, Munich and Heidelberg, and then was flown back to the United States. This tour received the blessing of the State Department, and the practical help in the matter of transportation and the costs of the tour in Germany from the Air Force. Blevins Davis underwrote all other costs—production, salaries and so forth. The venture was the first of its kind in American history in that, though privately financed, it received some official recognition. It was an important forward step in the general movement in the United States for national and international recognition of the arts. Again, as nationally with the Webster company, internationally also Shakespeare leads the way. ROSAMOND GILDER

Canada: Amateur Performances

As far as one can gather from reports received, these last nine months have been an exceptionally lean, indeed literally empty, period for Shakespeare productions in Canada by visiting professional companies. Even the comparatively populous and wealthy east, with two urban communities each over a million strong (and each with *one* public theatre) has drawn no visit of Shakespearians either from the United States or from Britain. Canada has had to rely on itself. One of its few semi-professional companies, the New Play Society of Toronto, acting on a small and simple stage, gave recently a very creditable performance of *King Lear*. Another, the Earle Grey Players, will produce *Measure for Measure* next month. In the summer, we presume, there will be both in Montreal and Toronto the usual series of Shakespeare plays, given in outside settings. In the number of amateur productions, staged in private halls and in the University theatres, there seems also to have been a falling off. There have been school plays in various parts of the country, but, as far as can be ascertained, Toronto alone among the Universities has produced Shakespeare

during the winter season. This was *Othello*, given in Hart House Theatre by a student cast under the direction of Mr Gill. An otherwise good performance was flawed by the commonest of amateur failings, an inability on the part of some to speak the lines distinctly. Too often the amateurs forget that all rests ultimately on the audience's reception of and response to the power and beauty of the language.

During the period under review the Canadian radio stations have done valuable work in their broadcasts of some of the plays; and in the near future we may have the opportunity of seeing Shakespeare produced by some of the competitors in the Annual Canadian Dramatic Festival. R. S. KNOX

U.S.S.R.: New Translations and Productions

The Sovetsky Pisatel (Soviet Writer) Publishing House in Moscow has put out a second edition of Marshak's translations of Shakespeare's Sonnets. The first edition was issued in 25,000 copies and this second in 50,000—totalling in all 75,000 copies. The book contains an article of mine on Shakespeare's Sonnets. The Leningrad branch of 'Goslitizdat' Publishing House has put out the eighth and last volume of the *Complete Works of Shakespeare*. Many new Soviet translations appear in this volume. The same publishing house has issued a one-volume edition in folio of selected works of Shakespeare edited by M. P. Alexeyev and A. A. Smirnov. Shakespeare translations by Boris Pasternak have been published in two volumes by the Iskusstvo (Art) Press. The Children's Publishing House has issued Pasternak's translation of *King Lear* in a separate volume (50,000 copies) for secondary school pupils. The edition is furnished with an essay on *King Lear* and explanatory notes by myself. The eleventh volume of the *Complete Works of A. N. Ostrovsky*, now being put out by the 'Goslitizdat' Publishing House, contains Ostrovsky's translation of *The Taming of the Shrew* and fragments from his translation of *Antony and Cleopatra*. The great Russian playwright never finished this translation—he was sitting at his desk and working on it when his end came.

Of theatrical productions of Shakespeare during 1949 I shall mention only a few. The Moscow Theatre of Satire has successfully staged *The Comedy of Errors*. One of the theatres of Gorky city brought its production of *The Merry Wives of Windsor* to Moscow audiences during its recent tour; the play was staged in a new translation by S. Marshak and myself. *Othello* was put on in Kaluga and, in the Azerbaijanian language, in Baku; *Romeo and Juliet* was put on in Dzerzhinsk (Gorky region) and, in the Georgian language, in Tbilisi; *The Taming of the Shrew* in Tambov; *Much Ado About Nothing*, in the Georgian language, in Sukhumi; *The Comedy of Errors*, in the Mari language, in the city of Yoshkar-Ola. I am planning to visit Tashkent soon where I shall see a new production of *Hamlet* in the Uzbek language (this by the way is not the first production of *Hamlet* in that tongue).

The above list of the productions of 1949 is far from complete. It goes without saying that all the dramatic schools in our country invariably work on Shakespeare.

MIKHAIL MOROZOV

Poland: Interest in the Elizabethans

The interest aroused in the Elizabethans by the Shakespeare Festival of 1947 has led to the production, for the first time in Poland, of Beaumont and Fletcher's *The Knight of the Burning Pestle* (Katowice, June 1949; see Plate XB) and has made *The Merry Wives of Windsor* one of Warsaw's greatest successes. Shakespeare's comedy, played from October 1948 to March 1949, was presented at the Polski Theatre by Richard Ordyński.

W. BOROWY

Germany: (1) Manifold Activities

There has been a noticeable increase in the production of Shakespeare plays in Germany during the last two years. *Hamlet* alone has been put on in no fewer than fourteen different productions in the past twelve months, the most outstanding and successful being that by Gründgens at Düsseldorf, with full houses booked for weeks in advance. In addition to *Hamlet* may be mentioned *Othello*, *Twelfth Night*, *A Midsummer Night's Dream* and *The Taming of the Shrew* among the plays which were most frequently performed during the last year. The list of Shakespeare plays produced in Germany in 1949–50 does not, however, include any of the Roman plays, and of the histories only *Richard III*, *Richard II* and *Henry IV* have been staged. A noteworthy production of *As You Like It* by Heinz Hilpert with the actors of the theatre of Konstanz toured many stages in the western zone. At Düsseldorf *Timon of Athens* was produced in the prose translation by Wieland (see below). Although in some German theatres improved stage conditions allowed a greater emphasis on setting and lighting, as well as elaboration of costume and decor, in general a tendency towards economy and spareness of setting seems to prevail. The tendency to popularize Shakespeare by providing for bold, even vulgar, effects and for a display of doubtful indecency became apparent in a challenging and provocative though greatly successful production of Shakespeare's *All's Well That Ends Well* at the Kammerspiele, Munich. A similar, but even worse,

distortion of Shakespeare was the much debated production of *The Taming of the Shrew* at Lübeck in April 1950, where an effort was made to modernize by means of motor-vehicles, bicycles, jazz-music and hyper-modern costumes. On the other hand, the Max Reinhardt tradition was continued in a lovely and exquisite open-air production of *Love's Labour's Lost* in the Schlosspark at Marburg. The famous, old tradition of Shakespeare production at the theatre of Bochum found expression in two remarkable productions of *Othello* and *Cymbeline* in 1949 by Saladin Schmitt (president of the German Shakespeare Society). The new director of the Bochum theatre (Schalla) has now inaugurated a rather different style of Shakespeare production, which was illustrated in two successful and noteworthy productions of *Measure for Measure* and *Macbeth* on the occasion of the German Shakespeare Society's annual meeting on 23–24 April 1950. This year's meeting was given special importance through the presence of Cardinal Archbishop Dr Frings who is patron of the society and who, in his address, spoke about *Richard III* and *Hamlet* in their relation to our times. The Society now has more than 2000 members, a remarkable fact in view of the general decrease of members in all other societies after the currency reform. The *Shakespeare-Jahrbuch*, of which the last issue was published in 1948, is to be continued this year under new editorship. All in all, it can be said that Shakespeare activity in Germany has almost regained its former vitality.

WOLFGANG CLEMEN

(2) For and Against Schlegel-Tieck

In the seasons 1948–9 and 1949–50 (to the end of February) eighty-four theatres at seventy-seven centres gave about 1675 representations of twenty-one plays of Shakespeare. As the season will not end before June or the first days of July there will be, during this period, at least 2000 representations of Shakespeare in Germany. Even in 1949, the year of the Goethe-jubilee, Shakespeare was the major dramatist of the German stage—and all zones are alike in participating in this activity.

Most of the theatres chose the Schlegel-Tieck-Baudissin translation. But German managers and scholars are convinced that this classic rendering is not at all ideal, that it romanticizes the figures and the verse of Shakespeare. Its romantic vagueness is far from Shakespeare's clearness, as far as the spirit of German romanticism is from the spirit of the Renaissance. The German public is, however, accustomed to it, and it is the rendering of true poets, whereas modern renderings often prove too 'scholarly' in their effort to follow

PLATE VIII

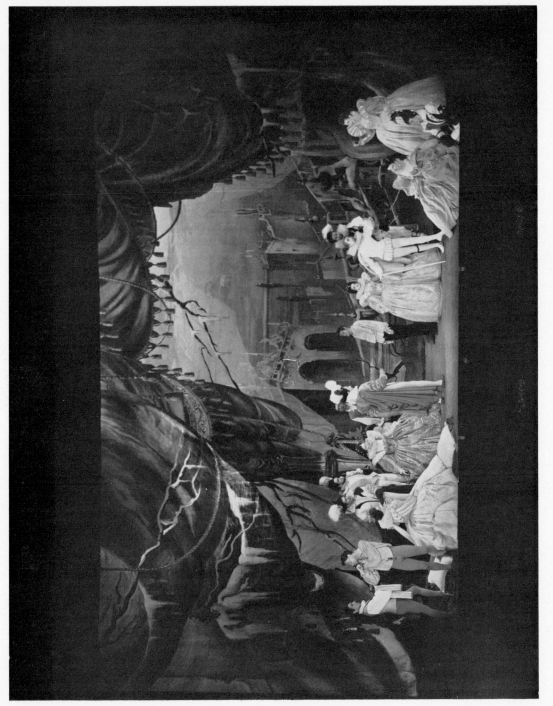

As You Like It, New York, 1949. Theatre Guild Production, directed by MICHAEL BENTHALL

PLATE IX

Kiss Me, Kate, New York, 1949. Based on *The Taming of the Shrew* by
SAM AND BELLA SPEWACK. Settings by LEMUEL AYERS

PLATE X

A. *Hamlet*, Elsinore, 1949. Production by BLEVINS DAVIS; directed by
ROBERT BREEN; settings by NAT KARSON

B. *The Knight of the Burning Pestle*, Katowice, Poland, 1949. Production by
KR. BERWIŃSKA-GOGOLEWSKA; settings by MARIAN EILE

PLATE XI

A. *Love's Labour's Lost*, Old Vic, New Theatre, 1949. Production by HUGH HUNT; settings by BERKELEY AND SUTCLIFFE. THE OPENING SCENE

B. *Love's Labour's Lost*. THE HUNT

PLATE XII

A. *Love's Labour's Lost*. THE ARRIVAL OF MARCADE

B. *Love's Labour's Lost*. THE LADIES' TABLEAU

PLATE XIII

B. *Measure for Measure.* THE PRISON

A. *Measure for Measure,* Shakespeare Memorial Theatre, 1950.
Production and settings by PETER BROOK. THE CONVENT

PLATE XIV

A. *Measure for Measure*. CLAUDIO AND JULIET HALED TO PRISON

B. *Measure for Measure*. THE CLOSING SCENE

Shakespeare's lines and words literally. They buy exactitude at the price of poetry.

Finding both the classic and the modern translations unsatisfactory, some producers have taken to literary experiments. Hans Schulla's production of *Timon* at Düsseldorf was in the early rendering of the classic Christoph Martin Wieland. Between 1762 and 1766, when the first discussion about Shakespeare began in Germany, Wieland had attempted to win his works for the German stage. Though he translated in prose and in spite of the incorporation of many features of the bourgeois morality of the Age of Enlightenment, his rendering makes its public feel something of the poetical fire of the original. Yet its interest is historical rather than intrinsic. The same must be said of Paul Rose's production of Gottfried August Bürger's translation of *Macbeth* at Tübingen. The prose of this master of the ballad, a poet of undoubted dramatic talents, shows still more of the dramatic fire of the original, more than most translations. It was written in 1778 and after its first performance at Riga in 1784 was popular until Schiller criticized it in favour of his own translation. A third experiment was made by the Kreistheater at Borna in Saxony. Here *The Taming of the Shrew* was played in the rendering by Johann Ludwig Deinhardstein, who was director of the Vienna Burgtheater from 1833 to 1840. Rejected by all scholars, Deinhardstein's *Bezähmte Widerspenstige* was as popular with the public as his *Viola*, a rendering of *Twelfth Night*. The performance at Borna proved the effectiveness of this rendering, but—though interesting—it is no better than the classic translation of Baudissin.

Modern translations were chosen by ten theatres for eleven productions. Less than ten per cent of all German Shakespeare productions were given in another translation than that of Schlegel-Tieck-Baudissin. Most poetic worth was attributed by the critics to the rendering of *As You Like It* by Rudolf Alexander Schröder, which was played at Frankfurt a. Main. The Stadttheater at Freiburg i. Breisgau will play *A Midsummer Night's Dream* translated by Richard Flatter, an Austrian scholar living in America. His translation has already been successfully given at the Burgtheater in Vienna. At Magdeburg *Macbeth* was performed in a translation by Walter Josten.

The most successful among the modern translators of Shakespeare still is Hans Rothe. His renderings of the early comedies, *The Two Gentlemen of Verona* and *The Comedy of Errors*, have won popularity, despite the fact that objection is frequently made to his modernization of the characters and his use of present-day slang. His

The Comedy of Errors was given at Wuppertal and Hannover (Theater am Ballnof). Gustav Gründgens produced at Düsseldorf *The Two Gentlemen of Verona* in Rothe's translation and for forty-four performances his public enjoyed the charming easiness and witty actuality of this production. The other prominent producer from Berlin, Heinz Hilpert, brought out *Much Ado about Nothing* and *As You Like It* in Rothe's translation at Konstanz and this production gained fame all over Germany as Hilpert and his players toured through many towns. At Berlin and at the Ruhr-Festspiele at Recklinghausen the critics compared the style of Hilpert's production, its delicacy, harmony and serenity, with Mozart's chamber-music. Rothe's translation was used in Hans Schweikart's production of *All's Well That Ends Well* at Munich, while his *Measure for Measure* and *Henry IV* were performed at Ulm and Gelsenkirchen.

(3) *Post-war Study of Shakespeare*

Since the war no complete edition of Shakespeare's works has been issued, though the public badly needed and wanted it. Many editors have sought to bring out such a set of volumes, but none had capital enough for the venture. There have been, however, numerous editions of one or several of his plays, some of them published in the first number of *Mitteilungen der Deutschen Shakespeare-Gesellschaft*.

A list of works about Shakespeare was published in the second number of the *Mitteilungen*. The most important and greatest among these is Ernst Leopold Stahl's *Shakespeare und das Deutsche Theater* (noticed in *Shakespeare Survey*, 2). Stahl gives a complete and lively history of the reception of Shakespeare in Germany and of his position and influence on the German stage from the time of the Englische Komödianten down to 1947.

The German Shakespeare Society published two *Year-Books* (80/81, 1946 and 82/83, 1948). In 1949 the two editors, Max Deutschbein and Ernst Leopold Stahl, died. The new editors, elected in January 1950, are Hermann Heuer (Münster), Wolfgang Clemen (München) and Heinrich Stamm (Zürich). The next *Jahrbuch* is being published in 1950. The German Shakespeare Society also published some essays about Shakespeare, some of them being the main lectures at its annual meetings. These are:

(1) Frank Thiess, *Shakespeare und die Idee der Unsterblichkeit* (Dortmund, 1947).

(2) Max Deutschbein, *Die kosmischen Mächte bei Shakespeare* (Dortmund, 1947).

(3) Gustav Friedrich Hartlaub, *Prospero und Faust* (Dortmund, 1948).

(4) Rudolf Alexander Schröder, *Goethe und Shakespeare* (Bochum, 1949).   KARL BRINCKMANN

Austria: A New Edition of Schlegel-Tieck

This year's report on Shakespeare performances and Shakespearian scholarship in Austria is very meagre indeed. None of the leading theatres had a new performance, although the Vienna Burgtheater kept last year's *Julius Caesar* in its repertory. Only the popular Vienna Scala Theatre tried its hand on *Othello* (October 1949), with actors not much used to playing Shakespeare. Nevertheless, the performance was well spoken of, but neither the acting nor the producing showed new ideas.

The Klassiker Verlagsgesellschaft, Vienna-Baden, announces the first complete reprint of the well-known Schlegel-Tieck (1839-40) translation of the plays in any German-speaking country since the last war. It will come on the market during 1950, nicely printed, on good paper, and handsomely bound. E. Zellwecker has contributed scholarly introductions to the various dramas, and the present writer has written a short introductory biographical sketch.   K. BRUNNER

Norway: A Contrast to Ibsenian Realism

Since the production of *As You Like It* at Trondheim in April-May 1949, Shakespearian activities in Norway have been very slight. The only event worth mentioning was the guest performance of *A Midsummer Night's Dream* by the Young Vic Company of London. This took place at Det Nye Teater, Oslo, on two successive nights in November 1949. Stein Bugge, late director of Den Nationale Scene, Bergen, has enthusiastically written about the English production (two articles in *Morgenbladet*, 11 and 25 November), pointing out that here was an admirable and useful object-lesson in theatrical idealism; he contrasts it with the Ibsenist realism which has long kept a stranglehold on the art of the Norwegian stage.

At the moment of writing, rehearsals for *The Merchant of Venice* are in progress at Nationaltheatret, Oslo, and this is likely to be the next Shakespeare event of major importance.   KRISTIAN SMIDT

Greece: Shakespeare in Athens

The Taming of the Shrew, translated by K. Karthaios, was produced at the Royal Theatre of Athens, by the National Theatre Organization, in autumn 1948. Producer: D. Rondiris. The same performance was revived at the Municipal Theatre of Piraeus.

Richard II, translated by K. Karthaios, was produced for the first time in autumn 1947, at the Royal Theatre of Athens, and revived in January 1949. Producer: D. Rondiris.

Antony and Cleopatra, translated by M. Skouloudis, was produced in Athens, at the Ideal Theatre, by the Katerina Company, in October 1949. Producer: S. Carandinos.   GEORGE THEOTOKAS

Italy: Stages Great and Small

During the course of this year Shakespeare has been performed on the widest and on the smallest stage in Italy—the Roman theatre of Verona (*Julius Caesar*, produced by Guido Salvini, with a simultaneous setting, August 1949), and the tiny Teatro dei Satiri of Rome (*Hamlet*, December 1949). In the production of *Hamlet* an attempt was made to give an equivalent of the apron stage, but the severe cuts in the text and the indifferent acting deprived the performance of real value. The translator of the Verona *Julius Caesar* was C. V. Ludovici, who is preparing a new complete verse translation of Shakespeare's works.

Renzo Ricci, who is making a speciality of Shakespearian roles, has appeared again as Richard III at the Piccolo Teatro of Milan (February 1950). Giulio Coltellacci designed the costumes both for this and for the Verona performance of *Julius Caesar*. The translator of *Richard III* was the poet Salvatore Quasimodo, whose light-heartedly undertaken translation of *Romeo and Juliet* (performed in Verona; see *Shakespeare Survey*, 2, p. 129) has been severely criticized by Gabriele Baldini in the review *Belfagor* for 31 January 1950 (article: *Come viene tradotto Shakespeare*).

The poet Eugenio Montale has produced a good acting version of *Hamlet*, neatly published in November 1949 by Cederna, Milan: the translation was made at the suggestion of the actor Romano Cialente, who, however, has been prevented by death from putting it on the stage. Montale's translation is mostly in prose; he finds that blank verse 'in narrative passages demands almost irresistibly that prose should be used in the Italian translation'.   MARIO PRAZ

SHAKESPEARE'S COMEDIES AND THE MODERN STAGE

[A study of production problems with particular reference to 'Love's Labour's Lost' (at the New Theatre, 1949–50) and 'Measure for Measure' (at the Memorial Theatre, Stratford-upon-Avon, 1950)]

BY

RICHARD DAVID

Dr Johnson was the last critic who dared to say that Shakespeare's most characteristic and most inspired work lay in his comedies. The Romantics, putting an exaggerated value on tragedy as in some way nearer to the heart of the matter, degraded the comedies to the status of pot-boilers; and even to-day we have hardly escaped from the Romantics' spell. We have one expounder of the comedies for every ten on the tragedies; and for a Granville-Barker to stoop to *A Midsummer Night's Dream*, or an Edith Evans to Rosalind, is exceptional.

We may not agree with Johnson that the comedies deserve more effort than the tragedies, but clearly they require more if they are to make a comparable impression on a modern audience. Tragedy is large in gesture and effect, and even when its overtones are lost and the subsidiary strokes bungled, its main import can hardly be missed. Comedy depends much more on detail, on delicate adjustments of balance and of contrast; it seeks to reproduce the climate rather than the actual predicaments of real life and its method is rather allusiveness than direct presentation. Comedy has more and finer points of attachment to the world in which it is composed than has tragedy. For this reason, comedy dates the more rapidly and the more thoroughly, and after a lapse of years a tragedy based even on so fantastic a convention as Fletcher's is easier to grasp than a comedy of Jonson or Middleton, for all its firm grounding in human nature. Tragedy can be understood in the original, as it were, even by those unacquainted with the tongue; whereas comedy, to be appreciated by a modern audience, must undergo some degree of translation into modern terms.

The difficulties that face the would-be translator are broadly of two kinds. Some old comedies have remained crystal clear in intention, though the details of the action and of the language through which that intention is conveyed are now largely incomprehensible without a gloss; in others, language and action are perfectly plain and yet the point of the whole has become obscure or capable of various interpretations. These peculiar difficulties are well exemplified in two distinguished recent productions, the *Love's Labour's Lost* directed by Hugh Hunt for the Old Vic Company in the winter of 1949–50, and Peter Brook's *Measure for Measure*, with which the Stratford Memorial Theatre opened its 1950 season. Whatever may be the topical implications of *Love's Labour's Lost* its main point is plain—the gentle ragging of youthful priggishness and affectation, as measured against natural good sense and natural good feeling—and it is a point that time has not dulled. Dons and donnishness are to-day even more popular as butts than they were in the 1590's, and the vivacity controlled by a good heart that Shakespeare praises is a virtue that does not grow stale. On the other hand, the almost Joycean reduplication of puns and the obscure allusions of the play are a byword. *Measure for Measure* is by comparison straight-forwardness itself as far as the text goes; but the arguments as to whether the piece is comedy or problem-play, Isabella heroine or caricature, are unending.

Even though the intention of *Love's Labour's Lost* may be plain enough, some skill is required in the presentation to convey it to a modern audience. The point or moral of the play (as of so many comedies) is a code of manners, a demonstration of what rational behaviour should be by a comparison with irrational behaviour. Nathaniel is unwittingly providing an ironic commentary on himself and his peers when he says of Dull:

> ...such barren plants are set before us, that we thankful should be,
> Which we of taste and feeling are, for those parts that do fructify in us more than he.
>
> (IV, ii, 29–30)

The standards set are those of taste and feeling, aristocratic standards, and the ladies must live up to them—the lords, too, once they have come to their senses. Moreover, the audience must be conscious throughout that the action is enclosed in a coherent and self-contained world defined by these standards.

The coherence of the play was admirably preserved in the Old Vic production. The sets perfectly suggested the self-contained world of Navarre's park, shut away among steep hill-slopes down which the hanging woods cascaded, excluding the everyday world and blanketing every sound that might penetrate from it. Among the trees showed the turrets of castles and hunting lodges, each retreat and secret corner of the domain isolated from the others by the waters of a spreading lake that was at the same time the means of communication between them. One may criticize the elaboration and heaviness of this set. It was no doubt suggested by the backgrounds to Elizabethan miniatures, the more extended works of Hillyard or of Oliver; but enlarged to backcloth scale the effect was baroque rather than renaissance, more Jacobean than Elizabethan. It accorded well with the autumnal ending of the play, but hardly with the green goose season of its opening. The devotees are solemn enough, but their solemnity must be seen to be against nature; the landscape (if we must have one) should be a laughing landscape that mocks their sober suits and matches the frills and freshness of the ladies through whose eyes we judge them. And yet the sense of a private and self-sufficient world, so successfully achieved in this production, owed much to the swathing and insistent scenery.

The structure of the play is uncomplicated. The first three acts present the situation and the opposing parties in bold and simple colours. Act IV is a helter-skelter with everyone at cross purposes, diversified by the to and fro of the hunt and the entrances of the comics. The long last scene builds up slowly but steadily, becoming more and more fantastic and ebullient until the appearance of Marcade bursts the bubble in an instant; this is one of the greatest *coups de théâtre* in Shakespeare, and it brings, after the whirlwind of fooling that has preceded it, the still small voice of sincerity and actuality before the play dissolves in thin air and bird-song. Hugh Hunt divided the whole naturally enough into three movements, each set in a different part of the labyrinthine park. In the first the nobles of Navarre made their pact to forgo female company, and rated Costard the clown for his transgression of it (Plate XI A); at the same spot Armado wandered ashore, from a boat paddled by Moth, to meet the disquieting vision of Jaquenetta; here too the ladies of the French embassy, advancing through the forest glades, were intercepted by Navarre and his courtiers. The focus of the second movement was a rustic cottage, again by the waterside, which provided shelter for Armado's lovesick meditations, and a prison for Costard; after the hunt arranged for the entertainment of the French ladies had swept by (Plate XI B), it served as a convenient hiding-place from which the eavesdropping lords could overhear each other's confession of forbidden love, and a rendezvous for Armado and the other devisers of his pageant. The last movement (that is, the last scene of the play) opened with the ladies idling outside their pavilion; to them the masques of the Russians and of the Nine Worthies; and over the lake at their back, when the merriment was at its height, loomed the barge that brings the funereal Marcade with his news of the French King's death to cloud the scene (Plate XII A). The management of this effect was overwhelmingly successful, as was the quiet recapitulation of the lovers' problems that follows, and the final fading of the play in trills and falling darkness. This by itself was full justification for both setting and production.

Such elaborate dressing and marshalling of the action, though foreign to Shakespeare's theatre, is legitimate as the just translation of his intention into modern terms. The original audience of a coterie play or a play of manners (and *Love's Labour's Lost* is in some sense this) is specially conditioned, by the community of interests it shares with the author, to appreciate the mood of his work and accept his illusion. A modern audience, unused even to the unifying and sharpening effect of verse, may well be encouraged to draw the same sense of characteristic atmosphere from scenery and direction. In some of his efforts to this end Hunt nevertheless went outside his brief.

The play must open with a tableau of the lords signing their solemn declaration. It is tidy and elegant to balance this, at the point where the ladies are to take over the lead, with a similar tableau of the feminine party, and the last movement in the Old Vic production accordingly opened with a 'still' of the ladies outside their pavilion (Plate XII B). Shakespeare, however, has made no allowance for this, nor has he provided accompanying action. What are the ladies to do? They shall sing a song in chorus. This is 'pretty and apt', but something irrelevant has been added to Shakespeare.

There were other instances of this striving to impose an extra formality on an already formal play. The second movement was rounded off—after Armado and Holofernes had completed their plans for the pageant—with a burlesque dance in which *all* the comics joined. Now it may be appropriate, as Granville-Barker has suggested, that Dull should here dance a few steps of his hay to show what he thinks is a suitable entertainment for the gentlefolk; but for Armado or Holofernes, who has just expressed his disgust at Dull's low suggestion, to take part in it is to deny their nature, and at this point of the play they must still be true to themselves. At the end, when comedy slips imperceptibly into vaudeville, let them dance their jig if you will. A more blatant, though less serious, reversal of Shakespeare's intention for the sake of spectacle occurred in the last movement, when the Russian maskers are begging the ladies for a dance. "Play music then," says the mock Princess. "Nay, you must do it soon. Not yet? No dance. Thus change I like the moon." In the Old Vic production a formal dance did in fact follow the words "Play music then", and continued some time before Rosaline, resuming her broken speech, brought the measure to an end. Yet it is clear that the lords, though constantly tantalized into thinking that the ladies may dance with them, are as constantly put off. Ten lines later the King is still begging the 'princess' to begin.

Such dislocations, the first of dramatic propriety, the second of literal meaning, could hardly be justified even if the added dances succeeded perfectly in reinforcing the tone or continuity of the action. Here they had the opposite effect. The movements were perfunctory, the music feeble and banal to a degree. Yet even perfectly designed music and choreography would here have been an intrusion, a formal element introduced just where the text avoids it. Shakespeare has given plenty of opportunities in this play for formality, and we have now to see the opposite error, of trying to break down a given artificiality and make the scenes of spectacle 'come to life'. The tableaux, or scenes of ceremony, demand some supporting cast, and no doubt Shakespeare gave his king and princess as large a train of attendants as his company could muster. The sole function of these extras, however, is to add weight and volume to the dignity of their masters, and any attempt to give depth to the scene by making individuals of them is totally un-Shakespearian. A tendency to 'work up' the crowd is one of the most dangerous features of modern productions of Shakespeare. In *Love's Labour's Lost*, it is true, there was nothing to equal the horrors of Komisarjevsky's *King Lear*, in which the hundred knights, vociferously echoing their master's "Return with her?", effectively broke not only the rhythm but the mounting tension of one of Shakespeare's greatest dramatic crescendos. The interpolations which the ladies were allowed to make in Boyet's reading of Armado's love-letter were exactly similar, but in this context harmless; while the caperings and posturings and beard-waggings of the burlesque philosophers in Navarre's train, which were employed to 'lighten' the King's first speech and his reception of the ladies' embassy, were not so much destroying Shakespeare's intention as grossly over-playing it. The solemn performance of Navarre and his peers has indeed its anti-masque; but that is later provided by Armado, Holofernes and Nathaniel and no duplication of it is needed. It was again an over-zealous striving for vigour and variety that made a pantomime of the hunting scene.

Finally, a rather different form of over-emphasis. At the beginning of the last scene the ladies' light-hearted chatter about Cupid suddenly steadies as Rosaline says to Katharine:

> You'll ne'er be friends with him, a' killed your sister.

Katharine's reply introduces the first note of seriousness into the play:

> He made her melancholy, sad, and heavy—
> And so she died: had she been light, like you,
> Of such a merry, nimble, stirring spirit,
> She might ha' been a grandam ere she died.

Hunt properly seized on this as a forecast of the serious mood of the end of the play. For a moment the sun is hidden by a forerunner of those clouds that are later to overcast the scene, and we get a premonition of love's labour *lost*. This is admirable; but the mood was unduly prolonged in the repartee that follows between the two girls, which was worked up into a real quarrel, so that the Princess' "I beshrew all shrows" had to be delivered *tutta forza* in order to quell it. This gave a change of tempo and colour, and showed us a new side of Rosaline's character, a hard shrewish side; but at this stage of the play neither the action nor the character has been sufficiently developed to bear this elaboration, and the only result was to turn the audience against so viperish a heroine.

SHAKESPEARE'S COMEDIES AND THE MODERN STAGE

This prolonged analysis of faults has been undertaken to show how the producer with the very best intentions—of giving continuity or variety to his play—may achieve the exact opposite. In general, however, the total mood of the play—buoyant, lyrical, penetrating, extravagant—had been so firmly and truly established by both producer and actors that it could not be shattered by incidental 'wrong notes'. As Elizabethans and as courtiers the ladies were perhaps more convincing than the men, who had a touch of the hobbledehoy about them; but that did little harm in a play wherein the ladies must show a superiority of wit and grace throughout, for all that their task is the harder, since there is less of substance in their badinage and only an exactly calculated bravura of speech and movement can carry it off. The greater delicacy of the ladies' playing was, however, counterbalanced by Michael Redgrave's performance as Berowne. He succeeded not only in conveying the wit, the wisdom and the vitality of the man, but in making him completely sympathetic to the audience. The great set speech of act IV, scene i—"And I forsooth in love", in which he takes the audience into his confidence, was a *tour de force*. The speech is by no means easy, for many of its terms and turns of expression are obsolete to-day; but by treating it simply and directly, by trusting himself to the words (and his confidence clearly grew with practice), he made its point clear and its effect captivating.

The comic performances in no way betrayed the standard set by those of the straight parts, although (as, alas, so often happens) their unnecessary business seemed to increase and to get more out of hand as the run of the play proceeded. George Benson gave us the perfect Costard; would that all players of Shakespearian clowns were as direct and bold and true to the text as this. On the other hand, the Holofernes and the Nathaniel were rather translations into modern equivalents—a Will Hay or a Groucho Marx with his stooge. This is legitimate; the Crazy Gang or the Itma comics are to-day the closest in line of descent to the figures of the Commedia dell'Arte from whom the fantastics of *Love's Labour's Lost* derive. The only characters that were totally off key were Armado and Moth, presented as a seedy Don Quixote and a ragged urchin. Now it is of the essence of both figures that they are of the Court (Dull and Costard are quite enough to represent the bumpkins). Armado is as much an exquisite as Osric. It is part of the joke that his finery is only on the surface (he cannot afford a shirt) but his every effort goes into maintaining the *appearance* of finery, and finery it is. Moth is the cheeky page boy, a 'cit' if ever there was one, and a diminutive echo of his master's finicking fashion. The humour of their interchanges, already precarious after the lapse of three and a half centuries, fades utterly if they are presented not as the lightning duels of court rapiers but as the rustic's solemn game of quarterstaff.

This brings us to the consideration of the topical jokes and private humours that make up so large a part of the dialogue, particularly between the farcical characters, and present the second and more troublesome problem to any would-be translator for the modern stage. There would seem to be four ways of dealing with this largely dead wood: (1) to cut the passage altogether; (2) to accompany it with some entirely extraneous piece of business, in the hope that this will distract attention from the words, which are 'thrown away' as best may be; (3) to have the words spoken against music which will render them inaudible; (4) to try the passage straight and hope that *someone* will see, or pretend to see, the joke—at least the purists will be satisfied. The purists of course will object strongly to the first solution, but I do not see how with some passages it can be avoided if the performance of the play is to be living entertainment and not merely a (possibly edifying) ritual. Solutions two and three are clearly abominable, and though one would like always to see the direct method given a trial there are some things it cannot save. The trouble is that producers will differ in their judgement of what can be saved and what must be cut, and most of them are likely to err on the side of pessimism.

The Old Vic production used all four methods. Of the seven cruces that have notoriously baffled or divided commentators only two, the 'envoy' of the fox, the ape and the humble-bee, and the play of Holofernes and Moth on 'piercing a hogshead', were cut (and rightly cut) *in toto*. The 'tender juvenal', the 'school of night', and the 'charge-house on the mountain' were all given their chance, perhaps in the belief that their ill-fame was too great for them to be ignored. Armado's odd salutation—'Chirrah'—was also left in, together with the reference to an eel that so strangely annoys him on his first appearance. This proved a dangerous course, however, at least in the case of the eel, for with the disappearance of the real occasion of the joke it was necessary to drop Armado's inexplicable irritation at it ("Thou heat'st my blood") and invent a new cue for it. Moth therefore made his entrance carrying a real eel, which he might be supposed recently to have fished out of the encircling lake; and I suspect this detail conditioned the producer's whole view of Moth's (and, with him, Armado's) appearance and status, which I have already tried to show were misconceived.

Some other jokes, of which the point is known but cannot be explained without a considerable gloss, were also wisely cut: Moth's play with the four complexions, his skirmish with Holofernes over sheep and vowels, and most of the 'greasy' talk between Boyet and Maria at the end of the hunting scene. There was little excuse, however, for devoting to the same extinction such simple puns as those on style, stile and climbing in the merriness, or the frequent and pertinent comments on the fantastics' inability to count; and it was surely strange, if these were to go, that such obvious interpolations as the duplicated versions of the lovers' first dialogues, and Costard's comments on a vanished entry for Armado and Moth in the hunting scene, should have been spared to puzzle us.

Of the second method of dealing with an obscure passage, the introduction of distracting business, there were three prominent examples, two of them particularly unhappy. It was perhaps allowable that Dull, in the midst of Nathaniel's wordy tirade on his insensitivity, should be discovered to be carrying, apparently without being aware of it or discommoded by it, an arrow from the hunt still firmly embedded in his posterior. This is at least a fair gloss on Nathaniel's "only sensible in the duller parts"; but the disproportionate laughter it aroused in the audience shattered the continuity of the scene and the delicate balance between its actors. The other two instances of this technique were unhappy because the jokes so painstakingly masked remain perfectly valid ones to-day and if allowed to make their own effect would have raised greater and more relevant amusement than their substitutes. When Jaquenetta brings Berowne's letter to Nathaniel to interpret, Holofernes is consumed with curiosity to see it but feels it would be beneath his dignity to look over the Curate's shoulder. He therefore pretends to be very much absorbed in his own thoughts, on a plane far above mere mundane affairs. He murmurs (incorrectly) a verse from Mantuan, hums the notes of the scale (again wrongly) all the time striving, under cover of this pretended abstraction, to get a glimpse of the letter. In the Old Vic production all this was thrown away to the accompaniment of a stupid piece of byplay in which Nathaniel tried surreptitiously to put his arm round the trusting Jaquenetta and found himself embracing Costard instead. This is entirely out of character for the Curate, while the Pedant's itch to meddle, sacrificed for it, is a typical and essential trait. Again, when the comics return from the dinner to which Holofernes has invited Nathaniel to witness his eloquence, the Curate is more than ever impressed by his host's superior learning. When Holofernes utters a particularly choice word Nathaniel, according to a direction in the original First Quarto text, draws out his notebook and with admiring comments records the *trouvaille*. In place of this characteristic and revealing action, Hunt made his players enter as if tipsy, and for the unction and the notebook of the toady substituted slurred syllables and some sorry business with a bottle. This is presumption.

To resort to the third way out, on the other hand, is the rankest cowardice, and it speaks well for the Old Vic production that this all too popular device was only used once, for the admittedly involved and paradoxical lines in which Boyet describes to the ladies how, Navarre having fallen in love at first sight, all his faculties are concentrated in his longing gaze. This speech was half chanted to a musical accompaniment to which Boyet's audience swayed in time. The effect was odious, but it was certainly impossible that many words should be caught, much less interpreted. It was perhaps surprising that the producer should have funked this passage when such teasers as "Light seeking light doth light of light beguile", and many of the "sets of wit", were left to take care of themselves, and did so very nicely.

Measure for Measure has no comparable problems. The niceties (if they may be so called) of a few passages of bawdry are unintelligible without notes, but their general drift is plain and in any case does not affect the action. There are some startling leaps of imagery and syntax, but nothing to nonplus an audience acquainted with *Hamlet* and *Lear*. A dozen textual confusions require straightening out. Peter Brook did not scruple to make cuts in all these, and emendations in the last, but he made them fairly and firmly. The worst sufferers were deservedly the banter of Lucio and his two gentlemen, and the long-winded prose in which the Duke expounds his plot to Isabella—at worst reviser's stuff, at best an experiment, superseded by Shakespeare's later work, in contriving a measured prose to link scenes of highly-wrought verse. There was less excuse for the drastic compression of the last scene (no apology by the Duke for the circuitousness of his proceedings, no Barnardine); the aim here was clearly to remove anything that might dull either the climax and point of the play, or the Duke's nobility. In this it was no longer the minor difficulties of his text that the producer was tackling but, with equal hardihood, his main problem—what *is* to be the total effect of the play?

The simplicity of the text of *Measure for Measure*, as compared with that of *Love's Labour's Lost*, is a function of its more serious mood. It is a play of ideas rather than of impressions and is concerned more with lines of conduct followed out to their logical conclusions than with the confusions and compromises of real life. There is still controversy as to how far these ideas form a coherent argument, and *Shakespeare Survey* has already given space to notable pleadings on either side. The one maintains that *Measure for Measure* is Shakespeare's considered opinion on the apparent conflict in Renaissance theory between the Christian duty of the Ruler to secure Justice, and that of the individual to be merciful. The other finds in the purpose and character of Isabella and the Duke as many dislocations as in the time-scheme, and holds that Shakespeare, here more even than usual, was concerned only to contrive a series of fine dramatic moments, heightening the effect of each as best might be, without regard to the philosophic or

K

psychological coherence of the whole. A modern producer is apparently faced with the alternative of abandoning any totality of effect for the sake of the incidental beauties, or of clouding these by the imposition of a 'programme' that will be bewildering to his audience.

Peter Brook's solution of the conundrum was symbolized in the setting that he himself devised for the play. This was a double range of lofty arches, receding from the centre of the stage on either side to the wings upstage. These arches might remain open to the sky in those scenes where some air and freshness is required—the convent at night (Plate XIII A) where Isabella hears from Lucio of her brother's plight, Mariana's moated grange, and the street scene in which all odds are finally made even; or, in a moment, their spaces could be blanked out, with grey flats for the shabby decorum of the courtroom, with grilles for the prison cells (Plate XIII B). Downstage, at either side, stood a heavy postern gate, also permanently set, serving as focus for the subsidiary scenes to which the full stage would have given undue emphasis, or those, such as the visiting of the imprisoned Claudio, which gain by a cramped setting. The single permanent set gave coherence to the whole; its continuous shadowy presence held together the brilliant series of closet-scenes played on a smaller section of the stage, that glorious succession of duets, Lucio-Isabella, Isabella-Angelo, Claudio-Duke, Isabella-Claudio, in which Shakespeare conceived the action. These were given all the more definition, and urgency, by the apparently confined space in which they were played, although their scope was restricted more by lighting than by any material barrier, and at any moment the whole span of the stage might spring to life and remind us of our bearings in the play. The occasions for such a broadening of effect are not many, but the producer made the most of them. To the progress of Claudio and Juliet to prison, with all corrupt Vienna surging and clamouring about them (Plate XIV A), and to the final marshalling of all the characters for judgement (Plate XIV B), he added a third full-stage scene, in which the prisoners, processing through the central hall of the prison, brought its holes and corners for a moment into relation with each other. Shakespeare's text gives only the slimmest pretext for this, in Pompey's enumeration of the old customers whom he has met again in his new employment; but the expansion—in both senses—came happily as a central point of relief in a chain of scenes each requiring a confined attention.

The great duets largely play themselves. It is they that make the play memorable, and such tense and moving writing is found elsewhere in Shakespeare only in the great tragedies. There is of course the notorious danger that to a modern audience Isabella may appear unbearably self-centred and priggish. Isabella knows, and a Jacobean audience took for granted, that there can be no compromise with evil, that, though the only road to right may appear to lie through wrong, the taking of it can do no one any good. Claudio acknowledges it, when not blinded by his panic, for he finally begs his sister's pardon for suggesting otherwise; and we know it, too. But we are shy of being dogmatic about it in the manner of the Jacobeans; though we may admit Isabella's reasons we find it hard to swallow her matter-of-fact schematization of them—"More than our brother is our chastity".

The producer and Barbara Jefford together saved our faces. Miss Jefford's was a young Isabella, a novice indeed, with no mature *savoir-faire* with which to meet her predicament, but only the burning conviction that two blacks cannot make a white. When she came to the perilous words she turned, from speaking full to the audience, to hide her face passionately against the wall behind her, as if herself ashamed that her intellect could find no more adequate expression of her heart's certainty. In the same way her tirade against her brother, when he begs her to save his life at any cost, was made to appear as much anger with her own failure as a witness to truth, her own inability to communicate it to others. It was indeed skilful, and a good illustration of one kind of 'translation', to substitute the pathos of the inarticulate for an affronting insensitivity, and convert what is often an offence to modern playgoers into the very engine to enforce their sympathy. Altogether it was a moving performance, that found its perfect foil in the suppressed and twisted nobility of John Gielgud's Angelo. With such interpreters the producer could risk the boldest effects. The climax of the play was breath-taking. Mariana has passionately implored Isabella to kneel to the Duke for Angelo's pardon; the Duke has warned her that to do so would be "against all sense"—"He dies for Claudio". The pause that followed must have been among the longest in theatre history. Then hesitantly, still silent, Isabella moved across the stage and knelt before the Duke. Her words came quiet and level, and as their full import of mercy reached Angelo, a sob broke from him. It was perfectly calculated and perfectly timed; and the whole perilous manœuvre had been triumphantly brought off.

Yet it is not Isabella, still less Angelo, that is the crux of the producer's problem, but the Duke. If the play is to mean anything, if it is to be more than a series of disjointed magnificences, we must accept the Duke's machinations as all to good purpose, and himself as entirely wise and just. Peter Brook presented Vincentio rather as Friar turned Duke than as Duke turned Friar, and maintained throughout the impressiveness of his appearance at the cost of rendering his disguise completely unconvincing. He had found in Harry Andrews a Duke whose commanding presence could dominate the play, as the half-seen arches the stage, and whose charm of manner could convince us of his integrity and wisdom. If his speaking could have been more measured, more confident, more natural ease and less careful manipulation, we might have had the Vincentio of a generation.

It remains (since *Measure for Measure* is still a comedy) to say something about the comics. In refreshing defiance of tradition, Pompey, Elbow, and Abhorson were left to make their proper effect as natural English 'characters', instead of being reduced, as in most productions of the play, to circus clowns and fantastics. Peter Brook has not always escaped censure for that over-emphasis on 'business' which I have already denounced as the fatal Siren of modern producers. Here, where so much depended on control, the supporting elements in the play were not allowed to get much out of hand. The Viennese mob was extremely loud and energetic, but then the outrageousness of its manners (a motif echoed in the Brueghelesque grotesquery of Brook's costumes) is an essential contrast to the nobility of the play's main themes. Pompey was assiduous in distributing advertisements of Mistress Overdone's establishment to all with whom he came in contact, a 'turn' for which the cue can only be wrung from the text with difficulty; but it is in character, and was carefully confined to those moments when no "necessary question of the play was then to be considered". It was permissible, too, having provided a pit from which an admirable Barnardine emerged with his true effect, to use it for a tumultuous 'exeunt omnes' at the end of the scene. The only real excrescence was some buffoonery with Pompey's fetters that for a moment put the Duke's dignity in jeopardy. This must be forgiven a producer of such restraint elsewhere that he could keep the crowd in the background of his prison scenes silent and motionless through almost an entire act; could dispense with music, save a tolling bell and the herald's trumpet; and at the close could allow his couples merely to walk, "hand in hand, with wandering steps and slow", in silence from the stage—and to what great effects!

These two productions have been set out as complementary, yet in essentials they were working to the same ends: the presentation of a coherent, intelligible, and acceptable whole that should be true to Shakespeare's text; and the marshalling of exuberant and occasionally obstreperous episodes to serve that purpose alone. As regards the subsidiary problem, Hugh Hunt must claim the greater extravagance of his material as excuse for his greater lapses; of the main, whereas his solution was workmanlike, Peter Brook's was masterly, for here his task was infinitely the harder. The difficulties that both producers have so clearly had to face are evidence that a Shakespearian comedy requires at least as much painstaking study and sensitive perception devoted to its staging as does a tragedy; their successes, that the comedies are worth the attention, and that there is now again good hope that they may sometimes get it.

THE YEAR'S CONTRIBUTIONS TO SHAKESPEARIAN STUDY

1. CRITICAL STUDIES

reviewed by J. I. M. STEWART

Roy Walker has followed up his full-length study of *Hamlet*, noticed in the last number of *Shakespeare Survey*, with a similar study of *Macbeth*.[1] His method is essentially imaginative, the full significance of the tragic pattern revealing itself through a pondering of the processes of free association which one or another poetic image sets in motion. The hazards are obvious, and the book comes to a good many conclusions with which few will agree: for example, that the problematical Third Murderer is a "dramatic personification of Macbeth's guilt", and that Hecate (put into the play by Shakespeare himself, but without a speaking part) is correspondingly the guilty spirit of Lady Macbeth. But Walker tells us that although he fully expects to be assailed on particular judgements, he nevertheless believes that his "method of interpretation is genuinely in communication with Shakespeare's creative activity"; and that it is, moreover, "somewhat akin to an X-ray examination, in which the normal surfaces are rendered transparent and almost invisible so that the inner structure may be observed and knowledge of the organism and its functioning increased". This bold claim is justified. Walker combines an ability to view the play as a whole, ranging swiftly and sensitively over its whole surface and through its various depths, with an answering ability never to lose contact with its serial nature, its weight and impact as action. The pattern he discovers is in consequence always dramatic as well as philosophical. His commentary on the first act of the play in itself sufficiently evidences a quite unusual range of critical powers. For example, he understands the theatre.

Hamlet begins with the Ghost, *Macbeth* with the Witches, and the poetic purpose, I have noted, is to strike at once the keynote of the tragedy in each case. But there is also a careful dramatic construction evident in this ordering of the incidents. When Hamlet confronts the Ghost, we observe him and not the Ghost, whom we have seen twice already. When Macbeth confronts the Witches we observe him, not the Witches, whom we have seen twice before....Likewise, we have heard Ross and Angus tell the King about Cawdor's treachery and the King's directions as to how they are to greet Macbeth. When they come to repeat these words, we watch Macbeth, not Ross and Angus, since our interest is in seeing the effect of the news upon him....I therefore suggest that the very fact that we know what Ross and Angus are going to say in scene iii—because we have heard it in scene ii—is evidence for, not against, the authenticity of scene ii.

This last observation is only one stroke in a brilliant defence of the Folio text of the first act—an act throughout which Walker finds woven an unbroken sequence of significant images and subdued double meanings. Every student of the play is aware of the tremendously effective places in which its irony, as it were, breaks the surface ("He was a gentleman on whom I built An absolute trust"), but Walker shows how strong a current of this irony flows steadily beneath

[1] *The Time is Free* (Dakers, 1949).

K*

the dark waters of the tragedy. Of his larger findings it is not possible to write here. He has produced an interpretation set beside which much intelligent and devoted study must show as decidedly inert, and his further essays in Shakespeare criticism will be awaited with the keenest expectation.

Three other full-length studies of single plays are available for review. In the first of these, Ernest Jones, who is President of the International Psycho-Analytical Association, has brought to what is presumably its final form the Freudian interpretation of *Hamlet*.[1] This has a long history, which began in a footnote in Freud's *Traumdeutung* as published in 1900, and was given considerable substance by Jones himself as early as 1910. We now have little sense of discovery in reading that the Hamlet-legend is a highly elaborated and disguised account of a boy's love for his mother and consequent jealousy of and hatred towards his father. But Jones's comprehensive handling of the subject, which includes some subsidiary discussion of the Oedipus complex as it is operative in other plays of Shakespeare's, will continue to be of great interest to those curious in the psychogenesis of imaginative creations. On the other hand, his inquiry into the personal circumstances that may have prompted Shakespeare's special concern with the theme involves biographical speculation that grows progressively less convincing with the years. As if aware that the comment of depth psychology on the tragedy is now a little in need of freshening up, Jones has discussed in a separate paper the significance, from a psycho-analytic standpoint, of murder by means of poison poured in the ear.[2] This is certainly startling enough. The medical view of *Hamlet* has progressed far from that age of innocence in which an American doctor could see the Prince's hesitancy as indicative of his suffering from fatty degeneration of the heart. It remains to be remarked here that Jones's command of *Hamlet* criticism as a whole stands as a shining example to many professional students.[3]

Richard Flatter, whose *Shakespeare's Producing Hand* was reviewed last year, has published substantial studies of *Hamlet*[4] and *Othello*[5]. Both books suggest markedly original interpretations of the plays they discuss. Whereas it has been the general tendency of *Hamlet* criticism in recent years to see the hero as overwhelmingly preoccupied with the fact of his mother's adultery, Flatter views him as primarily concerned with the problem of her possible complicity in her first husband's murder. There is a point, Flatter thinks, at which Hamlet actually meditates matricide ("O heart, lose not thy nature"); and the mere knowledge of Gertrude's adultery, "partly absolved by time and subsequent marriage", could not in itself drive him to that. He goes to his mother's closet to wring a confession from her; and this he would succeed in doing (for she is in truth guilty) did not the Ghost intervene. The Ghost's "Do not forget: this visitation Is but to whet thy almost blunted purpose" is, in fact, a mere pretext for creating a hasty diversion in the interest of obscuring the truth and preserving the Queen's reputation. But if

---

[1] *Hamlet and Oedipus* (Gollancz, 1949).

[2] 'The Death of Hamlet's Father', *International Journal of Psycho-Analysis*, XXIX (1948), 174–6.

[3] *Shakespeare Association Bulletin*, XXIV (January 1949), prints three substantial papers on *Hamlet*: 'Hamlet's "All but Blunted Purpose"' by George Detmold (pp. 23–36); 'Current Fashions in *Hamlet* Criticism' by R. M. Smith (pp. 13–21); and 'Horatio's Hamlet' by J. D. Spaeth (pp. 37–47). In the same volume (October 1949) G. Blakemore Evans has a note on 'Belleforest and the Gonzago Story' (pp. 280–2). *The Listener* has two essays dealing with the play: John Bamborough's 'The Missing Speech in *Hamlet*' (14 July 1949, pp. 74–5) and T. S. Gregory's 'I hold You Up a Glass' (7 July 1949, pp. 19–21).

[4] *Hamlet's Father* (Heinemann, 1949).   [5] *The Moor of Venice* (Heinemann, 1950).

Gertrude must not be aspersed Hamlet's task of executing revenge upon Claudius is impossible. And we have here the true explanation of Hamlet's entering with such seeming blindness upon the fencing match. He realizes that his mother has his father's forgiveness; it becomes his only wish to spare her pain—even the pain of knowing that he has detected her guilt; he therefore goes open-eyed to his death, having first conveyed to her (under cover of appearing to address Laertes) the declaration that his suspicions and accusations have been the issue of lunacy. Flatter always argues closely and cogently from the text, but it is perhaps in other parts of his book, where he is less concerned with achieving drastic reinterpretation, that his work will appear most valuable to many readers. It would be interesting to see whether his conception of the play's final scene could be made intelligible and convincing on the stage. And the same curiosity is prompted by his views on the right manner of playing the close of *Othello*. How did Shakespeare design that the hero here should respond to the eventual revelations of Iago's devilry? "Those disclosures", writes Flatter, "do not make the Moor despair; on the contrary, they cannot but restore his self-esteem. And when he exclaims 'O fool, fool, fool!' he does so…with an almost blissful feeling of relief." Othello's final emotion "is that of a husband who, overwhelmed with joy, welcomes back his wife whom he had feared lost". He should die "laughing with relief and jubilation". And if we ask why, if this be so, Othello should appear to forget all about Desdemona in the interest of painting a romantic picture of himself at Aleppo, Flatter has his answer ready: this celebrated speech is a rigmarole invented on the spur of the moment to deflect the attention of his auditory and enable him to wrench a dagger from one of those around him. Here again the critic may be judged more impressive in earlier parts of his study— particularly in his discussion of the character and motives of Iago, and in his exposition of the dramatic significance of the first act of the play.[1]

King Lear has a small volume to itself by John M. Lothian.[2] In a series of well-balanced and lucid essays the writer deals with Shakespeare's handling of his sources, the spiritual progress of Lear, the role of the Fool, and the character of Edgar. A final essay is concerned to refute Bradley's suggestion that the King is not throughout the leading figure in the tragedy. The course of Lear's thought and the development of his attitude to life are central to the play's movement and are brought repeatedly to our notice; in all but the narrowest sense, then, Lear is steadily at the centre of the action. This is sound criticism, if slightly old-fashioned in tone. A more modern idiom and technique is brought to the illumination of the play, as of the major tragedies in general, in a remarkable essay by Robert B. Heilman, 'The Lear World'.[3] A major

[1] *Othello* has further been the subject of a number of articles in journals. In 'Three Notes on Donne's Poetry with a Side Glance at *Othello*', *Modern Language Notes*, LXV (February 1950), 102–6, D. C. Allen makes the curious observation that in Othello's "If heaven would make me such another world, Of one entire and perfect chrysolite" (v, ii, 144–5) the reference may be to that vitrification of the earth which current speculation supposed would be the consequence of the Great Combustion. In an earlier number of the same journal, LXIV (June 1949), 415–17, V. H. Anderson touches upon one of the play's *cruces* in a note, 'Othello and Peregrina, Richer than All his Tribe'. To *English Studies*, XXX (October 1949), 175–84, G. Bonnard contributes a valuable critical article with the challenging title, 'Are Othello and Desdemona Innocent or Guilty?'. And a further significant essay in interpretative criticism is that by John Wilcox, 'Othello's Crucial Moment', *Shakespeare Association Bulletin*, XXIV (July 1949), 181–92.

[2] *King Lear: A Tragic Reading of Life* (Toronto: Clarke, Irwin and Company, 1949).

[3] *English Institute Essays, 1948* (New York: Columbia University Press, 1949).

theme of the tragedies, Heilman suggests, is that of the disastrous consequences attending the release of positivist or mythoclastic attitudes to life. Shakespeare, in fact, like Sophocles in the *Oedipus Rex*, is concerned with the apparent decay of the mythic habit of mind; his tragedies are about the myth in crisis. Gloster in his blindness comes to a new vision; Lear in his madness to a new understanding; Lear's madness has a secondary level holding overtones of extraordinary clarity. Lear, Edgar and the Fool are in essence the three wise men of the play, the burden of which is that insight must be sought by a denial of the ordinary sense and logic of the world and must be found in the intuitions, even those of madness. And this theme of reason-in-madness is balanced by that of madness-in-reason. Goneril, Regan and Edmund are eminently rational, but their reason is madness since it is destructive of the values upon which all order depends, and since their seemingly clear-sighted rationalism must in fact lead them to destruction. In addition to being rationalists these characters are individualists; in them we see a revolt against the traditional, communal order of life. They suggest the collapse of the myth of governance, and also of the myth of love, which in Goneril and Regan is replaced by lust. Lust is a symbol of anarchy as opposed to harmony, and is the counterpart therefore of their unscrupulous calculations which signify the decay of governance. They have passed outside the myths; and the myths alone *order* experience. Lear himself, moreover, exemplifies man's liability to destroy mythic values unintentionally. He tries to measure his daughters' love; he tries to quantify it; he tries to secure a rational computation of what is not susceptible to this kind of estimate. And he thereby sets loose in the world, all unwittingly, a spirit of hard calculation which is to be employed remorselessly against him.[1]

The volume to which Heilman contributes contains three further essays of interest here, collected under the general heading *Myth in the Later Plays of Shakespeare*. In 'The Argument of Comedy' Northrop Frye, after discussing how the New Comedy "unfolds from what may be described as a comic Oedipus situation", examines the genetic relationship between comedy and tragedy, finds that "the ritual pattern behind the catharsis of comedy is the resurrection that follows the death, the epiphany or manifestation of the risen hero", and proceeds to a brief analysis of Shakespeare's comic world in terms of these formulations. Leslie A. Fiedler in 'The Defense of the Illusion and the Creation of Myth' declares that "in any age a work of art is on one level about...the threat to the illusion it attempts to create". Shakespeare, we are told, "seems to have felt the illusion of his art imperiled on four main fronts, and to have evolved, in response to those four threats, four essential myths that come to full flower in the last plays: the myth of the *Cosmic Drama*, the myth of the *Cosmic Dream*, the myth of the *Beardless Beloved*, and the myth of *Qualitative Immortality*". These the writer proposes to make the subject of a fuller study, and meanwhile offers some curious observations—for example, that if Claudius had not called for lights, into the Tragedy of Gonzago there would presently have had to come a Hamlet-

---

[1] Several articles have appeared on the sources of *King Lear*. William A. Armstrong (*Times Literary Supplement*, 14 October 1949) finds a passage in *The Arcadia* concerned with distinctions between beneficent, amoral and malevolent aspects of Nature; and these, he suggests, may have influenced Shakespeare's conception in the play. Fitzroy Pyle (11 November) judges the argument unconvincing. Kenneth Muir and John F. Danby, writing in *Notes and Queries*, 4 February 1950, suggest a further general indebtedness to *The Arcadia*, book II, chapter XII, where there occurs a debate on the rights and wrongs of suicide, the justice of the gods, and the slaughter of the innocent. In *Studies in Philology*, XLVII (January 1950), 42–50, Robert Adger Law discusses 'Holinshed's Leir Story and Shakespeare's'.

character to contrive another play to catch the conscience of the murderer, and in that play *another* Hamlet, and so on. In the final essay here, 'Three Shakespearean Myths: Mutability, Plenitude, and Reputation', by Edward Hubler, the writer remarks: "Perhaps one day we shall be able to say that we are not so sophisticated as we once were. On that day we shall be nearer Shakespeare." With this voice in the wilderness anyone committed to the examination of much contemporary Shakespeare criticism is likely to feel a good deal of sympathy.

Of books dealing with groups of Shakespeare's plays, or with aspects of his art, the most comprehensive is by T. M. Parrott.[1] So all-embracing, indeed, is this volume that, although its concern is with Shakespearian comedy, it contrives to discuss every one of the thirty-six plays in turn and devotes more than 2000 words to *Titus Andronicus*. Where comedy is present, the author expounds it, and if it is absent he inquires the reason. Thus he supposes that when writing *Richard II* Shakespeare may have recalled being obliged to act in *Woodstock*, a play the comic element in which would not improbably make him determined that his own handling of Richard's reign should be wholly serious. Parrott's treatment of *Much Ado About Nothing* is characteristic of the thorough-going nature of his book: there is an account of the story as treated by Bandello, Ariosto and Spenser; a careful examination of the changes made by Shakespeare in the interest of romantic comedy; a full appreciation of Beatrice and Benedick; a similar appreciation of Dogberry; and a discussion, with illustrative passages, of the various excellence of the play's prose. It is a pleasure to reflect that the author of this vigorous and copious book was a university professor a full decade before many of us, now ageing rapidly, were born.

The comedies have been studied also in a stimulating volume by E. C. Pettet.[2] Here, as with Parrott, the approach is conservative, as a single sentence will reveal. "Possibly", Pettet writes, "there is a certain amount of symbolism in Shakespeare, in the tragedies as well as the romances; but this must, surely, be slight and incidental, since Shakespeare was first and foremost a dramatist (and a dramatist of the theatre, not of the study)." When perplexed by elements in the plays, we should look for "the obvious and common-sense explanation". And the history of Shakespeare's dealings with romantic material is straightforward. He judged it at the beginning of his career the best matter to exploit in attempting to elevate the drama—to substitute for the rough 'laughter' which Sidney condemned that 'delight' proper to a refined comedy. But almost from the first he developed within the framework of his romantic comedies a criticism of the romantic assumptions, and in the 'dark' comedies his deepening sense of vehement real life took him away from them altogether. Later, when the fiery compulsion of his tragic mood was spent, he returned—partly perhaps under the influence of Beaumont and Fletcher—to his first love, so that his final plays are essentially romantic comedies once more, although the impress of his life's experience naturally differentiates them from his early work in various significant particulars. Pettet is at his best in defining the romance tradition; in expounding in some detail its two outstanding English epitomes in Spenser's poetry and in *The Arcadia*; in tracing its assimilation into comedy by Lyly and Greene; and in exposing what may be termed the ambivalence of Shakespeare's attitude to it. His estimate of the final plays will appear to some to be more open to question. These, he holds, are characteristically romantic in that the mass of incident is quite unhampered by any considerations of verisimilitude; and the emphasis upon presenting a number

[1] *Shakespearean Comedy* (New York: Oxford University Press, 1949).
[2] *Shakespeare and the Romance Tradition* (Staples, 1949).

of sensational situations makes the characterization thinner, the motivation more deficient, and the emotion more strained and false in the romances than in the comedies. Moreover, while the comedies are bound together by one dominant tone—the sentiments, boldly reflected or humorously criticized, of romantic love—the final plays are by a man no longer seriously interested in this material, with the result that they lack emotional cohesion, and tend to resemble Beaumont and Fletcher's plays as described by Coleridge—'mere aggregations without unity'. The emotion, again, is often spurious because inadequately or artificially occasioned, inappropriate to what is known of a character, and 'untrue to real life'. Such as it is, it is frequently dissipated through verbal decorativeness, and the prominence of this in *Cymbeline* in particular may be evidence of that play's special debt to the younger dramatists. Pettet, then, is unable to accept E. M. W. Tillyard's view of Shakespeare's last plays as integral with the tragedies, and as representing, indeed, 'the final regenerative phase' of the tragic experience. The last plays are in essence comedies once more. The substantial identity of the two kinds is susceptible of experimental verification. Take *Much Ado*, excise a large part of the comic matter, expand the serious parts, and the result—provided you have Shakespeare's abilities—will be a play with the substance and much of the spirit of the romances.[1]

E. M. W. Tillyard has published a short series of lectures delivered before the University of Toronto on *Hamlet, Troilus and Cressida, All's Well That Ends Well*, and *Measure for Measure*.[2] F. S. Boas long ago classed *Hamlet* with the 'problem plays' rather than with the tragedies; but Tillyard's reasons for adopting this grouping are his own. "The sheer wealth and vigour and brilliance of all the things that happen" he considers to be what constitutes the dominant quality of *Hamlet*. And this rich variousness, the determination to present "the utmost variety of human experience in the largest possible cosmic setting," creates the peculiar sense of real life which for Tillyard characterizes the problem comedies proper; but which, he holds, runs counter to the 'very definite and formal' mode demanded by high tragic art. Moreover *Hamlet*, it is argued, does not quite get down to the roots of tragedy; the hero is as a tragic protagonist abundantly promising, but he does not in fact achieve the spiritual regeneration necessary to the attaining of full tragic stature. The case here is argued with all the skill and distinction that the critic so securely commands. Some, however, may hold that he considers too curiously. Formally his Class List may be impeccable. But outside the Examination Hall the Prince of Denmark will continue to consort with the Thane of Cawdor, the Moor of Venice and the King of Wessex rather than with Claudio, Bertram and Troilus. Tillyard remarks that his story, like theirs, is about a young man getting a shock; but we should get a greater shock ourselves if Shakespeare's supreme dramatic creation turned up in Vienna, Rousillon, or Asia Minor. It is in the last of these localities that Tillyard lingers longest—and to very good purpose, his skirmishing on the Trojan plain being a fine example of subtle and lucid manipulation of material perfectly at the writer's command. With *All's Well* and *Measure for Measure* he deals more succinctly, finding in the latter that the high and moving realism in the earlier part of the play is achieved at too great cost to its dramatic potentialities as a whole, so that Shakespeare is eventually constrained

---

[1] Mention should be made here of Warren Staebler's 'Shakespeare's Play of Atonement' (a substantial study of *As You Like It*), *Shakespeare Association Bulletin*, XXIV (April 1949), 136–75; and of W. Schrickx's 'Shakespeare and the School of Night', *Neophilologus*, XXXIV (January 1950), 35–44.

[2] *Shakespeare's Problem Plays* (Chatto and Windus, 1949).

to relax the poetical tension of the piece and fall back upon an abstract form of drama wholly out of key with the opening.[1]

There have been two books surveying the whole body of Shakespeare's dramatic output. Donald Stauffer's *Shakespeare's World of Images: The Development of his Moral Ideas*,[2] is more accurately described by its sub-title than by its title. All great works of art, the writer asserts, reflect the convictions of their creators; and the question "How did Shakespeare think human life should be led?" is one that can be answered with confidence and in some detail. Moreover, it is worth answering. The fashionable assertion that Shakespeare was not a profound thinker, or indeed was not a thinker at all, but rather one who merely assimilated or felicitously re-expressed well-worn truths, ignores the true relationship of thought and expression. "If, before a great writer phrases some idea, it was never so well expressed, then also it was never so well thought, no matter how often it was thought." These premises being granted, we shall find that there is a number of roads by which Shakespeare's moral ideas may be methodically and reasonably approached: "his choice of subject, his shaping of sources, the judgements implicit or stated in the outcome of his plots, his ventriloquism when characters speak out of key, his un-dramatic set speeches, his repetitive ideas, his recurrent images, and his choric or touchstone figures". When we have studied him in the light of all this we shall agree that there could be no greater error than to mistake his breadth of understanding and receptivity of mind for lack of moral conviction. His judgements are not suspended but complex. And "for all those who cannot go beyond the moral interpretation of life to the religious interpretation, it might easily be held that Shakespeare is the most precious of thinkers". His dominating themes are "integrity, loyalty, patience, love, forgiveness, humility", and his work is a final answer to all those who would assert the radical dissociation of art from the good life. All these round assertions come, however, from a postscript to the book, the body of which by no means represents a relentless hunt for edification. The development of that moral concern which is from the first implicit in the plays is allowed to expose itself in the course of a general critical argument tracing Shakespeare's progress from *Titus Andronicus*, in which only an intermittently-appearing delight in nature is genuinely his own, to the final romances. Of these last the thought "is eminently Christian—the wandering or sinful mortals, contrition, repentance, resignation, patience, prayer, forgiveness—but the thought is not expressed in Christian terms or even with a Christian certainty". Stauffer writes with vigour and appreciation throughout his long study; he nowhere neglects the virtues of one part of Shakespeare's work because they are not present in other and greater parts; his discernment has equal play in *Richard III* and in *The Tempest*. This is a book that can be read with constant interest by anyone reasonably familiar with the plays, and it would be a stimulating companion through a systematic perusal of them.

A companion of a more simply factual sort has been designed and largely written by F. E. Halliday.[3] It is claimed that here, for the first time between two covers, is all that the ordinary

[1] J. C. Maxwell's 'Creon and Angelo: A Parallel Study', *Greece and Rome*, XVIII (January 1949), 32–6, makes an interesting comparison between *Measure for Measure* and the *Antigone*. Neither play, he points out, has a heroine of much promise dramatically. Each is faced with a single task and neither falters in it; and criticism that would seek to complicate these characters, whether by the detection of a *hamartia* or otherwise, is misdirected. Angelo and Creon are the characters giving scope for the portrayal of human complexity, and the dramatic problems involved in presenting them are shown to have been treated by both dramatists after much the same fashion.

[2] New York: Norton, 1949.   [3] *Shakespeare and his Critics* (Duckworth, 1949).

Shakespeare-lover wishes to know and to keep by him for reference. The volume is certainly extremely informative. The first part contains a well-documented account of Shakespeare's life; a general survey of the Elizabethan theatre, with its playwrights and players; a discussion of Shakespeare's verse; a long section on the development of his style as shown in copious extracts; a similar section on characterization; 'a history of the various texts'; and an exposition and refutation of the theory that the plays were written by Bacon. The second part reviews the history of Shakespeare criticism at large; supplies selected critical passages from Robert Greene to Caroline Spurgeon; and then addresses itself to giving essential information about each of the plays and poems in turn, with a further substantial selection of critical passages in every case. Halliday's encyclopaedia—for it is virtually that—will have no particular appeal to those with well-furnished libraries and the habit of moving about among books. It may be welcomed, nevertheless, as likely to diffuse knowledge and stimulate enquiry. Unfortunately the reader will have to go elsewhere if he wants to acquaint himself with any of the more recent trends in Shakespeare criticism—which, after all, he is more likely to want than, for example, an exposition of the distressing cryptogrammatic aberrations of Sir Edwin Durning-Lawrence.[1]

Halliday's compendious volume must contain some 300,000 words. But this makes it no more than the baby brother of another, and truly astonishing, compilation by Bernard M. Wagner.[2] This marshals, in an odd variety of typographical uniforms adopted in the interest of inexpensive production, a notable company of Shakespeare critics, and allows them, each and all, the most ample ground for manœuvre. In Swinburne alone as here represented one could read from dawn till dusk; and should one seek either Maurice Morgann's *Essay on the Dramatic Character of Sir John Falstaff*, or Hazlitt's *Characters of Shakespeare's Plays*, or the late Charles Williams's *A Myth of Shakespeare*—why, here is the text *in extenso*! As a physical object this must be as hideous a book as was ever produced, and its justification is to be found in a footnote to the preface. "If the college library has a hundred books on Shakespeare, but only *one* copy of Emerson or Morgann, and four hundred students who are to read one small book or pamphlet a week for twelve weeks"—the answer is to get together what is needed at a price of $5. The history of American engineering, we are told, is full of feats of brilliant improvization. Here is something similar, planned on the Campus. We shall not all of us travel in Wagner's grand pantechnicon, but we are dull fellows if we do not pause to admire it.

In journals interest has been distributed somewhat unevenly over Shakespeare's work. The English historical plays, for example, have been comparatively little studied, although one well-conceived paper by Raymond Chapman insists that new knowledge of the philosophical background of these dramas should not be allowed to obscure their basis in the medieval concern with *Fortuna* and *Occasio*.[3] The Roman plays, on the other hand, have received much attention.

[1] A thoughtfully arranged anthology may be noticed here: Arthur Stanley's *The Bedside Shakespeare* (Gollancz, 1948). Well aware of the dangers of his task, the editor gives generous selections from the plays and poems, with introductory notes, which may well send readers on to a fuller study of the plays.

[2] *The Appreciation of Shakespeare: A Collection of Criticism—Philosophic, Literary, and Esthetic—by Great Writers and Scholar-Critics of the Eighteenth, Nineteenth, and Twentieth Centuries* (Washington: Georgetown University Press, 1949).

[3] 'The Wheel of Fortune in Shakespeare's Historical Plays', *Review of English Studies*, n.s., 1 (January 1950), 1–7. The same writer considers 'Double Time in *Romeo and Juliet*' in *Modern Language Review*, XLIV (July 1949), 372–4. J. W. McCutchan examines 'Similarities between Falstaff and Gluttony in Medwall's *Nature*' in *Shakespeare Association Bulletin*, XXIV (July 1949), 214–19.

On *Antony and Cleopatra* there have been maturely considered critical articles by J. F. Danby, L. C. Knights, and W. A. Bacon; and on *Coriolanus* by P. A. Jorgensen, and Sidney Shanker.[1] Horst Oppel's *Der Späte Shakespeare*, a stimulating and pleasantly produced *opusculum* from Hamburg, is a heartening token of restored communications with German Shakespeare scholarship.[2] And to this period of Shakespeare's work attention is further directed in two thoughtful essays by Kenneth Muir and Derek Traversi on *Pericles* and *The Tempest* respectively.[3] Numerous articles less easy to classify can receive no more than mention here, despite the varied interest of much that they contain. An essay by Leo Kirschbaum entitled 'Shakespeare's Stage Blood and its Critical Significance' turns out to be occupied not with genealogical speculation but with red paint.[4] Sir Henry Thomas's 'Shakespeare in Spain' is both erudite and entertaining; we learn from it that among the *Obras Completas* of Shakespeare *Romeo and Juliet* and the *Sonnets* enjoy the greatest popularity in the Peninsula; we learn too that in a second-hand bookshop in Barcelona the writer's attention was once confidently invited to a row of brown-paper parcels as containing, *inter alia*, the original manuscript of *Hamlet*.[5] Here too must be mentioned Benjamin Boyce's 'The Stoic *Consolatio* and Shakespeare'; Lily B. Campbell's 'Concerning Bradley's *Shakespearean Tragedy*'; Hardin Craig's 'An Aspect of Shakespearian Study'; P. H. Houston's 'There's Nothing Either Good or Bad But Thinking Makes It So'; Jane Mayhall's 'Shakespeare and Spenser: A Commentary on Differences' and Warren Smith's 'Artful Brevity in Shakespeare's Monologs.'[6] Work touching incidentally upon Shakespeare includes E. C. Mason's 'Satire on Women and Sex in Elizabethan Tragedy' and Alexander H. Sackton's 'The Paradoxical Encomium in Elizabethan Drama'.[7] In this connexion too must be mentioned Mary Crapo Hyde's comprehensive study of the principles of Elizabethan dramaturgy, *Playwriting for Elizabethans 1600–1605*.[8]

So much for the words of Mercury. But the record need not end untouched by Apollo. In *By Avon River* 'H. D.' has published in a single volume a perceptive essay, *The Guest*, on Elizabethan lyric, and a three-part poem, *Good Frend*—the record, itself finely lyrical, of her imaginative response to Shakespeare.[9]

[1] J. F. Danby, 'The Shakespearian Dialectic: An Aspect of *Antony and Cleopatra*', *Scrutiny*, XVI (September 1949), 196–213; L. C. Knights, 'On the Tragedy of *Antony and Cleopatra*', *Scrutiny*, XVI (Winter, 1949), 318–23; W. A. Bacon, 'The Suicide of Antony in *Antony and Cleopatra*, Act IV, Scene xiv', *Shakespeare Association Bulletin*, XXIV (July 1949), 193–202; P. A. Jorgensen, 'Shakespeare's Coriolanus: Elizabethan Soldier', *PMLA*, LXIV (March 1949), 221–35; Sidney Shanker, 'Some Clues for *Coriolanus*', *Shakespeare Association Bulletin*, XXIV (July 1949), 203–8.

[2] Hamburg: Heinrich Ellermann, 1949. Oppel has also published *Das Shakespeare-Bild Goethes* (Mainz: Kirchheim, 1949), an excellent expository and critical essay which will particularly appeal to those whose interest in Goethe has been quickened by the recent bicentenary.

[3] 'The Problem of *Pericles*', *English Studies*, XXX (June 1949), 65–83; '*The Tempest*', *Scrutiny*, XVI (June 1949), 127–57.   [4] *PMLA*, LXIV (June 1949), 517–29.

[5] *Annual Shakespeare Lecture of the British Academy, 1949*, Oxford University Press, 1950.

[6] Boyce, *PMLA*, LXIV (September 1949), 771–80; Campbell, *Huntington Library Quarterly*, XIII (November 1949), 1–18; Craig, *Shakespeare Association Bulletin*, XXIV (October, 1949), 247–57; Houston, *ibid.* (January 1949), 48–54; Mayhall, *Modern Language Quarterly*, X (September 1949), 356–63; Smith, *Shakespeare Association Bulletin*, XXIV (October 1949), 275–9.

[7] Mason, *English Studies*, XXXI (February 1950), 1–10; Sackton, *University of Texas Studies in English*, XXVIII (1949), 83–104.

[8] Columbia University Press (London: Geoffrey Cumberlege), 1949.   [9] New York: Macmillan, 1949.

2. SHAKESPEARE'S LIFE, TIMES AND STAGE

reviewed by CLIFFORD LEECH

The first paper in Leslie Hotson's new book[1] has led to prolonged discussion and remarkable difference of opinion. His case is that Sonnets 107, 123 and 124 contain topical references which date them *c.* 1589: the 'mortall Moone' of 107 is the Armada; the 'pyramids' of 123 are the obelisks which Sixtus V re-erected in the years 1586-9; the 'childe of state' of 124 is the French King Henri III. Of the three identifications, Hotson is most convincing on the first, and brings forward a number of contemporary references to the Armada as a moon-shaped formation as it advanced into the Channel. The reviewer in *The Times Literary Supplement*,[2] accepting the argument as a whole, wrote that the essay "may prove to be the most significant contribution to Shakespearian studies of recent years": the dark lady can, we are told, now be seen as causing only "the transient passion of youth". Not all correspondents of the *Supplement* have agreed: on 17 February Hugh Ross Williamson suggested that Sonnet 107 refers to the Third Armada, of 1597; on 31 March the Countess C. Longworth Chambrun expressed her continuing devotion to the Southampton theory. More important is the evidence brought forward by John Sparrow on 3 March and by I. A. Shapiro on 21 April that references to the crescent-formation of the Armada are frequent for many years after 1588. Even if we accept Hotson's identifications without cavil, it hardly seems to follow necessarily that the sonnets were written as early as 1589: the Armada remained as strongly fixed in men's minds as in our own day, for example, the Battle of Britain has done; the obelisks of Sixtus V could seem novel longer than Hotson thinks; the rather uncertain identification in Sonnet 124 does not demand a date immediately after Henri III's death.

If Hotson's date for the sonnets were accepted, we might also accept T. W. Baldwin's placing of *Love's Labour's Lost* in 1588.[3] But even if we find no difficulty in that, so early a date for Sonnet 129 seems incredible. Hotson has indeed assumed rather easily that the whole collection was written in the same year.

The 'Other Essays' by Hotson include several that have previously appeared in periodicals, throwing light on Shakespeare's friends, on Mercutio's phrase 'Dun's the mouse', and on the stage-popularity of Ancient Pistol. In this kind of research some degree of conjecture is legitimate, and Hotson would not claim that every one of his identifications is certain. We can be grateful for his interesting guidance through Elizabethan by-ways, though I. A. Shapiro[4] has put a convincing case against Shakespeare's association with the 'Mermaid Club', which Hotson has perhaps too readily assumed.[5]

---

[1] *Shakespeare's Sonnets Dated and Other Essays* (Hart-Davis, 1949).

[2] 'Dr Hotson's Arguments', *Times Literary Supplement*, 10 February 1950.

[3] *Shakspere's Five-act Structure* (Urbana, 1947), p. 629.

[4] 'The "Mermaid Club"', *Modern Language Review*, XLV (January 1950), 6-17.

[5] Alan Keen in 'A Shakespearian Riddle', *Times Literary Supplement*, 21 April 1950, has explored possible connexions between Shakespeare and a 'Shropshire circle' which included Sir Richard Newport, whose autograph appears in the copy of Hall's *Chronicle* which Keen believes that Shakespeare annotated. The article is confusing and full of promises of further revelations. We are warned of the existence of a 'W. H.' in William Hoghton, the

One other essay requires special mention, 'Love's Labour's Won', in which Hotson suggests that Meres's title should be assigned to *Troilus and Cressida*, which he thinks was written for performance at the Middle Temple. The case depends partly on the interpretation of 'love's labour': in *Love's Labour's Lost* 'labour' we are told means 'effort', in *Love's Labour's Won* it means 'sorrow' or 'pain': the two play-titles are 'associated' but not 'set in opposition'. But when one word in a title is changed to its opposite, attention is focused on that, and the implication is that the new play is in some way the reverse of the old: we have Elizabethan examples in *A Knack to Know a Knave* and *A Knack to Know an Honest Man*, and in *Every Man in his Humour* and *Every Man out of his Humour*. It is therefore difficult to believe that an audience going to see *Love's Labour's Won* would not expect a play with an ending diametrically opposed to that of *Love's Labour's Lost*. Hotson does not mention the possibility of later revision, but that would surely be necessary if *Troilus and Cressida* were first acted in 1598.

Shakespeare's biography is the theme of three authoritative articles in *Shakespeare Survey* 3: Charles J. Sisson[1] has surveyed the knowledge acquired and the conjectures hazarded since 1900; F. P. Wilson[2] has printed his lecture to the Fourth Shakespeare Conference; and James G. McManaway[3] has summarized recently expressed views on the dating of the plays.

Points of detail are the concern of a number of other articles. Abraham Feldman[4] puts forward the view that Chettle's apology in *Kind-Harts Dreame* is not to Shakespeare but to Peele: admittedly Shakespeare was not one of the 'playmakers' to whom Greene's letter was addressed, but Feldman is on dubious ground when he claims that Peele practised the 'qualitie'.[5] Murray Bromberg[6] has vigorously attacked and, I think, successfully destroyed the argument of Norman Nathan that Shylock was a satiric portrait of Henslowe. John H. Long[7] has suggested that Hortensio's love-poem presented to Bianca in *The Taming of the Shrew* makes use of Thomas Morley's *A Plaine and Easie Introduction to Practicall Musicke* of 1597: Long admits that the evidence is not conclusive, but it does something to strengthen the link between Shakespeare and Morley and may assist in the dating of the play. W. Schrickx[8] is mainly concerned with identifying Chapman as the 'rival poet', but his argument is impaired by the difficulty he has experienced in making out the sense of certain passages in *The Shadow of Night*: he is commendably cautious on the alleged association of Chapman with Ralegh.

With these explorations must be associated Sir Duff Cooper's essay in Shakespeare biography.[9] This is written with an engaging lightness, and it would be to consider too curiously to wonder how Shakespeare acquired a strong military consciousness (together with promotion to non-

nephew of Alexander Hoghton who had a William Shakeshaft in his household in 1581. Hotson, we may note, has also promised to produce a 'W.H.' who will be appropriate for his dating of the sonnets.

[1] 'Studies in the Life and Environment of Shakespeare since 1900', *Shakespeare Survey*, 3 (1950), 1–12.

[2] 'Shakespeare's Reading', *Shakespeare Survey*, 3 (1950), 14–21.

[3] 'Recent Studies in Shakespeare's Chronology', *Shakespeare Survey*, 3 (1950), 22–33.

[4] 'Shakspere and the Scholars', *Notes and Queries*, cxciv (24 December 1949), 556.

[5] Sir Edmund Chambers, *The Elizabethan Stage* (1923), iii, 458–9, rejects the tenuous evidence for this.

[6] 'Shylock and Philip Henslowe', *Notes and Queries*, cxciv (1 October 1949), 422–3.

[7] 'Shakespeare and Thomas Morley', *Modern Language Notes*, lxv (January 1950), 17–22.

[8] 'Shakespeare and the School of Night: An Estimate and Further Interpretations', *Neophilologus*, xxxiv (January 1950), 35–44.

[9] *Sergeant Shakespeare* (Hart-Davis, 1949).

commissioned rank) in the few months' service that is here suggested. Nor do we need to wax solemn over the references to the *Ur-Hamlet*, to the problems of authenticity, or even to the "shifty Lord Chancellor". We may suspect that Sir Duff could produce as good a case for the soldiership of other Elizabethan dramatists, if he had a mind to it. But we shall still be grateful for some shrewd observations on Iago and Hamlet, and for a demonstration of how to write on Shakespeare with simplicity and taste. Nothing here is arch, nothing facetious: here is no sad scholar wooing a popular market.

Studies of Elizabethan thought and historical event are continuing, and it is these that provide the basis for an adequate criticism. Hardin Craig[1] has ably summarized his thinking on the pre-Cartesian consciousness that he finds an all-important characteristic of Shakespeare's time. Though our debt to him increases, one may wonder whether Craig does not impose on the thought of the period a uniformity that the evidence does not bear out. "They were the children of God and they knew it", he says of the Elizabethans, but he might add that they knew it with a varying degree of sureness. They had an old paganism and a new doubt, as well as an orthodox body of faith. A. P. Rossiter,[2] in a book which discourages the reader with its blend of the delphic and the colloquial, has most profitably revealed the ambivalencies that lie everywhere in the Elizabethan heritage: even miracle and morality were no simple acts of faith. When we proceed to Marlowe and to Marston, to Shakespeare's *Troilus* and Webster's *Duchess*, we must recognize that these men had not the rock for their feet that their Spanish contemporaries knew. It was increasingly the way of Elizabethan and Jacobean dramatists to see both sides of a question: they might use an orthodox pattern in the shaping of a play, as Shakespeare in *Macbeth* or Tourneur in *The Atheist's Tragedy*, but the result reflects their own disturbance of mind. And at times their questioning could become overt, as with political issues in the anonymous *Woodstock* and with the larger philosophical issues in *Troilus*.

The need for recognizing the precarious balance in the Elizabethan attitude is stressed by Sidney Shanker,[3] who has seen a connexion between the mob-scenes in *Coriolanus* and the popular outbreaks in Warwickshire and Northamptonshire in 1607. He presents Shakespeare as caught in a dilemma, instinctively critical of a social threat yet aware that the old order could not endure. The relation of *Coriolanus* to contemporary social fears has also been pointed out by E. C. Pettet[4] and by Brents Stirling.[5] The treatment of the mob in *Henry VI*, *Julius Caesar* and *Coriolanus* has been shown by Stirling to derive largely from the frequent Elizabethan attacks on Anabaptists, who were associated in the public mind with all rioters and all nonconformists. In the two earlier plays, indeed, the presentation of the fickle and brutal multitude is in line with orthodox Elizabethan doctrine: the common people who took the law into their own hands were as blameworthy as the individual led by ambition to social wrong. But in *Coriolanus* the behaviour of the people is shown with a deeper scorn, a temper of mind that appears also in Timon's railing. In *Timon* it is significant that a rebel against the state, Alcibiades, is victorious and

[1] 'An Aspect of Shakespearean Study', *Shakespeare Association Bulletin*, XXIV (October 1949), 247–57.
[2] *English Drama from Early Times to the Elizabethans. Its Background, Origins and Developments* (Hutchinson's University Library, 1950).
[3] 'Some Clues for *Coriolanus*', *Shakespeare Association Bulletin*, XXIV (July 1949), 209–13.
[4] '*Coriolanus* and the Midlands Insurrection of 1607', *Shakespeare Survey*, 3 (1950), 34–42.
[5] *The Populace in Shakespeare* (Columbia University Press; London: Geoffrey Cumberlege, 1949).

welcomed on his return from exile, and *Coriolanus* itself may show the playwright driven towards a new passion for correction and discipline of the common man, and yet at the same time doubtful whether any human being can so escape from frailty as to qualify for the office of governor. Anti-popular feeling in *Coriolanus* significantly co-exists with the presentation of a man with the urge to command but unequal to the task. Paul A. Jorgensen[1] has interestingly noted Shakespeare's stressing of his hero's limitations both on the field of battle, where he is a good fighter but a poor general, and in the political arena.

The complexity of the Elizabethan attitude is also brought to our notice in two other articles. Raymond Chapman[2] shows that Shakespeare's histories displayed the operations of an amoral Fortune: we over-simplify the picture, in fact, if we see in the thought of these plays only a political lesson. Eudo C. Mason[3] emphasizes the change in tone and in style around 1595 in the dramatic comments on women and sex. He rightly stresses the key-position of Marston, but makes too easy a distinction between the cynical and the tragic figures: they overlap, surely, in Iago and Flamineo. We may doubt, too, whether Lear's sexual preoccupations are irrelevant to his position.

In an attractive book, C. W. Scott-Giles[4] has outlined the principles of medieval and Tudor heraldry, and has listed the arms of every historical figure in the plays. The common reader will learn much, and the producer will find the book invaluable. The author has designed arms for the Bastard Faulconbridge, and has not resisted the impulse to include a boar's head in Falstaff's: an uninstructed reader wonders why the brizure in Faulconbridge's arms is not a bend sinister. There is also a straightforward account of Shakespeare's arms and their acquisition. One reviewer has pointed out[5] that Scott-Giles gives too ready credence to the old identification of Shallow and Sir Thomas Lucy.

A great deal of knowledge and conjecture is brought together in a book by Karl J. Holzknecht,[6] which is useful in its general picture but often inaccurate in detail and over-simplified in the interpretation of the age and its drama. It is odd to find the Duke in *Measure for Measure* included, along with Duncan and Gonzalo, in a list of 'dignified old men', Prince Hal described as 'refreshingly sincere', Shakespeare blamed for Hamlet's conduct with the dead Polonius, and the phrase 'hearty affirmation of life' used to characterize Elizabethan tragedy. Holzknecht makes too clean-cut a division between Elizabethan and Jacobean, and attaches too much weight to the influence of the monarch. Misquotations and departures from accepted dates are noticeable.

George F. Reynolds[7] has briefly and cogently reminded us of the basic principles of Elizabethan staging, putting his emphasis on the fluidity of action and on the unchanging background

---

[1] 'Shakespeare's Coriolanus: Elizabethan Soldier', *PMLA*, LXIV (March 1949), 221–35. A less fruitful relation of a Shakespeare character to the life and thought of the age is to be found in Charles L. Draper's 'Falstaff's Bardolph', *Neophilologus*, XXXIII (October 1949), 222–6.

[2] 'The Wheel of Fortune in Shakespeare's Historical Plays', *Review of English Studies*, n.s., I (January 1950), 1–7.

[3] 'Satire on Woman and Sex in Elizabethan Tragedy', *English Studies*, XXXI (February 1950), 1–10.

[4] *Shakespeare's Heraldry* (Dent, 1950).

[5] *Times Literary Supplement*, 10 March 1950.

[6] *The Backgrounds of Shakespeare's Plays* (New York: American Book Company, 1950).

[7] 'Staging Elizabethan Plays', *The Listener*, 11 August 1949; reprinted in *Shakespeare Association Bulletin*, XXIV (October 1949), 258–63.

L

provided by the tiring-house wall. Leo Kirschbaum[1] notes the clear evidence in *Julius Caesar* and *Coriolanus* that blood was freely exhibited on the Shakespearian stage, in a way that later audiences would shrink from: he suggests, however, that certain recent productions have come nearer to the Elizabethan manner. A fresh approach to the stage-structure has been made by C. Walter Hodges,[2] who suggests that stage-level may have been head-high and that the stage was usually an open structure of posts or trestles, draped with hangings. He believes that the Fortune was exceptional in having a panelled-in stage. The exciting suggestion is made that on occasion part of the yard may have been cleared of groundlings and used for acting: perhaps, Hodges says, Marina's barge in *Pericles* was a practicable boat brought in through one of the gates of the yard; perhaps, too, an actor might similarly enter on horseback. We must be doubtful of this until evidence can be produced, but Hodges does indeed set our fancies spinning.

Contributions to our knowledge of seventeenth-century stage-history are made by Harry R. Hoppe,[3] who has noted performances by English players at Ghent between 1604 and 1665, and by James G. McManaway,[4] whose scrutiny of an auction-catalogue of 1827 has revealed that the Third Folio texts used for performances at the Smock Alley Theatre, Dublin, included *Troilus*, *The Tempest* and *Measure for Measure* along with the twelve other Shakespeare plays already known to have been acted there: McManaway has observed that the prompter's changes in the text in certain cases anticipate the emendations of eighteenth-century editors, and he suggests a possible link between editorial practice and the stage tradition.

Later stage-history is the concern of Miss Isabel Roome Mann,[5] who notes a benefit performance of *Othello*, with a special prologue, at Stratford on 9 September 1746; of Kurt Raeck,[6] who comments on the false romanticism encouraged by open-air performances; of Robert de Smet,[7] who describes the fortunes of *Othello* in Paris and Brussels from the eighteenth century to the present day; and of Alf Henriques,[8] who surveys Shakespearian scholarship, production and influence in Denmark during the last fifty years. Miss Muriel St Clare Byrne's detailed description of the 1949 Stratford production of *Henry VIII*[9] is a record of lasting value.

G. Wilson Knight's book on Shakespearian production has been reissued with two additional chapters and some incidental changes.[10] His basic assumption remains that a Shakespeare play is built round a 'central intuition', and that consequently the producer's first task is to find this centre. He will not indeed recognize ambivalency in the major plays or imperfect structure in the minor. Moreover, Knight is singularly assured of his own interpretations: on the nature of

---

[1] 'Shakespeare's Stage Blood and its Critical Significance', *PMLA*, LXIV (June 1949), 517–29.

[2] 'Unworthy Scaffolds: A Theory for the Reconstruction of Elizabethan Playhouses', *Shakespeare Survey*, 3 (1950), 83–94.

[3] 'English Actors at Ghent in the Seventeenth Century', *Review of English Studies*, XXV (October 1949), 305–21.

[4] 'Additional Prompt-Books of Shakespeare from the Smock Alley Theatre', *Modern Language Review*, XLV (January 1950), 64–5.

[5] 'The First Recorded Production of a Shakespearean Play in Stratford-upon-Avon', *Shakespeare Association Bulletin*, XXIV (July 1949), 203–8.

[6] 'Shakespeare in the German Open-air Theatre', *Shakespeare Survey*, 3 (1950), 95–7.

[7] 'Othello in Paris and Brussels', *Shakespeare Survey*, 3 (1950), 98–106.

[8] 'Shakespeare and Denmark: 1900–1949', *Shakespeare Survey*, 3 (1950), 107–15.

[9] 'A Stratford Production: *Henry VIII*', *Shakespeare Survey*, 3 (1950), 120–9.

[10] *Principles of Shakespearian Production with Special Reference to the Tragedies* (Penguin Books, 1949).

Measure for Measure, he tells us, "there is scarcely room for divergence of opinion". His skill in conveying his ideas through the medium of Shakespeare production is evident from this book, but it is perhaps significant that he has no wish to use an Elizabethan stage.

3. TEXTUAL STUDIES

reviewed by JAMES G. McMANAWAY

Unless a work of art is to be studied in absolute terms as a timeless contribution to human culture, there can be no thorough understanding and appreciation of it until it has been fitted into a chronological pattern that will relate it to the other works in the canon and throw light on the development of the mind of the artist. Nor can a writer be studied intelligently without reference to the age in which he lived, the other writers of the time, and the events and movements which moulded, or were moulded by, them. It is the neglect or ignorance of this fundamental truth which leads to the framing of the questions one frequently hears: "What does it matter who wrote 'Shakespeare'? We have the plays, haven't we?" No rational account of the development of Elizabethan literature can be written unless we recognize that the author of 'Shakespeare' was a man who flourished at precisely the time of William Shakespeare of Stratford—neither earlier nor later—and accept the overwhelming evidence that William Shakespeare of Stratford is the author of the works then and now attributed to him. But the biographical records of playwrights of that age being scanty, there are gaps in the history and puzzles in the chronology of all the writers which continue to challenge our best efforts.

In particular, there is the blank in William Shakespeare's history which represents the years between the birth of Hamnet and Judith in 1585 and the penning of Greene's *Groatsworth of Wit* in 1592. Somehow during that interval, Shakespeare became an actor and acquired what Greene considered a dangerous proficiency in writing plays. Now comes Leslie Hotson[1] with the proposition that in that interval Shakespeare flowered as a lyrical poet and wrote over a hundred of his Sonnets. For his assumption that we fail to understand the topical allusions of the Sonnets only because we do not know the detailed history—and I should add the intimate gossip—of the times, he finds support in the prefatory remarks of John Benson, publisher of the *Poems* in 1640:

In your perusall you shall finde them Seren, cleere and eligantly plaine, such gentle straines as shall recreate and not perplexe your braine, no intricate or cloudy stuffe to puzzell intellect, but perfect eloquence....

Benson, presumably, lived close enough to Shakespeare's time for the allusions to be recognized, and so for him as for other cultured readers, the Sonnets and their story are supposed to have been pellucid. If this be true, editors should accord a more profound respect than is usual to the order in which Benson reprinted the Sonnets, which varies radically from that in the Quarto of 1609.

But how credible is Benson's statement? Doubt has been expressed by Hallett Smith[2] who

[1] *Shakespeare's Sonnets Dated and Other Essays* (Hart-Davis, 1949).
[2] '"No Cloudy Stuffe to Puzzell Intellect": a Testimonial Misapplied to Shakespeare', *Shakespeare Quarterly*, I (January 1950), 18–21.

shows that the quoted words were adapted by John Benson from a commendatory poem addressed by Thomas May to Joseph Rutter in praise of his pastoral tragi-comedy, *The Shepheards Holy-Day*, a book published by Benson in 1635. It is conceivable that when Benson read the Sonnets in the course of reprinting them he was struck by the remarkable applicability of Thomas May's phrases; but it seems much more likely, as Smith says, that while writing a publisher's blurb for his book Benson came upon or remembered the passage and, finding it good, adapted it with no thought that three hundred years later his plagiarism would win him esteem as a serious critic of literature.

The contemporary events to which Hotson finds specific references in Sonnets 107, 123 and 124 occurred during the years 1586-9; for the allusions to be most effective, the Sonnets in question should, he thinks, have been written almost at once; and he argues that if these three Sonnets can be dated before 1590, the hundred odd which precede them in Thorpe's edition must have antedated them in composition. Let us examine the Sonnets in turn. In number 107, the crucial lines are in the second quatrain:

> The mortall Moone hath her eclipse indur'de,
> And the sad Augurs mock their owne presage,
> Incertenties now crowne them-selves assur'e,
> And peace proclaimes Olives of endlesse age.

Rejecting the identification of the 'mortall Moone' as Queen Elizabeth, Hotson revives the unexplained suggestion of Samuel Butler that the reference is to the Armada and by quoting from English and Continental books published from 1588 to 1642 in which the line of battle of the Armada is likened to a moon, he attempts to show that Sonnet 107 celebrates the great naval victory of '88.

It is not always possible to pin down an Elizabethan poet when he plays at topical allusions. In the first place, it is unsafe to assume that he would employ the allusion only in the months following the event; and in the second place, he may have two or more events in mind. The conduct of Edmund Spenser may be cited, who in the political allegory of Book v of the *Faerie Queene* lets his hero Artegall represent now Lord Grey of Wilton and now Sir John Norris; and an interval of some twenty years separates the events which Spenser works into his narrative. Perhaps Shakespeare did have in mind the crescent-shaped alinement of the Armada, but his patriotic emotion at its mortal eclipse may easily have been recollected in the tranquillity of a later decade. He may just as readily have been thinking of his queen, for as the Countess de Chambrun reminds us,[1] Mrs Stopes long ago discovered that courtiers could and did speak of the waning and even the eclipse of Elizabeth, within her lifetime, as in the letter of 9 July 1595 from Sir Thomas Cecil to Sir Robert Cecil, his brother (Hatfield MSS, v, 273):

I left the moon in the wane at my last being at the Court; I hear now it is a half moon again, yet I think it will never be at the full, though I hope it will never be eclipsed, you know whom I mean....

This was written when Elizabeth was approaching the dangerous period of her grand climacteric. The Virgin Queen would have blazed with anger against the author, if the letter

---

[1] *Times Literary Supplement*, 31 March 1950.

had ever come before her eyes; but it passed between brothers, and the writer risked no more in using the phrase than Shakespeare did in the Mortal Moone Sonnet, which circulated only among his private friends until six years after it was beyond the power of the Queen to do him injury.

It is the belief of the Countess, furthermore, that Hotson has mistaken the theme of the Sonnet, which is, as J. R. asserted as long ago as 1848, the deliverance of the Earl of Southampton from the Tower by James as soon as he learned of Elizabeth's death. This and other interpretations of the supposed allusions are given at length by Rollins in his Variorum Edition of the *Sonnets*.

A lively controversy has been provoked. The reviewer in the *Times Literary Supplement* of 10 February allows "that Dr Hotson's arguments for accepting 1589 as the date of these three sonnets are convincing" and considers that the essay "may prove to be the most significant contribution to Shakespearian studies of recent years". John Sparrow[1] finds a reference to the crescent-shaped naval formation in *Eliza Sive de Laudibus Augustissimae et Serenissimae Principis Elizabethae*, which Augustus van Dans dedicated in 1619 to Sir Dudley Carleton, where, after Philip II has been speaking of the Armada, occur these lines:

> Dixit, et ex oculis rabidi iam flabra favoni
> Lunatas pepulere rates.

This tends to strengthen Hotson's case. But Sparrow's citation of Phineas Fletcher's *The Locusts*, canto IV, stanza 13, raises a serious question. Hotson had quoted only the first three lines, with their reference to the Armada as a 'Moone of wood'. The concluding lines of the stanza express the Pope's dismay that though "That long wish't houre, when Cynthia set i' th' maine" has come, it has brought Rome no gain, for though "One bright star fell, the Sun is ris'ne, and all his traine." "In this single stanza, therefore, the moon is made to do duty not only for the Armada ('Moone of wood') but also for the death of Queen Elizabeth ('when Cynthia set i' th' maine')." Sparrow points out that the planetary image is used in the corresponding passage in *Locustae* only with reference to Elizabeth and James. A version of *Locustae* was in existence as early as 1611, and if Langdale be correct *The Locusts* took shape about 1612. Thus can the poetic memory turn back across many years and light up great events with ambivalent imagery. And thus may Shakespeare have done in Sonnet 107.

Peter Leyland[2] objects that a crescent moon cannot suffer an eclipse and denies that the Armada can be the subject of the sonnet. Alfred Harbage[3] revives the arguments of Eccles and Mattingly in favour of 1603 as the date of composition and quotes Dekker's statement in *The Wonderful Year* that "88...was a yeare of Jubile to this". In addition, he quotes from E. L.'s contribution to *Sorrowes Joy* (1603) the pregnant phrase, "our Sunne eclipst did set".

In Sonnet 123, which Hotson calls 'The Riddle of the New-Old Pyramids', he finds a reference to the four Egyptian obelisks which workmen of Pope Sixtus uncovered where they lay in ruins in Rome and at his behest re-edified between 1586 and 1589. Several commentators have demurred that, when Shakespeare wrote 'pyramids', he may well have meant pyramids and not obelisks, even though Elizabethans used the term 'pyramids' loosely. Harbage is reminded of

---

[1] *Times Literary Supplement*, 3 March 1950.   [2] *Ibid.* 17 February 1950.
[3] *Shakespeare Quarterly*, 1 (April 1950), 57–63.

L*

the pyramid erected at the Royal Exchange to welcome James to the City; and Hugh R. Williamson[1] calls to mind the ornamental pyramids that frequently deck Elizabethan tombs, such as that of Sir Thomas Stanley, embellished by verses attributed to Shakespeare (see *English Church Monuments: 1510–1840*, p. 60).

Sonnet 124 Hotson attempts to date 1589 by explaining that "the childe of state", suffering "in smiling pomp", and eventually falling "under the blow of thralled discontent" is Henri III of France. Hugh Williamson is of the opinion that the lines might as readily be applied to the Earl of Essex. Neither interpretation deals satisfactorily with the concluding couplet, which calls to witness "the foles of time, Which die for goodnes, who have liv'd for crime".

Hotson's proposed dating is momentous, because it confronts us with the proposition that Shakespeare's lyric genius matured as early as 1589. We need go no further than Chatterton and Tennyson for proof of the early flowering of the lyric poet. The dramatist, in contrast, matures slowly, gaining skill in his craft only after repeated trials, and producing great drama only with the slow acquisition of insight into the hidden motives of mankind and an almost godlike comprehension as well of Cressid's frailty as of Lear's purgation. An early date for the Sonnets would clear away the rivalry between advocates of Pembroke and of Southampton as the fair youth, for in 1586 each was too young; and if Hotson can produce a convincing candidate for this honour, he will go far towards establishing his dates.

Some problems yet remain, however. *Venus and Adonis* and *Lucrece* bear every sign of having been published as soon as written. And few will be inclined to agree, as Hotson urges, that their poetic immaturity, as compared with the Sonnets, is the result of Shakespeare's having 'written down' to the level of appreciation of the youthful Earl of Southampton, to whom they are dedicated. It is difficult to believe that the man who possessed the metrical skill and emotional power to write Sonnets 71, 73 and 87, for example, could have done no better four years later than the 'unpolisht lines' of *Venus and Adonis*.

If Shakespeare wrote his Sonnets by 1589, he was indeed, as Hotson says, not following the vogue of sonnet-writing but rather was the leader of the fashion. A revolutionary thesis, this; but can it be sustained by a close comparison of the early sonnet cycles? Could Shakespeare's sonnets have circulated before 1590 among his private friends without leaving recognizable traces of their influence on the other sonnet writers? Sidney is indebted to Watson, and after the publication of *Astrophel and Stella* in 1591 there is a sudden outpouring of sonnets, each poet learning from his predecessors. Shakespeare, too, seems to learn, and some of his Sonnets, as 130, are an expression of his reaction against conventions that have become stereotyped. But this sonnet, too, along with the others to the Dark Lady, must apparently be put back 'in the poet's youth' (p. 35). I am reluctant to believe that Shakespeare could at the same time set the fashion in sonneteering and ridicule its conventions. Until grounds more relevant can be established, I shall adhere to a more conservative dating.

Julius Caesar presents the editor with comparatively few textual problems, as J. Dover Wilson has discovered in his New Cambridge edition.[2] Except for the duplication of text in IV, iii, which may result from the compositor's failure to heed a mark of deletion, the play runs smoothly, with only a few abrupt short lines, possibly caused by cutting, to break the regularity.

[1] *Times Literary Supplement*, 17 February 1950.
[2] Cambridge University Press, 1949.

The very simplicity of the editorial task arouses distrust. This unusually short play, which appears only in the Folio, was obviously not printed from Shakespeare's fair copy or even from his foul papers. Here are no equivalents of 'Enter Will Kemp' for 'Enter Peter'. What we have is a strictly edited text set from a scribal transcript. Yet despite the fact that the normalizing was probably done after the manuscript had left Shakespeare's hands, Wilson has been able to penetrate the iron curtain set up by the unknown first editor and with Ben Jonson's assistance recover an original Shakespearian line (cf. *Shakespeare Survey*, 2, pp. 36–43):

> Caesar did never wrong, but with just cause.

It would be interesting to know whether it was Shakespeare or another who deleted the line that had caused Jonson such offence.

Not the least virtue of Professor Duthie's edition of *Lear*, which was considered in this place last year, is that it is forcing scholars to re-examine the textual problems of the play in all their ramifications. W. W. Greg, for example, accepts the main thesis that *Lear* is a reported text.[1] He finds the hypothesis of a communal report challenging, but objects that the book-keeper could hardly have written "a dogge, so bade in office". He inquires whether the proposed explanation of misassigned speeches is not in some cases too elaborate—might it not be better to assume that the book-keeper, writing at top speed, sometimes left out speech-tags, with the expectation of supplying them later from his unaided memory. There are other factors, however. It seems likely to Greg, for example, that the actor who played Edmund stole boy-Regan's "Let the Drum strike, and prove my title thine" and altered it to "Let the Drum strike, and prove my title good", i.e. that this corruption is a stage debasement. In a word, Greg would like to accept the communal hypothesis, but is not happy in doing so.

Greg withdraws his earlier suggestion that inequalities in the skill with which lines of verse are divided may be explained in terms of two or more compositors of unequal judgement, because Philip Williams has proved, just short of conclusively, that only one man set the whole play (see *Papers of the Bibliographical Society of the University of Virginia*, 1, 59–68). He is still troubled, however, by the line division, which Duthie thinks the book-keeper supplied. Why should a prompt-book need line division? Why would a book-keeper work so erratically? Confident that the manuscript was never intended for a printer's eye, Greg is forced to attribute the line divisions to a compositor.

The Folio text of *Lear* was set from a copy of the 1619 Quarto which had been corrected by reference to the playhouse manuscript. When the Folio differs from the Quarto, therefore, its reading must generally be preferred as being the result of a deliberate change. "Obvious oversights of the compositor", and "a number of purely formal variants like 'thou': 'y^u'", to borrow Greg's language, account for 68 out of the 184 variants. And after 42 other differences have been accounted for, such as deliberate cuts in the Folio, alterations in the speaker consequent upon the Folio's reduction in the cast, and omissions (or reductions) in stage directions, "there remain 74 instances of variation that possess critical significance and in which Duthie elects to follow" the Quarto. Greg finds himself in agreement about 58 of these but believes "that in at least 16 instances (rather over a fifth) Duthie's choice of the Quarto reading is open to challenge". There were many opportunities for corruption in the Folio, and it is a sophisticated text, but,

[1] Review in *Modern Language Review*, XLIV (July 1949), 397–400.

as Greg reminds us, in the course of its transmission the text of the Quarto has been subjected to the processes of normalizing and devitalization in the mouths of actors, and in consequence the rule of *durior lectio* has special applicability. The editor of *Lear* must beware that a smoother reading or a personal preference does not betray him into the unwarranted retention of a Quarto variant.

The Bad Quarto of *Romeo and Juliet* continues to receive attention. In reviewing H. R. Hoppe's book with this title, W. W. Greg [1] gives qualified acceptance to Hoppe's conjecture that the actors who played Romeo and Paris fabricated the text but points the need for an explanation of their lamentable failure in IV and V, where their lines are no better than the rest. He wonders whether Hoppe has sufficiently considered the possibility of the prompter having acted as reporter.

If *Romeo and Juliet* was written about 1596, who could have stolen the text, and for what purpose? Hoppe's very diffident suggestion is that Gabriel Spencer and Humphrey Jeffes were the culprits in 1596–7, at which time he thinks they were transferring from the Chamberlain's to the newly formed Pembroke's. Greg offers several weighty objections: we have no evidence that any of Pembroke's men had ever been with the Chamberlain's; at such a time actors would be unlikely to sell a pirated text for publication or bring one to the new company; and the text as printed in the First Quarto could not possibly have been intended for representation on a London stage. It remains, then, for scholars to determine who were the reporters, why memories failed in IV and V, and the purpose for which the piracy was effected.

In the same number of the *Review of English Studies* (pp. 8–16) that contains Greg's review of Hoppe, Sidney Thomas proposes a partial solution to some of the problems, namely that Henry Chettle is the author of a number of passages of so-called un-Shakespearian verse in this Quarto 1. Chettle was in close association with Danter, the publisher, from 1591 to at least 1596, as a sort of literary editor. He was quite capable of writing poetry as good as the best lines in the scene at Friar Laurence's cell when Juliet and Romeo met to be wedded, and some of the phrases and tricks of style are closely paralleled in Chettle. Thomas makes a strong case for Chettle, not as the reporter, but as the poet who wrote linking passages of text. Hoppe, indeed, had considered the possibility that Chettle might be the reporter-versifier, but expressed a preference for actor-reporters; and earlier Fleay had mentioned Chettle, only to reject him, while Harold Jenkins, Chettle's editor, had expressed the pious hope that his author was not involved in the printing of the First Quarto. Chettle, however, satisfies the requirements—he has been found acting as reviser in *Sir Thomas More* and supplying a missing speech in *Huon of Bordeaux*, a manuscript play which Hoppe has elsewhere denominated "a bad quarto that never reached print". In 1592 in *Kind-Harts Dreame* Chettle regrets that he "did not so much spare [Shakespeare], as since I wish I had...because my selfe haue seene his demeanor no lesse ciuill than he exelent in the qualitie he professes: Besides, diuers of worship haue reported his vprightnes of dealing, which argues his honesty, and his facetious grace in writting, that aprooues his Art." Now, only five years later, this same Chettle appears to be caught in the act of tinkering up a stolen version of Shakespeare's popular tragedy of youthful love.

If Danter did not commission the piracy of the play, it seems a necessary corollary that Chettle's involvement was limited to editorial patchwork; and we cannot even speculate what was the condition of the text in the passages which his verses displaced.

[1] *Review of English Studies*, n.s., 1 (January 1950), 64–6.

A topical allusion has stimulated Thomas to further researches,[1] in the course of which he has found a reference in William Covell's *Polimanteia* (1595) that emphasizes the importance of a long forgotten earthquake in March, 1584. Covell lists it as one of the great prodigies of the last twenty years, with never a glance at the quake of 1580. If Juliet's nurse was thinking with Covell, the eleven years she mentions at *Romeo and Juliet*, I, iii, 23, would date the play 1595. *Polimanteia* is one of the first books to praise Shakespeare by name, and it would be strange if that ambitious young author was not familiar with it. Possibly it supplies the date of Shakespeare's earthquake.

In two other notes, Thomas discusses the bad weather referred to in *A Midsummer Night's Dream*[2] and Elizabethan shorthand.[3] If Shakespeare is for all time, he was also of an age, and thoughtful readers have long fancied that in an allusion which is rather unnecessarily dropped into *A Midsummer Night's Dream*, II, i, they have found a very human Shakespeare complaining about bad weather. The circumstantial detail supports the belief that the play was written and first performed in a year when unseasonably heavy rains had damaged crops and inflated the costs of food. And not unnaturally scholars have attempted to identify the year and thus date the composition of *A Midsummer Night's Dream*. Such a year was 1596, in the opinion of Thomas, who observes that crops were apparently normal in 1595 and that the weather of 1594, while unusual, was not such as Shakespeare describes. In support of 1596, Thomas cites previously unnoted passages in Stow's *Chronicles* (1598; sig. Ee5ᵛ) and William Barlow's translation of Lavater's *Three Christian Sermons* (1596; sig. A3ᵛ–4ʳ, C7ʳ).

Thirty years before Heminge and Condell reminded purchasers of the First Folio that where, before, they "were abus'd with diuerse stolne, and surreptitious copies, maimed, and deformed by the frauds and stealthes of iniurious impostors, that expos'd them" (i.e. the Bad Quartos), an Elizabethan clergyman was complaining in very similar terms. According to the Reverend William Cupper, there existed in 1592 "certaine hungrie Schollers and preposterous noters of Sermons", and "betweene the Printer and the noter, we have in stead of sounde and profitable Treatises, diverse mangeled and vnperfect pieces, even according to the slow hand, slipperie memorie and simple iudgement of him that tooke them". As Thomas points out, the reference is obviously to notes taken in long-hand, a method that was too clumsy to have produced, for example, the good passages of text in the Bad Quarto of *Romeo and Juliet*.

The authorship of *Henry VIII* is the subject of a valuable essay by A. C. Partridge[4] which he seems to have written to counter the recent assertion by Peter Alexander[5] of sole Shakespearian authorship. After reviewing the scholarly publications on this subject, Partridge applies the familiar linguistic tests and several new ones to the units into which the play seems naturally to fall when tested stylistically. The results, presented in statistical or tabular form, confirm in general the surmises of Spedding and Hickson about the presence of two hands in the play and about the identity of the two authors. Shakespeare's work about 1612 shows a preference for the auxiliary *do*, for *hath* and *doth*, *them* and *you*, and for such contractions as *'tis, isn't, to't, o'th*, and

[1] 'The Earthquake in *Romeo and Juliet*', *Modern Language Notes*, LXIV (June 1949), 417–19.
[2] 'The Bad Weather in *A Midsummer Night's Dream*', *Modern Language Notes*, LXIV (May 1949), 319–22.
[3] 'A Note on the Reporting of Elizabethan Sermons', *The Library*, 5th series, III (September 1948), 20–21.
[4] *The Problem of Henry VIII Reopened* (Bowes and Bowes, 1950).
[5] In an essay read at the Shakespeare Conference in Stratford in 1948 but as yet unpublished.

let's. In John Fletcher, on the other hand, there is strong evidence of newer speech habits: he is not addicted to the use of *do* as an auxiliary verb; *has* and *does* occur almost to the exclusion of the older *hath* and *doth*; *'em* and *ye* are "extremely characteristic of the Fletcherian rhythm and cadence"; and the use of contracted forms is different in both quantity and quality. The result of Partridge's study is to reject Massinger and to name Shakespeare and Fletcher as the authors. The presence of intrusive elements throughout the play suggests that one author had the final oversight of the play. This accords with Greg's opinion that the Folio text was printed from a clear fair copy in a scribal hand, working from carefully edited manuscript. It confirms Caroline Spurgeon's belief that the imagery entitles Shakespeare to a claim to more of the text than was allowed by Spedding and Hickson. And it amounts to an assertion that Shakespeare, possibly in retirement, blocked out the play, wrote much of it in final form, and supplied preliminary drafts of other passages, which Fletcher was allowed to rehandle as he put the play in shape for production. The essay concludes with a challenge to scholars to ascertain the details of Shakespeare's habits of language, after first producing an old-spelling text of all his works comparable to that of the Herford-Simpson *Jonson*.

Ever since A. W. Pollard divided Shakespeare quartos into two categories, called Good and Bad, scholars have grappled with the problems of the Bad Quartos. The relations of *The First Part of the Contention* (1594) to the Folio text of *2 Henry VI* have been studied by Peter Alexander, Madeleine Doran and others with results that are valuable for their own sake and are also helpful in their exemplification of some of the newly developed textual and bibliographical techniques. A significant contribution has been made by John E. Jordan,[1] whose methods of procedure are likely to be adapted to the study of other Bad Quartos. The acute reasoning which leads to his rejection of Alexander's suggestion that the actors who played Warwick and Suffolk-Clifford compiled the reported text, and of Chambers's hypothesis that the book-keeper was the culprit is worthy of commendation. Figures are adduced to prove that the actor who 'doubled' the roles of Armourer, Spirit, Lord Scales, Mayor, and Vaux is the most likely reporter of the text of *The First Part of the Contention*. This bit player was a man trusted with several parts and doubtless the opportunity to examine the prompt copy (p. 1112). "He would have been able to see much of the stage business and know the action fairly well, but he would not be expected to know it so thoroughly as the prompter. He would have heard many of the lines and would probably remember ones that struck him, but only the general purport of many.... He would reasonably confuse prose and verse, as well as misplace lines and misascribe speeches..." (p. 1108).

On one minor point I disagree with Jordan and his predecessors. In the Folio, the Queen says to Eleanor: "Give me my Fanne"; the Quarto version is: "Give me my glove." "Since there appears to be no reason for making the change in business," writes Jordan, "the difference is probably a mistake, and certainly the stage manager would have known exactly what he had to have ready to be dropped, although someone else may have remembered only that something was dropped." I propose a very different explanation. A London producer would impress his sophisticated audience by supplying a fan suitable to be carried by a Queen: a touring company could hardly be expected to have such a property; and I fancy that the text and the business were changed accordingly.

[1] 'The Reporter of *Henry VI*, Part 2', *PMLA*, LXIV (December 1949), 1089–113.

Efforts to perfect Shakespeare's text by restoration or emendation do not often concern themselves with stage business. A rare example is Charles T. Prouty's contention[1] that editors err in changing the assignment of certain speeches in II, i, of *Much Ado About Nothing*. In the Quarto, Benedick and Margaret converse while dancing. After the latter's exclamation, "God match me with a good dauncer", Prouty thinks Balthasar 'cuts in' in answer to her prayer, only to be dismissed by her next words, "And God keepe him out of my sight when the daunce is done". It has been customary since Theobald to 'correct' the text and the stage business by assigning all the speeches of Margaret's partner to Balthasar or (by Dover Wilson alone) to Borachio. By sparing Benedick the additional humiliation of being called a poor dancer, the emendation robs us of an amusing piece of business.

A textual restoration is proposed by H. W. Donner,[2] who finds that from Theobald to J. D. Wilson, editors read "Rebellious head" or "Rebellion's head" at *Macbeth* IV, i, 97. The Folio reading, "Rebellion's dead", was favoured by Halliwell-Phillipps, for the reason that Macbeth, confident in the assurances of the Weird Sisters, considered the only threat to his life could come from one re-appearing from the dead (probably the ghost of Banquo). Schmidt, too, and Koeppel preferred the Folio reading, for the first appearance of Banquo's ghost had sent Macbeth to the witches. The matter is discussed at length in an article entitled, 'De Dödas Uppror' (in *Acta Academiae Aboensis Humaniora*, XVIII, 2, Åbo, 1949), which Donner is abstracting. Throughout the tragedy, Macbeth is tortured by the threat that Banquo or his progeny will wrest the 'barren sceptre' from his 'gripe'. His assurance that though Banquo had broken out of the tomb at III, iv, 78–83, he would be powerless at IV, i, 95 to affect Birnam Wood, is shattered ironically when Banquo does appear almost at once to point to the pageant of his royal progeny. Donner adds that a compositor could hardly misread secretarial *h* as *d*. Dover Wilson gives the proposal his hearty acceptance,[3] for to him it illuminates the whole text.

Another textual restoration is advocated by A. P. Rossiter, who wishes to retain without emendation *Henry VIII*, I, i, 72 ff.:

> and his owne Letter
> The Honourable Boord of Councell, out
> Must fetch him in, he Papers.

The Folio punctuation is acceptable, he says,[4] for the passage may be paraphrased as follows: "The Cardinal's mere letter, that distinguished and impudent mockery of the whole council whose rights it usurps, once [being] sent out, had the power to call up and fetch in whomsoever", as it pleases him, 'he papers' (i.e. puts down on paper).

The punctuation of *King Lear*, III, ii, 1–3, is the subject of a valuable note by George W. Williams[5] which makes it probable that Pope's emendation of the Folio punctuation is correct:

> Blow windes, and cracke your cheekes; rage, blow!
> You cataracts and Hurricano's, spout
> Till you have drench'd our Steeples, drown'd the Cockes.

---

[1] 'A Lost Piece of Stage Business in *Much Ado About Nothing*', *Modern Language Notes*, LXV (March 1950), 207–8.   [2] *Times Literary Supplement*, 23 September 1949.

[3] *Ibid.* 30 September 1949.   [4] *Ibid.* 15 July 1949.

[5] 'A Note on *King Lear*, III, ii, 1–3', *Studies in Bibliography: Papers of the Bibliographical Society of the University of Virginia*, II (1949–50), 175–82.

In the same volume,[1] I. B. Cauthen identifies the song of Sir Toby Belch in *Twelfth Night* as the old Christmas-Epiphany carol, 'The Twelve Days of Christmas'.

The use of the word 'gamut', which occurs only in *The Taming of the Shrew*, III, i, seems to John H. Long[2] to imply familiarity with Thomas Morley's *Plaine and Easie Introduction to Practicall Musicke*. If so, the scene in question must have been written (or revised?) in or after 1597, the year in which Morley's book was published.

Whenever an editor comes upon pentameters imbedded in a passage of Shakespearian prose the urge is strong to suspect corruption or revision and to attempt the reconstruction of the text. This tendency, which is particularly manifest in the New Cambridge volumes, is gently ridiculed by C. S. Lewis, who amuses himself[3] by citing J. D. Wilson's note (p. 103) on *Two Gentlemen*, v, iv, 89–90, in which are imbedded several lines of verse. Wilson confesses the fact,[4] but urges that he is not thereby disqualified from detecting fossil verses in Shakespeare's prose, for he finds it incredible that Shakespeare could write prose "entirely of his own invention" which contains lines of verse. This, it seems to me, ignores the readiness with which English writers fall into iambics. Spenser's *View of Ireland* supplied Charles G. Osgood with numerous examples of imbedded verse in an essay contributed some years ago to the first volume of *E L H*.

The First Quarto of *Troilus and Cressida* exists in two issues, in the second of which a half-sheet, signed ¶, containing title-page and an address to the reader, replaces the original title-page, A1. Since the text of the play begins on A2, it may be assumed that A was the first sheet to be printed off, yet at least part of the type remained undistributed long enough for the last seven lines of the title-page to be used in printing the cancel title. Philip Williams, Jr, seeks[5] to discover when and how the cancel half-sheet was printed. Examination of the head-titles on the three pages of text in the final half-sheet M² and of the watermarks in M² and ¶² satisfies him that half-sheet imposition was not used, but that George Eld printed the cancel on the unused half-sheet of M. Absolute proof of this is, I think, impossible, but Williams establishes its probability. He might have strengthened his case, in my opinion, by insisting that the decision to insert the cancel was made almost as soon as printing began, for otherwise the type of the original title-page would almost certainly have been distributed as soon as sheet A had been perfected.

The minor eighteenth-century editions of Shakespeare have been generally neglected, but under the scrutiny of editors and bibliographers many of them prove to have important relations to the major editions. Thus a neglected 1745 edition in six volumes assumes importance when Giles E. Dawson[6] discloses that its unnamed editor was probably Bishop Warburton and that it throws valuable light on his relations to Sir Thomas Hanmer and on the source of numerous emendations of Shakespeare's text.

While collating texts for his Variorum Edition of *2 Henry VI* Gwynne B. Evans has discovered[7] that the 1757 edition of Theobald is not, as Jaggard says, a mere reprint of the second edition

---

[1] 'The Twelfth Day of December: *Twelfth Night*, II, iii, 91', *Virginia Studies in Bibliography*, II, 182–5.

[2] 'Shakespeare and Thomas Morley', *Modern Language Notes*, LXV (January 1950), 17–22.

[3] *Times Literary Supplement*, 3 March 1950.

[4] *Ibid.* 10 March 1950.

[5] 'The "Second Issue" of Shakespeare's *Troilus and Cressida*, 1609', *Virginia Studies in Bibliography*, II, 25–33.

[6] 'Warburton, Hanmer, and the 1745 Edition of Shakespeare', *ibid.* 35–48.

[7] 'The Text of Johnson's *Shakespeare*', *Philological Quarterly*, XXVIII (July 1949), 425–8.

(1740); it has textual importance because Dr Johnson based his text upon it, at least for *1 Henry VI* and probably, for twenty-five other plays. This upsets the received opinion that Johnson rests exclusively upon Warburton. So he did in his early volumes, thinks Evans; but probably at *The Taming of the Shrew*, the first play in vol. III, he changed to the 1757 Theobald. Numerous readings now credited to Johnson originate in his source, a matter of some importance to both Shakespearians and Johnsonians. The identity of the man who introduced the new readings in the 1757 reprint of Theobald is still to be discovered.

Except to the specialist, the discovery of and application to textual problems of new techniques of bibliographical study are apt to seem vermiculate scholarship. Yet each new bit of information about the printing and publication of books is potentially as valuable to the literary critic as the products of pure scientific research may be to the physician. There are random allusions to the supposition that in the early days of printing each compositor was expected to possess a set of wooden composing sticks of varying measures. It is known that by the time of Moxon's *Mechanick Exercises* (1683) every compositor had one of the new adjustable metal composing sticks. In his bibliographical examination of Restoration plays, F. T. Bowers has utilized this knowledge to good advantage. In a report[1] he calls attention to several books in which marked differences in the length of line may be a clue to the proper allocation of the type setting to two or more compositors. The advantages are obvious, particularly in determining how and when cancels and anomalous leaves or gatherings were printed. It is also a little easier now to study the spelling and punctuation habits of compositors and to estimate their relation to apparent corruptions in the text. In two of the studies mentioned above, Philip Williams, Jr, and George W. Williams buttress their arguments about the printing of the cancel in *Troilus* and the correct punctuation of a difficult passage in *Lear* by taking note of the printer's measure in the relevant sections of the books. It is to be hoped that quartos printed while wooden composing sticks were still in use will also be studied systematically, for speech tags, marginal stage directions, and mixed passages of prose and verse in them present difficulties that have no close counterpart in most of the later play quartos.

[1] 'Bibliographical Evidence from the Printer's Measure', *Virginia Studies in Bibliography*, II, 153–67.

BOOKS RECEIVED

CLARKE, D. WALDO. *William Shakespeare*. Drawings by D. M. Rossolymos. Essential English Library (London: Longmans, Green, 1950).

COOPER, DUFF. *Sergeant Shakespeare* (London: Hart-Davis, 1949).

H. D. [HILDA DOOLITTLE] *By Avon River* (New York: Macmillan, 1949).

English Institute Essays, 1948. Edited by D. A. Robertson, Jr. (New York: Columbia University Press; London: Cumberlege, 1949).

HALLIDAY, F. E. *Shakespeare and His Critics* (London: Duckworth, 1949).

HOLZKNECHT, KARL J. *The Backgrounds of Shakespeare's Plays* (New York: American Book Company, 1950).

HOTSON, LESLIE. *Shakespeare's Sonnets Dated and Other Essays* (London: Hart-Davis, 1949).

HYDE, MARY CRAPO. *Playwriting for Elizabethans, 1600–1605* (New York: Columbia University Press; London: Cumberlege, 1949).

KNIGHT, G. WILSON. *Principles of Shakespearian Production, with especial reference to the Tragedies* (Penguin Books, 1949).

LOTHIAN, J. M. '*King Lear*'. *A Tragic Reading of Life* (Toronto: Clarke, Irwin, 1949).

OPPEL, HORST. *Der Späte Shakespeare* (Hamburg: Ellerman, 1949).

PARROTT, THOMAS MARC. *Shakespearean Comedy* (New York: Oxford University Press; London: Cumberlege, 1949).

PARTRIDGE, A. C. *The Problem of 'Henry VIII' Reopened. Some Linguistic Criteria for the Two Styles Apparent in the Play.* With a Foreword by Allardyce Nicoll (Bowes and Bowes, 1949).

PETTET, E. C. *Shakespeare and the Romance Tradition.* With an Introduction by H. S. Bennett (London: Staples, 1949).

SCOTT-GILES, C. W. *Shakespeare's Heraldry.* Illustrated by the Author (London: Dent, 1950).

Shakespeare Association Bulletin, The, vol. XXIV (Shakespeare Association of America, 1949).

STANLEY, ARTHUR (editor). *The Bedside Shakespeare; An Anthology* (London: Gollancz, 1948).

STAUFFER, DONALD A. *Shakespeare's World of Images: the Development of his Moral Ideas* (New York: Norton, 1949).

STIRLING, BRENTS. *The Populace in Shakespeare* (New York: Columbia University Press; London: Cumberlege, 1949).

THOMAS, SIR HENRY. *Shakespeare in Spain.* Annual Shakespeare Lecture of the British Academy, 1949. From *The Proceedings of the British Academy*, vol. XXXV (London: Cumberlege).

TILLYARD, E. M. W. *Shakespeare's Problem Plays* (London: Chatto and Windus, 1950).

WAGNER, BERNARD M. (editor). *The Appreciation of Shakespeare. A Collection of Criticism—Philosophic, Literary and Esthetic—by Great Writers and Scholar-Critics of the Eighteenth, Nineteenth and Twentieth Centuries* (Washington: Georgetown University Press, 1949).

WILSON, JOHN DOVER (editor). *Julius Caesar.* The New Shakespeare (Cambridge University Press, 1949).

Year's Work in English Studies, The, vol. XXVIII, 1947. Edited for the English Association by Frederick S. Boas (Oxford University Press, 1949).

INDEX

INDEX

Boece, Hector, 35, 39, 40
Bogdanović, M., 117, 118, 119, 121
Bonnard, G., 141 n.
Boswell, James, the elder, *The Life of Samuel Johnson*, 66 n.
Boswell, James, the younger, 80
Bowers, F. T., 163
Boyce, Benjamin, 147
Boyle, Roger, Earl of Orrery, *Henry the Fifth*, *Mustapha*, and *Tryphon*, 94
Bradbrook, Muriel, 11–12, 15–16, 22
Bradley, A. C., 10, 12, 16, 17, 18, 21, 23, 44, 141
 Influence on Shakespeare criticism, 3–5
 Miscellany, 4
 Oxford Lectures, 4
 Shakespearean Tragedy, 3–4
Brandes, Georg, 1
Breen, Robert, production of *Hamlet*, 124–5
Bridges, Robert, 2–3, 16
Bright, B. H., 86
Bright, Timothy, *Treatise on Melancholy*, 11
Bristol, *see* Theatre Royal, Bristol
British Museum, 72, 74 n., 79, 84, 85, 87, 93
Bromberg, Murray, 149
Brook, Peter, 129
 production of *Measure for Measure*, 135–8
Brooke, Arthur, *Romeus and Juliet*, 87
Brooke, C. F. Tucker, 8
Brooke, Stopford, 5
Brookes, Baldwin (*see also* Hall, Dr John and family), 70–1
Brooks, Cleanth, 19
Brown, Ivor, 6
Brown, S. J., 18
Budský, Joseph, 112–13
Bugge, Stein, 128
Bujnák, P., 115 n.
Bunyan, John, *Pilgrim's Progress*, 30
Burbage, Richard, 76
Bürger, Gottfried A., 127
Burke, Edmund, 80
Burton, Robert, 79–80, 88, 93, 96 n.
 Anatomy of Melancholy, 80
Butler, Samuel (1835–1902), 154
Byrne, Muriel St C., 11, 152
Byron, George, Lord, 65–6
Bywater, Ingram, 93

Caldecott, Thomas, 81
Calvin, Johannes, 78
Cambridge, St John's College, 91
Camerarius (*see also* Aesop's *Fables*), 65

Campbell, Lily B., 3, 11, 14, 147
Campbell, O. J., 13–14
Canada, report on Shakespeare in, 125
Cankar, I., 117
Canterbury, *see* Prerogative Court of Canterbury
Capek, Jaroslav, 120
Capell, Edward, 87
Carandinos, S., 128
Carey family, as patrons of Thomas Nashe, 60
Carleton, Sir Dudley, 155
Carleton, R., *The Concealed Royalty*, and *The Martial Queen*, 94
Cary, Sir Robert, 91
Cauthen, I. B., 162
Cecil, Sir Robert and Sir Thomas, 154
Chalmers, George, 91
Chamber Accounts, *see* Stanhope, John, Lord
Chamberlain's (King's) Men, *see* Theatre, Elizabethan
Chambers, R. W., 7, 9, 22
Chambers, Sir E. K., 1, 5, 7, 11, 58, 60, 67 n., 74 n., 160
Chambrun, Countess C. L., 148, 154–5
Chapman, George, 7, 25, 42, 149
 Bussy D'Ambois, 43
 The Shadow of Night, 149
Chapman, Raymond, 146, 151
Charlemont Library, 81
Charles I, King, 80
 as Prince Charles, 91
Charlton, H. B., 5, 23, 43
 Shakespearian Comedy, 4
 Shakespearian Tragedy, 4
Chatterton, Thomas, 156
Chaucer, Geoffrey, 52, 78, 94
Chekhov, Anton, 104, 120
 The Three Sisters, 106
Chester, Robert, *Loves Martyr*, 85
Chettle, Henry, 63, 68 n., 158
 Kind-Heart's Dream, 59–62, 149, 158
Cialente, Romano, 128
Cicero, *De Officiis*, 83
Clarke, George, 94
Clarke, Mary Cowden, 3
Clemen, Wolfgang, 18, 20, 127
Clutton-Brock, A., 24
Coleridge, S. T., 1, 3, 144
Collier, John Payne, 88
Collins, A. J., 74 n.
Collins, J. Churton, 9
Coltellacci, Giulio, 128
Commedia dell' Arte, 133
Compagnie des Quinze, La, 101

166

INDEX

M

INDEX

INDEX

Henriques, Alf, 152
Henslowe, Philip, 149
Hepburn, Katherine, 123
Herbert, Sir Henry, 91
Hergešić, J., 122 n.
Herringman, Henry, 91
Heuer, Hermann, 127
Heywood, Thomas, 29, 58
    The Wise Woman of Hogsdon, 41
Hickson, S., 159–60
Hillyard, Nicholas, 130
Hilpert, Heinz, 126, 127
Hiscock, W. G., 96 n.
Hobbes, Thomas, 25
Hodges, C. Walter, 97, 152
Hoghton, William and Alexander, 148 n.
Holinshed, Raphael, 27, 87, 142 n.
    Chronicle of England, 37
    Chronicle of Scotland and *Cymbeline*, 29–30
    Chronicle of Scotland and *Macbeth*, 31, 35–47
Holmes, Elizabeth, 18
Holzknecht, Karl J., 151
Homer, *Odyssey*, 31
Hooker, Richard, 25
Hoppe, Harry R., 152, 158
Horace, 68 n.
    Epistles, 65–6
Hotson, Leslie, 8
    Shakespeare's Sonnets Dated reviewed, 148–9, 153–6
Houston, P. H., 147
Hubler, Edward, 143
Hugo, Victor, 1
Humfrey, Duke of Gloucester, 93
Hunt, Hugh, 138
    production of *Love's Labour's Lost*, 129–35
Hunt, R. W., 88
Huntington Library, 84–5, 93
Huon of Bordeaux, 158
Hurok, Sol, 123
Hutten, Leonard, *Bellum Grammaticale*, 95
Hviezdoslav (Pavol Országh), 109
Hyde, Mary Crapo, 147

Ibsen, Henrik, 17, 98, 128
    Peer Gynt, 106
Iljovski, V., 118
Imagery and symbolism in Shakespeare, *see under* Shakespeare
Inns of Court, *see under* London
Irving, Sir Henry, 102, 105
Italy, report on Shakespeare in, 128

Jackson, Sir Barry, 106
Jakubec, Jan, 115 n.
James I, King, 10, 35, 36–7, 38 ff., 95, 155–6
    Basilikon Doron, 39, 40
    Daemonologie, 41, 42, 43, 47 n.
    treatises on government, 36
James, Henry, 50
James, Thomas, 78, 79
Jameson, Mrs A. B., 3
Jeffes, Humphrey, 158
Jefford, Barbara, 136–7
Jenkins, Harold, 158
Jennens, Charles, 81
Jesenská, Zora, 110–1
Johnson, Dr Samuel, 3, 4, 6, 10, 57–8, 66 n., 80, 86, 87, 129
    edition of Shakespeare (1765), 56, 162–3
    Proposals for Printing a New Edition of the Plays of William Shakespeare, 52
    Rambler, on *Macbeth*, 53
Jones, Ernest, 11
    Hamlet and Oedipus reviewed, 140
Jonson, Ben, 4, 29, 93, 95, 129, 149, 157
    The Alchemist, 95
    Herford–Simpson edition, 160
    Lovers made Men, 92
    Masque of Queens, 42
    Sejanus, 54
    Volpone, 95
Jordan, John E., 160
Jorgensen, P. A., 147, 151
Joseph, Sister Miriam, 9
Josten, Walter, 127
Jovanović, Lj., 121

Kalthoeber, C., bookbinder, 80
Karson, Nat, 124
Karthaios, K., 128
Keats, John, 10, 20–21
Keen, Alan, 148 n.
Kellett, E. E., 18
Kemble, John Philip, 81
Kendal, Mrs, 105
Kernodle, George, 100 n.
Killigrew, Sir William, *Siege of Urbin*, 94
Kirschbaum, Leo, 147, 152
Kittredge, G. L., 7, 8
Klain, Hugo, 120, 121
Knack to Know a Knave, A, 149
Knack to Know an Honest Man, A, 149
Knight, G. Wilson, 18, 152–3
    critical influence, 20–4

169

M*

INDEX

Knights, L. C., 10, 23, 147
Koblar, F., 118
Koeppel, Richard, 161
Kolbe, F. C., 18
Komisarjevsky, T., 103, 132
Kostic, L., 117
Kriśković, V., 122 n.
Križák, Bohuslav, 109

L., E., contribution to *Sorrowes Joy* (1603), 155
Lamb, Charles, *Specimens of English Dramatic Poets*, 24
Lane, Rev. Edmund, 69
Langdale, A. B., 155
Lathom, Lord, 106
Laud, Archbishop William, 79, 83
Lavater, Ludwig, *Three Christian Sermons*, translated by W. Barlow (1596), 159
Law, Robert Adger, 142 n.
Lawrence, W. J., 11, 98
Lawrence, W. W., 13
Leavis, F. R., 10, 23, 24
Lee, Sir Sidney, 1–2, 7, 10
Legge, Thomas, *Richardus Tertius*, 91
Leslie, Bishop John, *De Origine, Moribus et Rebus Gestis Scotorum*, 47
Lewis, B. Roland, 74 n.
Lewis, C. S., 24, 52, 162
Lewis, D. B. Wyndham, 6–7
Leyland, Peter, 155
Liddell, J. R., 96 n.
Lily, William, *A Shorte Introduction of Grammar*, 86
Lindsay, Sir David, *A Satire of the Three Estates*, 99–100
Livy, 28
Locrine, 92
Lodge, Thomas, *Rosalynde*, 87
London (*see also* British Museum; Haymarket Theatre; Theatre, Elizabethan), 70, 73, 79, 81, 83
  Blackfriars, 70, 76
  Gray's Inn, 69
  Middle Temple, 149
  Public Record Office, 88
  Scriveners' Company, 70
  Somerset House, 71, 73
London Prodigal, The, 92
Long, John H., 149, 162
Lothian, John M., *King Lear: A Tragic Reading of Life* reviewed, 141
Lounsbury, T. R., 2
'*Love lyes a bleedinge*', 88

'*Love's Labour's Won*' *see* Shakespeare, William, *Troilus and Cressida*
Lucy, Miss C. Hartwell, 69
Lucy, Sir Thomas, 151
Ludovici, C. V., 128
Lydgate, John, 78
Lyly, John, 29, 49, 143
  Euphues, 50
  Mother Bombie, 41
  Sapho and Phao, 95

MacCallum, M. W., 9
McCutchan, J. W., 146 n.
Machiavelli, Niccolo, 7, 14
McIlwraith, A. K., 92
MacKail, J. W., 5
McKeithan, D. M., 9, 34 n.
Mackenzie, Agnes Mure, 4,
McKerrow, R. B., 58, 67 n.
MacMahon, Aline, 124
McManaway, James G., 149, 152; Woodward and McManaway's *Check List*, 93
Macray, W. D., 91, 96 n.
Macrobius, 64–5
Madan, Falconer, 82, 83, 84, 85, 86
Madariaga, Salvador de, 10, 24
Malone, Edmond, 82, 85–6, 88, 91–2, 93, 95
  A Dissertation on the Three Parts of Henry VI, 56, 57–8
  Attempt to ascertain the Order of Shakespeare's Plays, 57
  editions of Shakespeare, 80–1
  interpretation of Greene's 'upstart Crow', 56–68
  Malone Society, 81, 95
  Shakespeare collection, 80–1
Mann, Isabel R., 152
Marcham, Frank, 70
Marlowe, Christopher, 7, 29, 50, 59, 60–1, 63, 150
  Dr Faustus, 27, 30, 41, 42, 43–4, 92
Marriage of Wit and Science, The, 92
Marshak, S., 125
Marston, John, 150, 151
  The Malcontent, 24
  Sophonisba, 42
Marx, Groucho, 133
Mary Queen of Scots, 39
Masefield, John, 2, 5
Mason, E. C., 147, 151
Mason, Rev. Robert, 94
Massinger, Philip, 160
  The Virgin Martyr, The Emperour of the East, 92
Matthews, Brander, 11–12
Mattingly, G., 155

170

INDEX

INDEX

INDEX